Blairism and the War of Persuasion

This book is dedicated to
'the Birmingham School' and
all who learned in it.

ISBN 0 85315 992 0

British Library Cataloguing in Publication Data.
A catalogue record for this book is available from the British Library

Typeset by e-type, Liverpool

Printed in Great Britain by the Cambridge University Press

Blairism and the War of Persuasion

LABOUR'S PASSIVE REVOLUTION

Deborah Lynn Steinberg and
Richard Johnson (eds)

Lawrence & Wishart
LONDON 2004

Contents

Acknowledgements

We owe considerable gratitude to a number of people who have supported us through the preparation of this book. We would firstly like to thank our contributors and our editor Sally Davison from Lawrence and Wishart for their kind patience and continued enthusiasm for the project during the unavoidable delays to this book caused by Deborah's illness. We would like to thank Stuart Hall and Debbie Epstein for the formative discussions that resulted in the shape of the current collection. We would like to thank members and associates of the Birmingham School (the Centre for Contemporary Cultural Studies, the Department of Cultural Studies and the Department of Cultural Studies and Sociology, formerly hosted and, in the summer of 2002, decimated by the University of Birmingham, England), for the intellectual and political approaches, debates, insights and values that helped form this book.

Richard would like to thank Mariette Clare, Bob Bennett, Becky Johnson, Paul Johnson, Jean-Pierre Boulé, David Jackson, Dan McEwan, Parvati Raghuram, Stephen Chan, Ranka Primorac, Mercedes Cabayo-Abengozar, Nigel Edley, Christopher Farrands, and Nahed Selemen Baba for personal and intellectual support over a period of particular 'pressure'. Thanks also to the members of several groups who have shared – and helped to develop – ideas in this book including the Aging Men's Group (who will never be 'dinosaurs'), the Narrative Group (the last of the Birmingham Sub-Groups?), and the Postgraduate Seminar in Sociology and Women's Studies at the University of Lancaster (especially Bob Jessop, Jane Mulderrig, Maureen McNeil and Jackie Stacey). Some ideas and interpretations in this book have been tried out – and sometimes bounced back – by members of the MA course group on Globalisation, Identity and Technology and of the Research Practice Programme for beginning Ph.D. students in the Faculty of Humanities at the Nottingham Trent University and, differently, at teach-ins and day schools on the Afghan and Iraq Wars at the same university, and at meetings of the Stop the War movement and of the Campaign for Nuclear Disarmament in the cities of Leicester and Nottingham.

For their kindness, intellectual and moral support, in many forms, Deborah would like to thank Gillian Bendelow, Tony Elger, Robert Fine, Joan Haran, Christina Hughs, Cath Lambert, Terry Lovell, Mike Neary, Andrew Parker, Ian Proctor, Jonathan Tritter, Simon Williams and Caroline Wright (and her other colleagues in the Department of Sociology at Warwick University); Cyndy Fujikawa, Beau L'Amour, Debbie Epstein, Elizabeth Ettorre, Cathy Humphries, Gillian Lewando Hundt, Eléni Prodrómou, Peter Redman, Maxine and Irwin Steinberg; members of the DCSS action group and participants in the 'Whose University?' day of discussion; and members of the Narrative Group.

Distinctiveness and difference within New Labour

Richard Johnson and Deborah Lynn Steinberg

W hat is distinctive about the politics of New Labour or Blairism? This was the question we set the contributors to this volume when we first commissioned the chapters that follow. When the book was conceived – before the election of 2001 – there was little convincing critical analysis of New Labour's politics and a strong tendency, on the political left especially, to identify New Labour with Thatcherism, with 'Thatcherism rebranded' or 'Thatcherism plus spin'. The nature and meaning of Labour's 'modernisation', impelled by four successive elec-toral defeats, was far from clear; nor were the differences between Blair and his predecessors as Labour Party leaders, Neil Kinnock and John Smith, both in their different ways 'modernisers'. During Blair's first term, from 1997 to 2001, the euphoria of 1 May 1997, when Thatcherite Conservatism was so soundly trounced, and the seductions of Blair's progressive-sounding language, could still bolster hopes of something better, perhaps more 'socialist', in the second term. Even today, critics like Stuart Hall (2003) and Alan Finlayson (2000, 2003) have to work hard to show that Blairism is a distinctive project, different from, or *more than*, Thatcherism, and that it has not, as Hall puts it, 'simply like Topsy grown higgledy-piggledy of its own accord'. If it is widely recog-nised, today, that New Labour has acquired a political character of its own, the question remains what kind of politics has it become?

INTERPRETATIONS OF NEW LABOUR AND BLAIRISM

Four main lines of interpretation, some referring to the earlier modernising moments, some specifically to the Blairite phase, have been offered to date. We can summarise these schematically as follows:

- New Labour as Thatcherism in disguise
- New Labour as a Labour's latest phase of modernisation
- New Labour as a response to social change and electoral imperatives
- Blairism (note the shift of agent) as the dominant fraction within a New Labour's 'broad church'.

While it is useful to lay out these interpretations abstractly at this stage, they are in practice often combined, especially in the most recent accounts (e.g. Hall, 2003; Finlayson, 2003; Kenny and Smith, 2001). Perhaps New Labour is new in its *combinations* or 'articulations' of elements, apparently contradictory, previously opposed?

1. The first strategy, adopted in most critical analysis, has been to focus on the relation of Blairism to Thatcherism – the coinage 'Blairism' itself suggesting significant analogies if not strong continuities between the two. Usually the continuities are stressed. Early left analysis, including the 'New Left' currents at first, sought to 'demystify' New Labour by showing, that despite the webs of deceit spun by spin, New Labour was fundamentally Thatcherism by other names, despite its social-democratic inheritance and 'centre-left' posture (e.g. Hall et al., 1998).

In academic analysis (e.g. Hay, 1999), this tendency was strengthened by the quality and extent of good critical analysis of Thatcherism itself. This had been undertaken both from the angle of a cultural politics (e.g. Hall et al., 1979; Hall and Jacques 1983; A.M. Smith, 1994) and from the perspective of political economy or theories of the state (Gamble, 1988, 1994; Jessop et al., 1989). Both types of analysis were complex: Thatcherism had a main transformative dynamic – the installation of a neo-liberal or market-led system – but was also politically mixed, typically split between an individualistic neo-liberal side and a neo-conservative stress on nation, family and traditional morality. Its transformative if not hegemonic character was widely recognised. How could it be overlooked when institution after institution was demolished or changed under our very feet? This included the institutions of organised labour and the Labour Party. More generally Thatcherism was seen, correctly, as a major break from the political consensus that had dominated the post- World War II decades, up at least until Labour made its own breaks in the 1970s (e.g. CCCS, 1981).

One way to make the argument about Blairism-as-Thatcherism more careful is to distinguish between neo-liberalism on the one hand and both Thatcherism and New Labour or Blairism on the other. While Thatcherism and Blairism are political and ideological formations, each of which has a 'project' for social change and conservation, neo-liberalism can be seen both as a doctrine or theory and as a larger, slower tendency to transformation, which Gramsci would have called 'organic'. This transformation is affecting, in fundamental ways, the nature of social and economic relationships in our world, and also the forms of subjectivity or individuality in relation to collective life and social solidarities. 'Neo-liberalism' expresses both an ideology (or an 'ism') and, rather abstractly, a major dynamic of social change, much larger than the project of any party or political grouping. It is a dynamic in which every national formation and every kind of social provision becomes entangled, though in different ways and through different political means.

From this perspective, Thatcherism was a set of discourses, social alliances and forms of politics that inaugurated a first or early phase of a longer neo-liberal transformation.[1] It *became* organic or hegemonic, connecting up especially with key capitalist dynamics – with the transition from Fordist to post-Fordist production for instance. Like all political formations, including New Labour, however, it held together or 'articulated' many other elements. These often contradicted the drive towards marketisation and privatisation. How organic to neo-liberalism, for example, was the stress on heterosexual familial conformity and the attack on gay and other dissident sexual identities? Certainly, as the studies of sexual politics in this volume suggest, some consistently neo-liberal MPs within the Conservative Party never subscribed to this part of the programme. Neo-liberalism, it seems, can come in different and 'impure' combinations, both across different national formations, but also in different historical phases.

According to this line of argument, then, New Labour's hegemony and the hegemony of Blairism *within* New Labour are best seen as *a new or different phase within the drive towards a neo-liberal world*. The breaks between New Labour and Thatcherism are therefore as significant as the continuities: Blairism is *not* 'Thatcherism by another name'.

We can now re-pose our original question. What is distinctively new about Blairism (or aspects of New Labour) as a type of neo-liberal politics? We can conceive of its project for example as the *deepening* and *extending* of neo-liberal social relations and individualism, as the bringing of all spheres of social life into market and commodity relations and as the expansion of these relations globally. We can ask how such a project, focusing on labour and 'the knowledge economy', transforms the regimes of management, state power and citizenship (see Part I below; Jessop, 1994; Gamble and Kelly, 2001); and how cultural questions in the largest sense – ways of living, forms of subjectivity as well as attitudes to creativity and art – might be central to this politics (Bewes and Gilbert, 2000; Finlayson 2000; 2003; and see especially Parts I and III below).

2. The second interpretative strategy is to view New Labour, somewhat more narrowly, within a longer history of the Labour Party and of social-democratic political traditions more generally. (For an excellent review of these approaches up to the end of the first term see Kenny and Smith, 2001.) Particularly important for some commentators is the long history of Labour's attempts at 'modernisation', the repeated patterns, especially post 1945, of attempts to take account, particularly, of the apparent successes of capitalist economic life and social organisation

Key moments in this history were not only the monetarist moves of the mid-1970s under Callaghan – predating the arrival and naming of Thatcherism – but the systematic 1950s revisionism of Hugh Gaitskell and Anthony Crosland, and the technophiliac modernising rhetorics of

Harold Wilson in the 1960s. The question then arises of whether there is anything fundamentally new about New Labour, or whether, for example, it takes up again, perhaps more effectively, the enduring problems of older Labour. More immediately, the recent drive to modernise the party is dated not from Blair's own accession to the Labour leadership in 1994 but from the party's earlier responses to the succession of electoral defeats from 1978 to 1992 (e.g. Ludlam, 2001).

Different versions of this perspective are critical or appreciative of New Labour. Some academic analysis comes close to repeating the self-analysis of New Labour itself. In the more apologetic writing, the meanings and necessity of modernisation are not questioned. The general mood is pragmatic or 'realist'. It is not recognised that there are different possible models of modernisation, nor that, beyond this, there are deeper problems deriving from modernisation if it is viewed as neo-liberal deregulation – environmental deterioration, increasing social and political polarisation, and a systematic intensification of worldwide struggles for resources and therefore over strategic and military control. Nor is it recognised that these are signs that the dominant models of economic growth and social progress are open to fundamental doubt.

More critical versions of the novelty of New Labour stress the extent to which it has departed from traditions of social-democratic politics in Britain and Europe especially, on such questions as public state social provision, the protection of labour and even human rights. For some writers, Labour has never been a socialist or even a social-democratic party but rather a particular kind of alliance between 'social reformers' (as likely to be Liberals as Socialists) and 'reforming socialists'. Within this context, more recent modernisations – including those of Kinnock – are seen as moving the party nearer to the US Democratic Party rather than to a (weakened) European social democracy (e.g. Elliott, 1993).

A third interpretative strategy, with a long history, is to stress Labour's 'broad church'. Labour has always contained elements of working-class trade unionism and a kind of socialist professionalism or 'Fabian' expertise, a pragmatic defence of working-class interests and a zeal for the 'efficient' and reformed social institutions, as well as tendencies of the anti-capitalist left and the social-reforming centre. Even those authors who have stressed, correctly in our view, the long conservative under-tow of Labour's attachments to electoral politics and to 'Parliamentaryism', and its lack or loss of educational or counter-hegemonic popular potential, have stressed that it is not a unified politics (e.g. Miliband, 1973). Although it is arguable that Labour is a more homogeneous (and certainly more disciplined) political formation now, under Blair, than ever before, distinctions within the party and its social constituencies are an important strand of argument within this book. Several chapters in this book insist, for example, that Blairism is a narrower and a more specific political agency than New Labour generally. Blairism refers to the hegemonic fraction within New Labour, and to a particular project with strong transnational features, associated with the Prime Minister, his (expanded) office and his closest associates and political allies (see especially the chapters by Campbell, Epstein, Johnson and Steinberg, Steinberg and Johnson, Tincknell). By comparison, the drive to change the party was a broader project, including demands not so much to streamline it as to make it more democratic, as a first step in democratising a deeply hierarchical and 'traditional' political system. This version of the project could involve those politicised by the new social movements and cultural currents of the 1970s. From this perspective Blair has hijacked a process already underway under his predecessors, but not necessarily headed in the same directions. Under his Prime Ministership, it could be argued, both party and governments have become more and more 'Blairite', subordinating or shedding many of the currents that contributed to both optimism and success in 1997. The fate of gender politics, in and around the party and the political system, is a salient example here. It may be that sexual politics, by contrast, is an area where modernising options have remained more open (see Weeks in this volume).

4) Fourthly, there are a number of interpretative moves that have in common the identification of an underlying rationale for Labour's modernisation. They are usually employed to defend New Labour's 'newness' even in its Blairite version. They hinge on the practical conditions of electoral and political success. The first, most obvious, argument is that modernisation was a necessary response to the four electoral defeats from 1979 onwards. A second, more structural, argument stresses how Labour's traditional constituencies, the manufacturing working class concentrated in its cultural redoubts in the Midlands and the North, has been in serious demographic decline, so that some adaptation, including re-negotiation of the historic link to trade unionism, was inevitable. Third, it is argued that a necessary electoral strategy was to occupy the centre of British electoral politics by wooing a (different kind of) 'middle England'. Finally, it is argued that contemporary capital and especially global financial networks can destroy or blow off course any socially-radical government that seems likely to challenge its economic interests or its continued political weight. Labour, like all other national parties, has therefore to come to terms with what is all too accurately described as ' the *world* of business'.

CRITICAL PERSPECTIVES: 'PASSIVE REVOLUTION'

From a more critical perspective, these arguments about the necessity of particular modernisations presuppose an equally particular conception of the relation between political agency and social change. A sharp separation is made between underlying tendencies and dynamics and the pursuit of political strategies. Politics is then seen less as constructing a particular social order, more as reflecting or expressing social change. At most politics is seen as giving birth to or 'delivering' changes already

matured. It *follows* social change and does so with a logic that it would
be irrational to gainsay. This closes off arguments about the full
complexity of causes and the possibility of different solutions. Similarly,
in the realm of 'values' these are likely to be derived from the reading of
existing social 'realities'. These types of explanation are typical of Blair's
own rhetorics and the social theories on which he draws.[2]

Many of the chapters in this book are posited on different assumptions: that there are different versions of possible futures, even of
'modernisation'; that politics always plays a part in constituting the
realities with which it deals; and that popular mobilisations may shift
the relations of force in favour of the marginalised and unregarded
majorities. Moreover, all political and economic projects can be questioned for their cultural definitions and their preferred forms of human
identity. The kind of *cultural* analysis pursued in many chapters in this
book is therefore crucial in actual processes of social change, showing
how relative to values and conceptions of social interests all political
actions are. A major question, for example, concerns the political work
of extending and developing neo-liberal forms of individuality – 'individualism' in that sense.

In Gramscian political theory this difference is expressed in two key
terms: 'passive revolution' and 'counter-hegemony'.[2] Hegemony
involves not only the winning of consent, by political and ideological
contestation, but also the development of particular social relationships, forms of economic production and their 'corresponding' forms
of human life. For Gramsci, the communist counter-hegemony
involved going beyond existing social relationships, towards the possibility (that nonetheless lay within them) of a more co-operative and
egalitarian future. It necessarily involved the leading agency of popular
social groups, in the Italy of his time, first industrial workers and
second peasants and other rural social groups. This was an agency
always present in social life, but which could be organised politically
into a 'collective will' for a better world. Really 'organic' change, in this
sense, involved programmes that were based in the conditions of everyday life and in the 'common sense' or 'good sense' of those
subordinated groups who were also necessary to capital's reproduction
and (and here is one of Gramsci's limits) to the life of the nation.

'Passive revolution', by comparison, was Gramsci's term for 'revolution from above' or 'revolution without revolution' (see especially 1971:
59-60, 105-20). It was a key category in his understanding not only of
Fascism in Italy, but also the Risorgimento, and Napoleonic solutions
in post-revolutionary France. The term has a historical reach well
beyond the circumstances of interwar Italy. In political terms, passive
revolution is the demobilisation or disorganisation of forms of popular
agency and therefore of the possibility of organic change. This can be
achieved, for instance, by what Gramsci calls 'transformism', in which
elements of the programmes or the leaderships of popular movements

are incorporated into those of the ruling alliance (see especially 128 note 4, 227-8). Transformism does not, however, develop or 'educate' these currents, does not 'bring out the best in them', as it were. It does not base itself within them. Rather it seeks to contain and control popular forces from outside. This may involve making real concessions, but always within the limits of existing social arrangements. At this more 'structural' level, involving socio-economic relations and whole ways of life, passive revolution is an attempt to solve structural problems within the terms of existing structures. An example today might be trying to solve environmental problems without curtailing the production of commodities or contesting the power of big corporations.

Passive revolution is, therefore, a political strategy with many contradictions. It is 'revolution', but also 'restoration'. It often involves grandiose national projects – unifying the nation, 'purifying the race', defending the national culture, fighting a war on behalf of civilisation, generally achieving national 'greatness'. Yet at the same time, it puts a premium on 'politics' in its narrowest and 'dirtiest' meaning: striking deals, presenting issues cleverly, not giving too much away, a certain instrumentality or 'realism' in the 'machiavellian' sense.

Although several authors in this book make direct use of the idea of passive revolution (see especially Jones, Johnson and Steinberg, Smith below), we have not tried to construct a whole book around this idea. Our contributors have pursued the brief of New Labour's distinctiveness in different ways. Gramscian notions have been taken up alongside other overarching themes.

THE PLAN OF THE BOOK

We begin this book with an attempt to distil the key tendencies, often very contradictory, of Blairism and New Labour. We draw on the other chapters, but we also attempt our own substantive synthesis, providing an interpretation of the overall character of a complex political formation. The chapters that follow, while often developing general arguments of their own, are also case studies of specific aspects or themes. We group these contributions into four main parts.

First, in Part I, we explore the distinctiveness of New Labour by analysing different aspects of its reconstructions of citizenship and the state. Active state intervention is often seen as a key feature of Blairism as distinct from Thatcherism. Many of New Labour modes of state action have their origins in the Thatcherite recasting of local and national government, but the targeting of particular social groups, their 'inclusion' then their regulation, the setting of tightly specified 'standards' for citizens, especially for public workers and state professionals, the enhancement of many different forms of managerial auditing and control, and the stress on responsibilities as qualifying citizenship rights are all distinctive New Labour features.

Clarke and Newman's overview (as well as the more particular stud-

ies of race relations and migration policies, education, and sexuality)
suggests, however, that New Labour's practices of governance are
particularly contradictory. Again, New Labour embraces different
political elements and possibilities, even if the Blairite elements are in
dominance. These studies also suggest a certain 'passivity' in relation to
changes in economic organisation and social life. New Labour's most
active or 'revolutionary' side smoothes the paths of the global capitalist
economy, and acceptance of its main dynamics is the most constant
feature of Blairite definitions of the modern. On other, more 'social',
matters, especially on race relations, refugee policy and sexuality – as
also on issues of European union – New Labour follows rather than
forms public opinion. While in 'race relations', as in so many other areas
of policy, Labour began in a progressive mood – the uptake of aspects
of the Macpherson report on the murder of Stephen Lawrence for
instance – in its dehumanising treatment of refugees and asylum seekers
it reacted to popular conservative media campaigns in a deeply mistaken
attempt to pre-empt racist campaigning. In sexual politics, however, it
has certainly responded to liberal pressure groups, especially where its
central projects of global-economic projects are not threatened by
reforms. These two features – the fitting up of citizens for a global capitalist future, and uneven performances, often sliding into a certain
conservative passivity, on social reform – augur badly for another
apparent goal, the reduction of overall levels of social inequality.

In assessing New Labour's prioritisation of education, Ken Jones
(Chapter 2) takes his cues, explicitly, from Gramsci's 'passive revolution'.
He sees parallels between the defeat of progressive educational movements in England – though not in Scotland and Wales – and the situation
of the Italian Communist leader in the period of fascist insurgency.
While many progressive educators saw education as means of emancipa-
tion, New Labour's educational policies are centrally a pacification and
intensive regulation of the previous agents of educational reform, including parents, working-class pupils and teachers. The teachers' new
position is especially contradictory: 'they are operationally central but
strategically marginal'. They are pressured by a battery of controls that
reorder their everyday working lives. The spaces that opened up in the
1960s and 1970s for teacher-led curriculum innovation and creative
cultural negotiations with working-class pupils have been closed down.
Labour's main educational alliance, however, is with business, as shown
in its commitment to economic globalisation, to economically driven
educational goals and to public-private 'partnerships'. Jones identifies 'a
managerial-regulatory bloc that drives change and comprises both public
and private elements'. The alienation of the grassroots agents of education and promotion of major educational differences renders New
Labour's English model of educational modernisation vulnerable to
'damaging comparisons with Edinburgh or Belfast'.

'Modernisation' has been a keyword in New Labour's transformation of public institutions and the state. In Chapter 3, a wide-ranging review of the literatures and aspects of 'governance' and 'governmentality', Clarke and Newman stress that there are many versions of what a modern society and state should be, and that Labour's version is highly contradictory, in its policies and 'narratives' of progress. There are tensions between the ideal of 'a consensual inclusive society' and 'the agenda of neo-liberal economic reform', between the drive for central control and the encouragement of devolved local initiatives, between 'management' and 'participation', and between responding to citizens' claims and setting conditions for citizenship itself. New Labour's modernising project centres on this change in citizenship, the insistent emphasis on 'hard-working families' and enforcement of moralistic criteria of national belonging and exclusion.

In 'Labour's Loves Lost?', Jeffrey Weeks assesses Labour's record on sexual reform in relation to three main contexts: the longer history of the Labour Party's policy on issues of sexual citizenship; the 'long revolution' in sexual mores; and the emergence of new sexual discourses today. Weeks finds that the Blair governments have been more radical on sexual issues than any previous Labour government, but also subject to the same confusions and ambiguities as found among citizens generally at a time of rapid change in sexual mores. New Labour has been cautious not to alienate the 'middle ground' which it courts so assiduously, but it has responded to well-focused campaigning. This emphasises the importance of making the case 'from the grassroots upwards'. Weeks's relatively optimistic picture of sexual reform illustrates New Labour's continued power to attract activists in some socially progressive causes.

Lisa Schuster and John Solomos consider another contradiction of New Labour's policies: the tension between modest but real movements towards 'racial equality' and the increasingly draconian treatment of asylum seekers and would-be refugees. The authors see a shift away from the promises of opposition and of the first years in government, which included the first reception of the Macpherson Report, and the subsequent reform of the Race Relations Act of 1976. While the 2000 Race Relations Amendment Act may help to tackle institutional racism, there has been no real shift in the terms of the debate around immigration. Latterly Labour ministers and others have employed the racist and xenophobic language of 'swamping', and are also demanding that national minorities should 'integrate' or assimilate. This is a long way from the celebration of an achieved multiculturalism in other strands of Labour's rhetoric. Again, we see a pattern of early promise and of later reactions, which coincide with the increasing dominance of the Blairite wing within New Labour.

The chapters in Part II look at aspects of New Labour's social politics, or how it interacts with key social divisions, especially those of gender, class and sexuality. New Labour is approached through questions of social difference. This perspective is especially important since New Labour's own rhetorics, and an important strand of commentary, construct New Labour's politics in socially very *generalised* terms. It is either a politics of social inclusion/exclusion, or it is about 'the making of the neo-liberal subject', a new type of autonomous citizen, free-standing, self-educating, reflexive, mobile and infinitely adaptable (see Johnson and Walkerdine below). Here it is argued, rather, that the effects of New Labour also depend on social formations and processes which precede it; they do not depend uniquely on its own dynamics. The ideal neo-liberal subject implied by New Labour policies encounters historically formed subjects already embedded in social relations. These prior belongings affect how concrete individuals respond to neo-liberal models and managerialist incentives and sanctions. This perspective allows a more critical take on New Labour, drawing attention to its social boundaries, its inclusions and exclusions, its constructions of legitimate citizens and others. New Labour may offer greater levels of 'equality' and 'justice', but it certainly extends regulation, enforces new kinds of 'choice', and limits citizenship agency in important ways, often without a corresponding social equalisation.

As we have seen, sexual difference and citizenship is a domain where New Labour's claims to social progressivism have a certain seductive appeal and practical credibility. It is also a field where the view of New Labour as a 'broad church' embracing many differences can be seen most clearly, perhaps because party disciplines are relaxed. Here too its reforming impulses overlap with those of a still wider liberal alliance, including neo-liberal Conservatives. Focusing, in Chapter 6, on the reform of laws which discriminated against gay sex by setting a higher age of consent, Epstein, Johnson and Steinberg argue that Labour's 1997 victory secured a new hegemony, within the main legislative body, of different kinds of liberalism. These stretched from neo-liberal individualism and a discourse of rights, through Labour's mainstream 'social liberalism', to a more radical embracing of sexual diversity and interchange as a social good. The debates also reproduced, however, now in a more subordinated position, more conservative – and potentially homophobic – themes centred on the protection of the young, a component also within Labour's own ranks. Overall, the debates showed the limits of New Labour's reforming zeal, especially when liberalisation and sexual equality appear to threaten the privileged position of the heterosexual marriage. On the other hand, they also illustrate once more the potential for change in New Labour's early years, especially in an area relatively removed from its neo-liberal economic orthodoxies, but consistent with some neo-liberal concerns for individual rights and privacy.

Reading about these debates today suggests two rather different observations. First, it becomes clear just how different the political world of 1997 was compared with that of today, a major difference being the decisive turn of New Labour in the direction of its more Blairite variant. In 1997, pre-Blairite continuities can still be seen. Second, it also seems that some versions of lesbian and gay rights, and especially the acceptance of different but relatively separate 'communities', is far from incompatible with the main neo-liberal dynamics of possessive individualism and consumerist lifestyle.

In Chapter 7, Johnson and Walkerdine assess some of the social costs of neo-liberal policies by drawing on detailed research on the lives of young women in contemporary Britain. They show a continuation, perhaps a deepening, of social inequalities, which inevitably affects young women's 'opportunities'. Through the theme of the feminisation of both labour and the professions, they draw attention to the centrality of the construction of class-specific femininities in Blairite social politics. These more organic tendencies are considered in relation to Blairite social rhetoric, especially its redefinitions of key social-democratic or socialist terms: 'equality', 'social justice', 'civic society', even 'culture'. These redefinitions, they argue, amount to an active reinvention of all the key terms of an older socialist politics, and disorganise a politics based in a recognition of class and other inequalities, while attempting to retain the loyalty of some of these elements in New Labour's electoral coalition. Blairite redefinitions, however, make it still more difficult to address the more structural inequalities. Indeed, by encouraging a bland meritocratic disregard for 'failure', they help to reproduce them.

In Chapter 8, Haywood and Mac An Ghaill characterise New Labour through the forms of masculinities that it approves and, especially, disapproves. New Labour politics is defined in part by its promotion of a type of middle-class masculinity that they describe as 'protective paternalism'. This form of meritocratic respectability for men is juxtaposed to its 'others', who are the constantly reiterated sources, equally, of its own definitions. Thus protective paternalism and its forms of responsible fatherhood are defined particularly against working-class laddism, as a form of disorderliness and pleasure-seeking behaviour. Haywood and Mac An Ghaill also seek to relate the heightened social anxieties over paedophiles and 'stranger danger' to the privileging of forms of fatherhood that are far from always innocent of different forms of abusiveness.

Again this chapter provokes interesting reflections about the way we evaluate New Labour, especially in its 'broad church' versions. On the one hand, in the later Blairite phases especially, there is a stress on socially regulative interventions which impose strongly normative conceptions of what it is to be a man. On the other hand, the content of these norms, the characteristic emphasis on fathering for example, while invariably contradictory and often (middle-) class based, nonetheless show advances on more oppressive and predatory masculine models.

There is a general agreement among commentators that the distinctiveness of New Labour lies at least in part in matters of political style and the 'cultural' character of its project. The essays in Part III focus on New Labour's cultural politics and style. Spin, rhetoric, the art of politics and the politics of art are not trivial or superficial aspects of New Labour's repertoire. They involve, centrally, the type of relationships it seeks with ordinary citizens and with 'popular politics' – that is the active, collective political participation of ordinary citizens. From the angle explored in Michael McKinnie's chapter, they involve different allocations and definitions of 'creativity'. The relationship between representative democracy, with its institutions and elites, and participatory or direct democracy with its creative forms of citizenship, is critical in modern political systems. So are official attitudes to critical artistic or intellectual practice. Active and responsible citizenship is a key theme in New Labour's rhetoric. These chapters show, however, that its governing conception is not very democratic and that it is positively adverse to social criticism and alternative imaginings.

In her essay on 'Virtual Members', Estella Tincknell argues that specifically Blairite party 'reform' involves a particular conception of membership. This she places historically within Labour's positive relationship to modernity and its alliance with a masculinised and largely white industrial working class. In its pragmatism and stress on being modern, Blairite reform fits the longer history of Labour; it departs from it in constructing a 'post-modern politics'. In its earlier Kinnockite phase, modernisation promised a less exclusive, more democratic and more culturally sensitive political style, attractive to activists, who, like Tincknell herself, joined in the early 1980s, influenced by feminist and anti-racist movements. By the later 1990s, however, party members were being redefined as supporters, to be wooed and rewarded, rather than activists with convictions of their own. This redefinition affected all aspects of the party: the management of annual conferences, communications between centre and locality and the forms of electioneering and policy-making. The outcome has been 'an emptying out of the politics from the political' which is having disastrous effects, even, on the baseline practice of voting, helping to explain, perhaps, the startlingly low poll in the General Election of 2001.

Lisa Smyth approaches similar questions by analysing the relation between Blairism in government and grassroots movements of active citizens. Her main example – the People's Fuel Lobby of September 2000 – provides fascinating points of comparison with the government's later treatment of the much bigger movements against the Iraq war and US/British occupation. In the fuel strike, local activists, mainly drawn from transport businesses, and allied with sections of the media, mounted a sharp but short-lived challenge to a previously popular government – vulnerable however to charges of 'softness' on law and order matters. Smyth shows how much Labour's hegemony depends on the disorganisation and marginalisation of alternative forms of popular politics. In this case, the government worked hard to appear to be listening to complaints about fuel tax, insisted it must govern 'in the round' for all the people, and presented the fuel strikers as a minority threat to democracy and law and order. It did not draw on the environmental arguments that might have mobilised opposed forms of the popular. Its defensive strategies were, in this sense, passive, or pacifying, not hegemonic in a more expansive sense.

Joe Kelleher's close examination of Tony Blair's political rhetoric centres on his bids to 'win trust'. 'Trust me' is, he argues, a characteristic Blairite figure, but insistence upon it also marks a point of vulnerability. Much more than narrowly 'spin', this political rhetoric is a kind of drama or theatre, which prepares set roles for citizens and achieves crucial inclusions and exclusions. It defines in fact the parameters of politics, typically excluding an independent popular agency. Thus, while Blair's rhetoric asks us to sympathise with a parade of victims of ethnic cleansing in Kosovo, it excludes the same or similar people as refugees or asylum seekers in Britain. More generally, as Kelleher puts it, 'this is a rhetoric that already knows best' and does not hesitate to speak on other's behalf. His analysis of the vulnerabilities of this style, especially when faced by forms of independent witness, anticipates the profound crisis of trust, the cracks in consent and hegemony, that opened wide during and after the Iraq war.

The issue of policies for 'the arts' is critically positioned within the general question of political style. As Michael McKinnie argues, cultural critics have distinguished between forms of artistic practice that affirm the existing limited forms of 'community' and those that critically open up alternative social possibilities. Although New Labour has a more positive view of the arts than its Conservative predecessors, it values them in very particular ways: as 'creative industries' and parts of 'the new economy', as sources of inclusion, and, especially, as instruments for creating social consensus, identity and belonging. These criteria guide Labour's evolving and distinctive management of the public arts, as neither old-style marketisation or the Reithian promotion of 'civilisation', but as a particular version of the civic arts which is affirmative, disciplinary and regulative – though there are still evidently anxieties that a more subversive form of art might surface.

The chapters in Part IV focus on Blairite views and Labour legacies of the nation, and of international relations within a post-imperial, post-Cold-War context. Overall, the three studies reveal the conservative nature of Blairism as a form of international relations – its steady alignment, that is, with the main forms of military power and economic privilege within the world. One important aspect of this is the persistence of colonial structures of thinking and discourse at the heart of Labour's policies of development, its international alliances, and, in the case of Ireland, even in its forms of attempted de-colonisation. As Pat Noxolo argues very clearly, this is not so much a matter of explicitly racist or imperialist discourse, but rather of the ways in which agency and passivity are defined and distributed internationally. Blairism's appreciative alignment with the spaces of the powerful applies to the alliance, even fusion, with US power; and it also influences Blair's wholehearted endorsement of the worldwide projects of transnational capital, and, more domestically, his side-taking with forces of law, order and the unionist status quo in Northern Ireland. The other side of this stance is a refusal to listen to, and learn from, let alone ally with, the struggles of the subordinated, or the less powerful. This is most striking in the refusal to take anything for Britain or for England from the radically democratic forms of the Northern Ireland peace process, or to see *anything* admirable in the independence struggles of Third World states, even 'rogue' ones, or to qualify a terroristic anti-terrorism with some attempt to understand how violence and counter-violence interbreed.

A second shared theme in this part of the book, however, is a re-emphasised stress on differences within New Labour. It is Blairism, and especially the figure of the Prime Minister himself, that announces the most grandiose post-imperial themes. Other elements within New Labour have been carried by the reforming Northern Ireland Secretary Mo Mowlam, or by the wavering internationalist Clare Short, or the resigning ex-Foreign Secretary, Robin Cook, as well as by many Labour MPs who rebelled on the issue of the Iraq war. Here a less patrician notion of the party is often allied with a less accepting stance towards transnational big business and the Super Class, and a belief in a more pacific, more environmentally aware, and less imperialist insertion into the world's disorder.

Pat Noxolo's account of Labour's early policies of development and aid focus on the continuity of an imperialist division of the world between active, developing parts and passive circumscribed regions where all impetus to improvement must come from outside. This repeats the spatial and temporal organisation of the world as envisaged from the metropolis in late empire, and especially perhaps under that form of liberal imperialism which stressed the civilising mission of the colonial powers. The persistence of imperial ambition can be seen in the figure of Britain as a 'pivot' or 'fulcrum' nation, and in the reduction of the Caribbean or Africa to the status of passive victims in the need of aid, but prone to squandering it. The grandiosity and superiority of ambitions in 'aid and development' are matched by Blair's own assumption of transnational mission, his sustained evocation and wooing of 'the international community'. Such claims to influence are themselves an aspect of continuing rivalries, for they coincide with heightened competition with international agencies and other 'donor' states, not to say a loss of independence (from the USA) in military and other matters. As in earlier imperial moments, claims to influence are associated with decline.

The mixed fortunes of the peace process in Northern Ireland throw as much light on New Labour as on contemporary Irish history. By comparing the strategies and styles of Mo Mowlam and Peter Mandelson as successive Labour Secretaries of State for Northern Ireland, Beatrix Campbell exposes the inner diversity of New Labour, as well as the deep complicities of the British state in histories of assassination. Mowlam's alliance with democratic and egalitarian forces in Northern Ireland is contrasted with Mandelson's colonial alignment with the law and order preoccupations of the Northern Ireland Office; and her willingness to go among the people (on both, or all sides) with his patrician stance. Thus while Mowlam protected and pursued of the Peace Agreement of Good Friday 1998, Campbell shows, in detail, how Mandelson stymied the early movement towards its implementation. By stressing the potential of the equality aspects of the Agreement as a 'dialogue between direct and representative democracy', Campbell also strengthens the argument that Blairism consistently opposes popular claims that threaten to escape its direction and control. Along with failures to learn from the different experiences of Scotland and Wales, the stalling of the Northern Ireland peace process shows how Blairism fails to learn from its own margins, or dares to challenge the powers of the secret state.

As several essays in this volume argue, globalisation is a keyword in Blairite vocabulary. In the final chapter of the book, Richard Johnson argues that the service of transnational or global power is another distinctive feature of Blairite politics. Blair's own circle and the Prime Minister's Office have a very particular role in the internationalisation of parts of the British state, including the military. So whose globalisation might this be and how does it impact on 'national' policies? In some ways, as Noxolo argues, this 'global' is an old British universality which has fallen on hard times, but, it is also an American universality, with Blair's Britain in a subaltern role. Though it continues to surprise even his critics, Blair's American loyalty, latterly so risky to his national hegemony, is a heavily over-determined or 'inevitable' aspect of his politics, consistent with his neo-liberalism, his commitment to 'bridging' the United States and Europe, and matching his conception of British national interests. His critics can exploit the considerable 'blood price' to the nation of supporting of a neo-Conservative President, but it is more important, perhaps, to construct an alternative globality, in opposition to the policies of permanent war and worldwide domination.

NOTES

1. We are especially grateful to Bob Jessop for discussion concerning the phases of neo-liberalism as a way of understanding both Thatcherism and Blairism.
2. The adoption of a Gramscian framework as one key editorial feature of this collection grew out of our preliminary discussions with Debbie Epstein and Stuart Hall. We are especially grateful to Stuart for his early

suggestion that we look closely at 'passive revolution' as a way of making sense of New Labour.

REFERENCES

Bewes, Timothy and Gilbert, Jeremy (eds) (2000) *Cultural Capitalism: Politics After New Labour* London: Lawrence and Wishart.

Centre for Contemporary Cultural Studies (1981) *Unpopular Education: Schooling and Social Democracy in England Since 1945*, London: Hutchinson.

Elliott, Gregory (1993) *Labourism and the English Genius: The Strange Death of Labour England?*, London: Verso.

Finlayson, Alan (2003) *Making Sense of New Labour*, London: Lawrence and Wishart.

Finlayson, Alan (2000) 'New Labour the culture of government and the government of culture' in Timothy Bewes and Jeremy Gilbert (eds) (2000) *Cultural Capitalism: Politics After New Labour*, London: Lawrence and Wishart.

Gamble, Andrew (1988) *The Free Economy and the Strong State*, Basingstoke: Macmillan.

Gamble, Andrew (1994) *Britain in Decline* (4th Edn.), London: Macmillan.

Gamble, Andrew and Kelly, Gavin (2001) 'Labour's New Economics', in Timothy Bewes and Jeremy Gilbert (eds) (2000) *Cultural Capitalism: Politics After New Labour*, London: Lawrence and Wishart

Gramsci, Antonio (1971) *Selections for the Prison Notebooks* (edited and translated by Geoffrey Nowell-Smith and Quintin Hoare), London: Lawrence and Wishart.

Hall, Stuart (2003) 'New Labour's Double Shuffle', *Soundings* No 24 (Autumn), pp10-24.

Hall, Stuart et al (1979) *Policing the Crisis: Mugging, The State and Law and Order*, Basingstoke: Macmillan.

Hall, Stuart et al (1998) 'Wrong': *Marxism Today Special Issue*, London: Marxism Today.

Hall, Stuart and Jacques, Martin (1983) *The Politics of Thatcherism*, London: Lawrence and Wishart.

Hay, C. (1999) *The Political Economy of New Labour: Labouring Under False Pretences?*, Manchester: Manchester University Press.

Jessop, Bob (1994) 'The transition to post-Fordism and the Schumpeterian workfare state', in Brian Loader and Roger Burrows (eds), *Towards a Post-Fordist Welfare State?*, London: Routledge.

Jessop Bob et al. (eds) (1989) *Thatcherism*, Cambridge: Polity.

Kenny, Michael and Smith, Martin J. (2001) 'Interpreting New Labour: constraints, dilemmas and political agency', in Steve Ludlam and Martin J. Smith, *New Labour in Government*, Basingstoke: Macmillan.

Ludlam, Steve (2001) 'The making of New Labour', in Steve Ludlam and Martin J. Smith, *New Labour in Government*, Basingstoke: Macmillan.

Miliband, Ralph (1973) *Parliamentary Socialism* (2nd Edn.), London: Merlin.

Smith, Anna Marie (1994) *New Right Discourse on Race and Sexuality*, Cambridge: Cambridge University Press.

Blairism and the war of persuasion: Labour's passive revolution

Deborah Lynn Steinberg and Richard Johnson

A t the time of writing, we are approaching the completion of a second term of New Labour government in Britain, with a third term very probable. This is a significant cultural moment: the hegemony of the party, of Tony Blair himself and of the modernising project of Blairism are arguably at their least stable, and most unpopular on the domestic front, yet seem secure for the foreseeable future. This security exists against rather daunting odds, threatened not least by what has been widely perceived as an ethical minefield, if not fiasco, with respect to the recent war in Iraq. The contestatory tensions accruing to the Blairite project make this a particularly fruitful moment for reflection on the cultural politics of New Labour.

Following the substantive case studies undertaken by the authors in this collection, several things about the British political landscape become manifestly clear.

First, New Labour has clearly broken the 'curse' of single terms of office that haunted 'old' Labour. Not only does there continue to be an overwhelming New Labour parliamentary majority, but the possibility of meaningful opposition has been undermined by two key accomplishments of the new politics. One is New Labour's success at appropriating the political centre, which includes a significant portion of the terrain that used to be dominated by the Conservative Party and, indeed, by the New Right, including: the definition of national morality; the ready deployment of the means to war; the preoccupation with discipline and regulation; and the embracing of market-led discourses and solutions. The second is New Labour's skilful appropriation of much of the language of progressive liberal traditions, including those that have underpinned the liberal-social democratic alliance (that is, the old centre-left middle ground of British politics).[1] These include their oft-cited preoccupations with social inclusion, community and fairness. This latter phenomenon has been compounded by a long-term contraction and dispersal of both old and new lefts, notwithstanding some arenas of vigorous contemporary revival and emergence.[2] Indeed,

Blairism has effectively transformed the terrains of both moral traditionalism and social progressivism.

Second, 'Blairism' has emerged as a definite political-cultural formation. As time moves on it is becoming dramatically less tenable to
suggest that New Labour/Blairism are simply Thatcherism rebranded
or distinguished only by their dependence on 'spin' – claims that
continue to overshadow some analyses of the emergent features of the
current regime. At the same time, Blairism/New Labour are far from
being entirely new. Rather they represent a site of reinterpretation and
re-articulation of a range of pre-existing political tensions and tendencies. Indeed, Blairism has foundationally involved an extension and
deepening of neo-liberal political economy as well as a re-visioning of
the subjectivities it requires.

Third, New Labour is not one politics, but rather a political
constellation, of which 'Blairism' is the dominant fraction. Like
Thatcherism before it, it can be argued, the hegemonic dominance of
the new politics is shored up by its tensions and contradictions. The
seductions (for some) of Blairite social progressivism, for example
(which refer in part to earlier social democratic projects), seem to
underpin a 'period of hope' described by Gramsci that both distracts
from and fuels popular investments in the State appropriation of 'the
struggle for renewal' (Gramsci 1986 [1930]: 105). Hope, in other
words, has been fuelled (even as it has been, in significant ways,
betrayed), not just by rhetorical practices aimed at persuasion, but by
the ways in which the Blairite project has pursued (appropriated)
projects of popular progressivism. As both the Weeks & Epstein and
Johnson & Steinberg studies suggest, this is perhaps most concretely
in evidence on the terrain of sexuality and the widening of certain
citizenship rights.

Finally, there are the twin themes of modernisation and (neo)moder-
nity that underpin a number of key elements of the Blairite/New
Labour project. First is the distinctive brand of managerialism characterising what might be described as the *statist neo-liberalism* of New
Labour domestic policy. This is a 'modernisation' that is explicitly
invested in a 'big' state apparatus rather than the residualised state of
Thatcherism. Modernisation, secondly, also refers to a re-visioned
moral discourse of nation, invested, on the one hand, in an assimilationist social liberal repertoire of community, most evidently directed
to the arenas of sexuality and ethnicity, and, on the other, in the
eschewing of popular forms of political dissent. This informs, in part,
the exclusionary subtext of the new inclusivity – that is, as Kelleher &
Epstein and Johnson & Steinberg argue, the summoning of ostensibly
expansive constituencies often relies on both old and new terms of
disassociation – along lines of political ideology, as well as disap-
proved/approved social identities/lifestyles (within and outside the
party; within and outside the nation). Finally, modernisation involves

the redefinition of the place of the nation in the world in several respects: as a nation whose 'third way' is a model for others; as a fulcrum around which pivots the cross-Atlantic alliances of the richest nations; and as a managing agent in the service of corporate branding and global capital. At the same time, the global is often opposed to the nation, with the former in the ascendant as a main source of 'reform-ing' dynamics. This, as will be discussed further below, is the obverse of Thatcherite post-Empire nostalgia in which nation and nationalism were always superordinate.

In this chapter we shall attempt to further distil and map out the emergent themes of Blairism identified by the authors of this collec-tion. We shall focus particularly on the points of distinction highlighted above: the Blairite reworking of neo-liberalism, drawing on and in distinction from Thatcherism; its simultaneous appropriation of the political terrain of 'left'; and the contestatory factions of Blairism and the oppositional currents of New Labour – the terrain on which a new war of position (in Gramscian terms) or effective counter hege-monic challenge has failed, so far, to consolidate. Finally, there is the question of persuasion, arguably the most powerful marker of what we shall argue is Labour's passive revolution.

NEW NEO-LIBERALISM

> These objectives are clear, right and achievable. They define our national purpose. They mean a politics no longer scarred by the irrelevant ideo-logical battles of much of the 20th century. Most of the old left/right tags today are nothing but obstacles to good thinking. We have to concen-trate on the things that really matter – what I call the big picture – not the periphery (Blair, Speech at the Lord Mayors Banquet, 10.11.02).

All of the authors in this collection argue that Blairism/New Labour are not Thatcherism, rhetorically repackaged. What emerges strongly from the studies explored here is that we are witnessing the composi-tion of a new political formation that deepens and transmutes already existing processes and discourses and, at the same time, forges signifi-cant shifts of both political style, and the material relations that this summons, suppresses and supports. What can be claimed legitimately is that the common terrain of this constellation of consistencies and distinction between the previous and current regime is neo-liberalism. Indeed, it might be useful to interpret Thatcherism as neo-liberalism phase 1 – what might be termed *social authoritarian neo-liberalism*; and Blairism as neo-liberalism phase 2 – *statist (or managerialist) neo-liber-alism*. These points of continuity-rupture emerge in relation to a number of themes including: the nexus of work, discipline and class; the relationship between the state and the market, and between the nation and the world; the dis/investments in populism and the popular in the production of the neo-liberal subject; and the meanings of 'modernity' and 'modernisation'.

New Labour discipline: re-making the middle class

As has been widely acknowledged, Thatcherism was characterised by a number of distinct tendencies and tensions that were quintessentially 'New Right'. In the context of questions of class and labour discipline, this included a sustained drive to decimate and disorganise traditional working class occupations and the structural referents of working class identity. This was effected by, among other things, the radical restructuring of the economy away from manufacturing; the razing of trade unionism and 'left' leaning political activism (through a combination of legislative restriction and militaristic policing); and the reversal (through the radical residualisation of state services through wholesale privatisation) of the post-war social democratic 'consensus' which favoured a strong welfare state. These tendencies, among other effects, produced a profound swell of unemployment (composed largely of redundant workers from heavy industries and their collateral service industries as well as from former state service sectors). The Thatcherite ethos was captured in a brutalist, neo-Darwinian discourse of competitive individualism and entrepreneurialism. The new underclass was exhorted to stop 'whinging', to pull themselves up by their bootstraps, to start their own businesses (if they were male) or, if they were female, to absorb (unpaid) the service work formerly provided by the state.

As the authors of this volume have pointed out, in many respects, Blairite/New Labour domestic policies have intensified the neo-liberal economic trajectories of the Thatcher years. Certainly the emphasis on public-private funding initiatives for services once delivered by the state has, as discussed by McKinnie in relation to arts policy, been extended (indeed very aggressively fought for). So too has the driving deregulatory ethos that has embedded and reshaped the domestic economy in the globalising trends of mega-capitalism. Moreover, discourses of labour discipline and individual initiative (intimately linked to notions of social (il)legitimacy) continue to pervade the current cultural vernacular. But at the same time there are marked distinctions between the Blairite political economy (and political-economic vision) and that which characterised the previous government.

For example, and as many of the authors in this volume note (Clarke & Newman, Jones, McKinnie, Walkerdine and Johnson), there has been a marked shift in the configurations of class and labour. Where the disciplinary economies of Thatcherism were pointedly directed to the major industrial working-class occupations and identities (a state-led unmaking of the working class), those of New Blairism/New Labour are focused on middle class labour, and driven with particular vehemence toward public sector professionals and skilled/autonomous labour: (e.g. fire-fighters). The consequence of this, it can be argued, is a fracturing and re-composition of the conditions of middle-class life, labour and subjectivities. Indeed, it might be further argued that Blairism has signalled a new phase of class reconstruction, grounded in part in tendencies set in motion under the previous regime. The hallmarks of this transformation include firstly, the radical innovation of forms of institutional audit and surveillance. The administrative authoritarianism of New Labour projects to 'reform' across public sectors (schools and higher education, social services, health, transport, the fire service, the police and so on) differ from the Thatcherite willingness to rely on marketisation, virtually on its own, to deliver new subjectivities. New Labour's project is not one of state sector residualisation, notwithstanding the intensification of private finance initiatives.

Intimately interlinked with the inflationary machinery of audit is the 'standards crusade' (Blair 28.8.97) described by several authors in this volume (Clarke and Newman, Jones, McKinnie). This crusade is characterised by the pursuit of perpetual self-improvement with the criterion of 'excellence' continually reset higher as projected indicators and outcomes are (seen to be) achieved. Further, there is a radical and progressive intensification of workload and the reliance on the self-discipline (and expertise) of professionals/skilled labour to assertively invest in and enact the industrialising tendencies embedded in the New Labour reformation of professional life. Underpinning this crusade is a compact of distrust and disenfranchisement that undercuts the privilege and qualified autonomy formerly accorded to professional and skilled worker status: in particular rights of professional self-governance and the presumption of expertise and competence on the part of individual professionals.[3] At the same time, it must be noted that the extent to which these presumptions have characterised the range of professions targeted for reform has significantly differed: the conditions of labour attending 'lower status' professions like nursing (which was targeted for the residualising and the labour-discipline discourses of the Thatcher years) cannot be equated with those for doctors. Thus, what seems particularly significant about the current regime is its assertive incorporation of the more powerful professional sectors into disciplinary regimes from which they were, formerly, relatively protected. Yet at the same time that proletarianised labour practices have been expanded in this way, the cultural identities formerly associated with them have continued to be marginalised.

It is interesting, in this context, to consider why public sector professions/skilled labour have been such particular targets for 'modernisation' in these terms, and how Blairism/New Labour have come to be so preoccupied with the reconstruction of middle-class life. As suggested above, one of the most significant 'achievements' of the previous government was to radically alter not only the material conditions but also the available social and cultural referents for working class identities. In this context, it could be argued, there is little working class life to be remade that has not already been conscripted into the orbit of neo-liberal political economy. As Estella Tinknell notes, moreover, this period witnessed the decimation of the traditional sectors of alliance, particularly trade unionism, that had previously shaped the centre of Labour Party politics. The 'new realist' transformations within the party that have emerged have progressively shifted away from working-class alliances and agendas. Moreover, as the studies in this collection suggest, one of the key currents in common between Thatcherite Conservatism and the Blairite project is a visionary authoritarianism – although each is invested in distinctive constellations of morally authoritative discourse – that is characterised by aggressive investment in quelling (or overriding) dissent.[4] What has emerged is a party that is foundationally re-orientated to middle-class identities (even as it is subjecting key sectors to regimes of labour discipline that run contrary to traditional middle-class forms of privilege and responsible autonomy); and one that is at war with its own new constituencies, and – as we shall discuss further below – with those aspects of the state and grassroots social alliance that can be said to have social democratising or non-affirmative tendencies.

Transforming the gender/class nexus

As many commentators of the period have noted, the neo-liberal class and economic transformations of the Thatcher/Major era were held in considerable tension with a social authoritarian gender/sexual morality, foundationally inflected by an ethnocentric tribalism – the 'new racism' as termed by Barker (1982). The period witnessed the resuscitation of Victorian domestic ideology, emphasising the radical separation of public and private along traditional gender lines and figuring its ideal citizen in aggressive, jingoistically masculine terms. The period also witnessed the invocation of a panoply of folk devils ('unfit mothers', beggars, muggers and so on) that explicitly referred back to early eugenics/moral purity ideologies. Thus, as noted by Weeks and Epstein et al, even as the state was residualised in terms of service provision (and the increasing reliance on the unpaid labour of women to take up the slack), it was significantly expanded in relation to the regulation of private moralities.

Blairite/New Labour politics has witnessed a significant reworking of the nexus (and contradictory currents) of gender and class relations. New Labour modernisation has, on the one hand, explicitly incorporated a discourse of 'equal opportunity', particularly in relation to gender and work. If we consider the discussions of Heywood/Mac An Ghaill and Clarke/Newman together, the ostensibly egalitarian notion that everyone has a right (and duty) to work translates into an expectation that both men and women will be managing paid and unpaid labour. At the same time, the post-fordist transformations of paid work (which have actively been pursued under New Labour economic policy) in which women have figured as 'ideal' (contingent, flexible) workers are held in tension with a competitive, meritocratic, work ethic historically figured as masculine. In both public and private, moreover, the intensification of work alongside the inflationary standards against which work is measured and valued are normative. This normative expectation of excellence (Walkerdine and Johnson) incorporates both traditional feminine (self-abnegating and altruistic) and conventional masculine (striving, hierarchically orientated) values. Thus it can be argued that the New Labour work ethic does not so much transcend traditional gender divisions, as devolve and disperse the labours of traditional masculinities and femininities to both men and women, who are expected to serve and embody the contrary tensions of traditional masculinities *and* femininities.

Reworking state and market

Blairism/New Labour has, it can be argued, explicitly re-invested in 'big' statism, but with many of the previous marketised trajectories of political-economic reform still much in evidence. For instance, during the past two terms, the managerial apparatus of the state has grown, and notwithstanding continued drives to co-opt private finance into public services, the regulatory jurisdiction of the state over those services has been unambiguously reasserted. Sub-contracting rather than selling off is the Blairite version of privatisation. The Thatcherite privatisation drive was marked by an underpinning and *prima facie* denial of both the social and the public as a site of collective popular ownership. The Thatcherite policy of selling off public utilities by means of mass-share offers was essentially selling people what they (e.g. as taxpayers; as citizens) already owned – and persuading them that they did not.[5] Blairism, by contrast, has clearly acknowledged the existence of both society and of the public sphere and public institutions as, legitimately, sites of popular 'stakeholding'. But in the Blairite vision of 'public', commodity relations and marketisation must be pervasive, must progressively define and structure all aspects of public and civic life. This is what marks the new formation as a politics emphatically on the side of big business and expansive capital; and, as Johnson with Steinberg notes, the relationship between the government and business constitutes New Labour's only egalitarian form of 'partnership'.[6]

This arrangement retains the work of moral visioning (ideology) as the province of the state (notwithstanding its intimate incorporation of marketised values) as distinct from operationalising functions, which are contracted out. At the same time, the Blairite formation has retained the hard line ('big state') approaches to law and order and to militarism cultivated under Thatcherism. Under both regimes, the State has been invested in (and with) the values of the market. However the parochial ethnocentrism of Thatcherite entrepreneurialism has given way to an explicitly globalised corporate orientation. Moreover, both Blairism and Thatcherism have figured moral regulatory states – but on the basis of significantly different moral repertoires and different means of compliance. In this context, the terms (and qualifications for) citizenship are perhaps one of the most salient points of both continuity and departure.

RE-ARTICULATIONS OF SOCIAL DEMOCRACY: POPULISM, POPULAR AGENCY AND NEW CITIZENSHIP

Perhaps the most powerful distinction between Blairite politics and the previous regime is its explicit investment in and reworking of a range of concepts associated with, in loose terms, the 'left'. The liberal/social progressivist rhetorics of community, social inclusion, partnership, devolution and so on describe a different neo-liberal constellation. If Thatcherism was invested in a monocultural, social authoritarian, 'little Englander' chauvinism, this has been rejected explicitly in Blairite repertoires of multicultural cosmopolitanism.[7] Beatrix Campbell suggests, however, that key strands of this aspect of Blairite 'modernisation' have been – at best – reluctant (and profoundly limited) concessions to wider shifts in popular values. She includes within this the early claimed investments in gender equalisation (within and beyond the Labour Party itself), as sought for by New Labour modernisers such as Mo Mowlam and Clare Short; and moves, early in the new regime, to 'devolve' power in Scotland and Wales, and to pursue (under the leadership of Mo Mowlam, later undermined by Peter Mandelson) a peace agreement in Northern Ireland.[8] Solomos and Schuster note a similarly contradictory commitment to anti-racist and aggressively racist policy (emblematised in the contrary tendencies of the Stephen Lawrence enquiry and New Labour's draconian anti-immigration policies, with their particular hostility to refugees). Weeks, and Epstein, Johnson & Steinberg point up real if significantly limited liberalisations of government policy towards sexual/lifestyle choices and multiple family forms (and the rights, at least of affirmatively orientated (pro-Blairite), gay and lesbian constituencies), while family policies (for example sex education in schools) remain deeply invested in familiar forms of compulsory heterosexuality.

It could be argued, however, that there is significantly greater duplicity in the invocation of these terminologies than a simple watering down of radical political values. As suggested throughout this collection, in the New Labour approach, 'rights' (invoked as inalienable) are often in practice qualified by a duty not only of work, but of aggressive conformity to the new disciplinary economies of labour, and to market values; political dissent is derided and overridden; 'stakeholding' is dispensed, like favours,[9] to the self-including; and 'partnership', as suggested by both Noxolo and Johnson with Steinberg, defines relationships of gross inequality (including on questions of military alliance with the USA and economic alliances with mega-corporate interests). Blairism (like Thatcherism before it) is a profoundly anti-democratic politics, that has successfully taken up (and redefined) terminologies and concepts across the spectrum of left, anti-Conservative, and anti-conservative movements.[10] The seductive (or at the least as we shall suggest below, disorganising) sense of social progressivism attached to New Labour/Blairite rhetoric has, moreover, been lent substance – it is not just spin – by its occasional concessions to social democratic/democratising values.[11]

The popular subject: the new citizen

It could be argued that what Thatcherism both addressed and summoned were subjects (of a monarchical state). The mode of address combined a hectoring dogmatism with a 'knowing' recognition (and summoning) of particular constituencies of the already converted, who understood (and did not aspire to transgress) their place in a fixed social hierarchy.[12] As argued by many commentators, the ideal subject of the Thatcher period was parochial, nationalistic, defensive and exclusionary; invested in the nostalgia of Empire and Victorian values; and in tribalised monocultural Britishness, and particularly Englishness. Such subjects included business sections of the middle class, lower middle-class aspirants and skilled, better-paid workers – not the professional middle classes and the rich (who most profited from the political economies of the period). Perhaps the most paradoxical objects of Thatcherite populism and spin were working-class masculine subjects – those, precisely, who had been contained, beaten back, and disinherited by the decimations of industrial/manufacturing occupations – with their resentments and defeats reconscripted in legitimated, abjecting (racialised, homophobic, misogynistic) aggression toward the myriad 'others' of the time.

Blairism, by contrast, addresses citizens.[13] And the mode is movement: as suggested above, the redefined discourses of social inclusion, democracy, justice, devolution and so on signal a meta-narrative (Epstein, Johnson and Steinberg) of social progress. Interestingly, the constituencies addressed are often the resistant rather than the converted (particularly the resistant on the left, including, as noted by Tincknell, those in the Labour Party itself) – the socially marginalised rather than the centre, and the sceptical rather than the already persuaded. The Blairite citizen is invited, rather than exhorted, to affirm, to assimilate, to include him/herself in the (neo)modernising project of state allied to market. This is the consumer citizen, who harnesses his/her own active agency in the exercise of market choices and branded identities; proletarianises his/her own labour; inserts him/herself into the marketised collectivity. This is the worldly, globalised citizen, of an intellectually muscular, arbitrating and moral nation, who does not hanker back to former glory in empire, but forward to a world of nations, a world community of markets and assimilationist values. This is the passive revolutionary citizen; who accepts (or will be persuaded of) the inevitability of both global capitalism and neo-liberal politic futures, even as s/he invests in the languages of (and is content with limited gestures toward) social progressivism, and who is prepared to continually up the ante in a perpetually inflationary economy of qualification (work) for (the rights of) citizenship.

BLAIRISM AND THE WAR OF PERSUASION

Much continues to be made of the question of 'spin' in relation to the current government, particularly as this is embodied in the figure of Tony Blair himself. Indeed, the (perceived) preoccupation with representation and (its potential to legitimate desired forms of) governmentality is, it can be argued, a specifically Blairite rather than more generalised New Labour phenomenon. Certainly there is much to substantiate this appraisal. As Joe Kelleher notes, the Blairite agenda of persuasion is articulated through a panoply of rhetorics and semiotic labour that constitute a foundational 'bid for trust', most prominently enacted by the figure of Blair himself. Thatcherism did involve notable strands of spin – perhaps most famously in the bid to motivate ordinary people to buy shares in privatised utilities, but also in strategic moments of story 'leaks' to fuel what seemed a never-ending stream of moral panics in the popular press (Hall et al, 1978; Epstein, 1997), in its party political broadcasting, and in its various mediatised educational campaigns.[14] However, as Kelleher argues, the intensity, prominence and character of the Blairite bid for trust reveals a relationship to popular representation and a hegemonic orientation that are distinct from the dictatorial-exhortative authoritarianism of the previous regime. Blairism clearly takes the work of culture and the arenas of mediated meanings as a primary task and terrain, of government and of party. But perhaps more importantly, the impetus to persuade carries, in itself, seductive connotations of democracy – of a contract perhaps – of not only the rights and responsibilities of citizenship but of reciprocities between 'the people' and the people's representatives.[15] Persuasion is, intrinsically, dialogic. Certainly the need to persuade not only offers recognition to oppositional currents, but an obligation to engage. There is a certain suggestive egalitarianism in such a bid for trust, a connotative construction of the political field as a democratic terrain, in which (all) dissenting contestants have a legitimate claim. That this runs counter to the substantive one-wayism of Blairite 'Third Way' politics, and to the passive revolutionary construction of the New Citizen, is, perhaps, the key paradox underpinning Blairism's achieved hegemony.

How important is the 'war of persuasion' in Blairite politics overall? It can certainly be argued that the material shifts in the political economies of nation, state and market that Blairite policies achieve or permit are decisive, and that they therefore somewhat moot the need for persuasion. Yet the *relation* of discursive redefinitions and persuasive rhetorics is crucial.

For example, the deskilling and partial proletarianisation of professional work which is currently underway, often experienced as a loss of autonomy, depends on the imposition of the audit culture and on the pressures of closer surveillance and administration. Consistently, these Blairite 'facts of life' are taken up by those of us working in public sectors, in our actual practices, whatever our conscious objections may be. (This is in part an effect of the dependence of these sectors on public funds.) The totalising tendencies of audit culture discipline erodes the potentialities for (imagination for, investment in) alternative ways of thinking and acting, so that objections increasingly seem 'impractical' if not dangerous. In this respect, the relationship of labour to the political field has taken on taylorised quality: what is done is (often radically) de-sutured from the values and beliefs of those doing the doing. If it is the case that to comply is to enact (at least a certain measure of) trust, the bid would appear to have been substantively won before it is offered.

PERSUASION, POSITION AND PASSIVE REVOLUTION

The unabated progression of its 'modernising' programme, and the continued re-confirmation of its hegemony, would seem to attest to the strategic success of Blairism's war of persuasion, notwithstanding considerable resistance from the ideologically (if not materially) unpersuaded. The fractures within the Labour Party itself, as Tincknell and Campbell discuss, mirror key moments and wider constituencies of protest (both within and – in the wake of the recent Iraq war – beyond Britain). Perhaps most painfully, these predominantly include constituencies most invested in the progressivist elements of the Blairite repertoire – whether these are carried within the Parliamentary Party, party activists in the country, or indeed a wider 'left' public. Considered in this context, it can be argued that Blair's war of persuasion is integral, not primarily to the immediate trajectories of institutional transformation described above and throughout this collection, but to the containment of tensions, to the disorganisation of a consolidated counter-hegemonic struggle. It is a project of seduction, of ideological interpellation, directed primarily to the range of constituencies who have historical alliances with the 'left' and who might be regarded as the 'natural' constituencies of a party ostensibly opposed to 'little englander', social authoritarian Conservatism and to the constellation of New Right politics that Thatcherism so significantly forged.[16] One very clear instance of the disorganising effects of the seductive promises of progressivism that come (though rather thinly now) from the Blairite wing is the continued difficulty for party (and other left) activists of deciding whether to try to re-reform Labour or to try to create a new left alternative from the small parties and wider movements. The war of persuasion is, in other words, integral to the foreclosing of an opposed war of position, which might otherwise emerge from the disparate currents of protest within and outside the Labour Party.

The distinctions outlined above witness a palpable and dramatic reorganisation of the political field, extending to the terms of citizenship; to the political economies of state and market and of nation and its place within the world; to alliances and oppositions in domestic and international spheres; to forms of subjectivity as they are materialised through shifting processes and networks of production and consumption; to the cultural repertoires of social (including national and global) identity; and to the meanings that accrue to (and parameters that delimit) democratic practice, popular agency and regimes of representation. As the studies in this book suggest, notwithstanding its intimate continuities with many strands of the previous regime, Blairism is 'revolution'. But it is a revolution that abhors popular activism, or, indeed, any active agency that is not affirmative of its own pre-defined values or purposes. It is a project that sutures and serves the fundamentally incompatible tendencies and values of right and left politics. And it is a foundationally anti-democratic project, that wields the hopeful languages of social progressivism in a bid for trust that seems, so far at least, to have secured its future against even globalised moments of protest.

NOTES

1. It has been well established by historians and political scientists that the post-world war two period in Britain was characterised by a cross-party consensus on the necessity of a welfare state, Keynsian economic policies and some incorporation into the state of trade union interests. It was precisely this post-war settlement that was decimated in Thatcher years, as well as the assumptions underpinning it about the potentialities and obligations of the state to compensate for, or provide a safety net against, the inequalities and waste of the market (see for example, CCCS Education Group, 1981).

2. The widespread and organised opposition to the Iraq War, which was distinctive for the ways in which it was institutionally validated and circulated – for example being televised virtually unedited on BBC News 24 (a phenomenon that would have been unimaginable under Thatcherism) – represented a significant revival of mass protest, involving a constellation of political-oppositional currents. The public mourning following the death of Diana in 1997, coinciding with the victory of New Labour, was also taken by some theorists to represent not only a revival of mass demonstration, but a significant shift in their form and potentiality (see for example Kear and Steinberg, 1999; Gilbert et al, 1999). Further examples include global justice and anti-globalisation movements, as well as forms of new unionism (harkening back in some respects to 'old' Labour').

3. This, of course, has varied depending on the public professional sector in question. Some groups, for example nurses, have arguably benefited under New Labour, with improved recognition and working conditions.

4. This was painfully brought home in Blair's singular justification for war in Iraq –without UN sanction, and notwithstanding overwhelming dissent on the part of the British people (and wider international communities) – in terms of the conscientious obligations of leadership (to be unpopular, to make the 'moral' decision, as he perceives it, notwithstanding democratic oppositions).

5. This was perhaps one of the most successful moments of Thatcherite spin: the British public were exhorted to purchase shares, on the (implicit) basis that what was public was not really public. I remember thinking to myself at the time, newly arrived myself in Britain, that the slogan for this process should have been: 'privatisation: because you don't really own it unless you've bought it twice'.

6. As Blair put it in the first months of the new government: 'The third way is to try to construct a partnership between Government and business to help us cope with change and success in the face of its challenge' (Blair 11.11.97).

7. Indeed, in his speech at the Lord Mayor's Banquet, Blair declared pointedly that: '...there is no place [in the New Britain] for misguided little Englander sentiment' (Blair, 10.11.02).

8. The reform of the House of Lords (in terms that many have regarded as significantly compromised) and the stated intention to pursue proportional representative voting in a reform of British electoral politics can also be included here.

9. This is captured poignantly, on a globalised stage, in Tony Blair's speech to the UN General Assembly Special Session on the Environment and Sustainable Development. He stated: 'First, we must give everyone a stake ...'. This use of the possessive 'we' (who legitimately own and control both stakes and stakeholding), versus the 'they' (who are passive recipients of their own interests, and who must be educated into their constructive investment), is characteristic of the Third Way rhetoric of citizenship.

10. Thatcherism also radically conscripted social-democratic and otherwise oppositional concepts. A notable example was the rewriting of the term 'reform'. (See discussion of the reactionary anti-feminist use of this term in the wake of the 1988 Alton (Unborn Children Protection) Bill in the Science and Technology Subgroup 1991). But Thatcherism never claimed to be a party of social progressivist values (rather it was explicitly in opposition to these).

11. In addition to certain liberalisations as discussed by Epstein, Johnson & Steinberg, Weeks and Solomos and Schuster, these include, for example, tax policies favouring poorer working parents and new initiatives to assist young people.

12. This is notwithstanding the narrative of social elevation attending Margaret Thatcher herself, whose relatively modest origins as a shop-keeper's daughter, and transformation into the social elect of traditional Englishness and social conservatism, was a pervasively cited allegory of the regime. (A certain element of social/economic mobility also attended the popular discourse concerning the rise of John Major.)

13. This is not to suggest that either Thatcherism or Blairism were/are singular modes of address. Rather, both were/are composite 'voices', composed of the varying styles (sometimes oppositional) of prominent figures close to the leadership. Blairism, for example, is an admix of brutalist political stylings reminiscent of the 'iron' politics of Thatcher herself (for example Home Secretary David Blunkett, Education Secretary Charles Clarke), the intellectual muscularities of Peter Mandelson, the muscular pragmatism of Gordon Brown, and the 'softer' (more marginal) political stylings of Robin Cook (now stepped down in his opposition to the Iraq war) and (even more marginally) Clare Short. It is interesting how, in both contexts, the personal styles of the leaders seem(ed) to embody (to contain, in both senses) contestatory constituent voices, signalled in the eponymous figurations of the political regime they front(ed). John Major was never able to replace 'Thatcherism' with 'Majorism' in this sense. It is also significant that both Blairism and Thatcherism were/are composite masculine styles – as oft parodied in figurations of Margaret Thatcher as a man in drag; and, as Beatrix Campbell suggests, this is emblematised in the jettisoning of Mo Mowlam from the peace brokering process in N. Ireland, and in so doing from the dominant axis of the Blair government.

14. The apocalyptic, fear-mongering AIDS education campaign (which exhorted that we 'Don't Die of Ignorance', against the image of a crashing tombstone, without providing any substantive and corrective information about HIV/AIDS transmission or safe sex) was a salient moment of Thatcherite spin (and euphemism) being brought into the service of its social authoritarian agenda.

15. It is no coincidence that the possessive form, 'the people's', became the early catch phrase of the new government, beginning with the significantly oxymoronic appellation of 'people's princess' (a term used by Tony Blair to describe Diana Princess of Wales in the wake of her death in 1997); it was deployed shortly thereafter in a perhaps similarly contradictory rhetorical 'leftism', to describe the 'people's fuel lobby' (Smyth) (see also Kelleher 1999).

16. As Kelleher suggests, the rhetoric and political stylings of Blairite persuasion summon 'us' into their dramaturgical terrain of moral agon and affirmative values.

REFERENCES

Brown, Phillip and Richard Sparks (eds.) (1989) *Beyond Thatcherism: Social Policy, Politics and Society*, Milton Keynes: Open University Press.

Campbell, Beatrix (1987) *The Iron Ladies: Why do Women Vote Tory?*, London: Virago.

CCCS Education Group (1981) *Unpopular Education: Schooling and Social Democracy*.

CCCS (1982) *The Empire Strikes Back: Race and Racism in 70s Britain*, London: Routledge.

Cohen, Philip and Harwant S. Bains (1988) *Multi-Racist Britain*, Basingatoke: Macmillan.

Epstein, Debbie (1997) 'What's in a Ban? The Popular Media, *Romeo and Juliet* and Compulsory Heterosexuality', in Steinberg, Deborah, Debbie Epstein and Richard Johnson, *Border Patrols: Policing the Boundaries of Heterosexuality*, London: Cassell.

Franklin, Sarah, Celia Lury and Jackie Stacey (1991) *Off-Centre: Feminism and Cultural Studies*, London: Harper Collins.

Gilbert, Jeremy et al (eds) (1999) 'Diana and Democracy', *New Formations Special Issue*, No.36.

Gilroy, Paul (1991) *There Ain't No Black in the Union Jack*, London: Routledge.

Gramsci, Antonio (1971) *Selections from Prison Notebooks*, London: Lawrence and Wishart.

Hall, Stuart *et al* (1978) *Policing the Crisis: Mugging, the State and Law and Order*, Basingstoke: Macmillan.

Kear, Adrian and Deborah Lynn Steinberg (eds.) (1999) *Mourning Diana: Nation, Culture and the Performance of Grief*, London: Routledge.

Kelleher, Joe (1999) 'Rhetoric, Nation and the People's Property', in Kear, Adrian and Deborah Lynn Steinberg (eds.), *Mourning Diana: Nation, Culture and the Performance of Grief*, London: Routledge.

Loney, Martin (1986) *The Politics of Greed: The New Right and the Welfare State*, London: Pluto Press.

Oakley, Ann and A. Susan Williams (eds.) (1994) *The Politics of the Welfare State*, London: UCL Press.

Riedman, Lester (ed.) (1993) *British Cinema and Thatcherism*, London: UCL Press.

Science and Technology Subgroup (1991) 'In the Wake of the Alton Bill', in Franklin et al, *Off-Centre: Feminism and Cultural Studies*, London: Harper Collins, pp147-221.

Solomos, John (1989) *Race and Racism in Contemporary Britain*, Basingstoke: Macmillan.

Steinberg, Deborah, Debbie Epstein and Richard Johnson (eds) (1997) *Border Patrols: Policing the Boundaries of Heterosexuality*, London: Cassell.

Tony Blair Speeches

Press conference in Denver, 21.6.97.

H. Morpeth School, Tower Hamlets, 28.8.97.

CBI Conference, Birmingham, 11.11.97.

Council of Europe Summit, Strasbourg, 10.10.97.

The Lord Mayors Banquet, 10.11.02.

1. A new past, an old future: New Labour remakes the English school

Ken Jones

There are four systems of schooling in Britain: those in Northern Ireland, Scotland, Wales and England. In three of them devolution post 1997 has strengthened tendencies that are broadly inclusive – a bias in favour of non-selective secondary schooling, a scepticism about market forces as drivers of worthwhile educational change (Jones 2002). This chapter is about the fourth system – the English system, in which the legacies of Conservatism are strongly felt, and in which government still ferociously pursues the war against public sector professionalism launched by its predecessor.

England is the exception, then. But it is a big exception, and a complex one. Much the largest of the four countries, it is also the most strongly linked to a new global policy community and to the emergent discourses which provide rationales for educational change (Hatcher 2001). So what from the viewpoint of Belfast or Cardiff may appear as something shaped by peculiarly English traditions, from an international perspective looks like a paradigmatic example of a system geared to the stratified societies of the knowledge economy – something which is better understood in terms of novelty rather than continuation.

This chapter attempts to understand New Labour's programme for English schooling in a way that grasps both its conservative and its radical elements. Doing so, it borrows from the insights gained by Antonio Gramsci, as he reflected from prison on the defeat of the insurrectionary left in the early 1920s, and the rise of fascism. These developments he set in the perspective of Italian and European history post-1789. Fascism for Gramsci was the latest episode in a long tradition of 'passive revolution' or 'revolution-restoration' – a process in which the ruling social groups, through state intervention rather than popular mobilisation, sought to promote sweeping institutional change and 'national renewal'; and in which reform was linked not to the extension of democracy but to the preservation of existing power structures in the face of a radical challenge which had been defeated, but had not been eradicated, either as memory or potential (Gramsci [1934] 1971: 59; 105).

Perhaps this summary is already enough to suggest how 'passive revolution' is a concept useful to the analysis of an educational programme in which dynamism and conservatism are closely linked, and which is haunted so powerfully by the possibility of a re-emergent opposition. It has further layers of meaning, also, that relate not so much to the substance of analysis as to the stance of the analyst. 'Passive revolution', in Gramsci's usage, is the basis of something difficult and unusual in any politics, and perhaps especially from within marxism: a recognition of the rationality and success of your antagonist's programme, and a coming to terms with the weakness of your own. In this sense, it is a concept self-consciously devised from the vantage-point of the defeated. Something of this sense of aftermath, together with a certain admiration for the scope and energy of the victorious party, shapes this chapter's evaluation of New Labourism in education. But, in the spirit of Gramsci, the piece aims to identify the limits and breaking-points of the new programme; its analysis – however subdued it appears in relation to the immediate prospects of the defeated – is directed towards that end.

DEFEATS

Like Gramsci's, my account of 'passivity' relates to once-influential forces that have ceased, in any strong sense, to be agents of social change. But where he had in mind the defeat of insurrection, I am concerned with setback and retreat among forces which were at one time powerful agents of social reform. Since New Labour is organised around a comprehensive 're-agenting' of policy, aimed at the sidelining of forces which previously had a role in the design, implementation and contestation of change, the field for analysis here is a wide one. We can begin with the Labour Party itself. Since its 1922 pamphlet *Secondary Education for All*, the party has been committed to institutional reforms intended to broaden equality of opportunity. In the immediate post-war years, party conferences opposed the Attlee government's preference for tripartite education and called for non-selective (comprehensive) secondary reform. When in 1965 Harold Wilson's government encouraged local authorities to move in this direction, it was the – diluted – culmination of the Party's long-standing support for universal comprehensivisation (Simon 1992); and the same principle underpinned the party's opposition to the Conservative transformation of schooling in the 1980s. The point here is not to glorify a tradition whose shortcomings have often been noted (CCCS 1981), but to indicate the existence until the middle 1990s of a kind of policy baseline, underwritten by constituency parties and affiliated unions, and operationalised by Labour-controlled local authorities, below which the party's programme could not slip. What has enabled the radicalism of New Labour's present educational project is, in the first instance, the eclipse of these forces. Unions and local authorities were defeated by Thatcherism in the conflicts of the 1980s. The anti-union laws and the rolling back of the public sector which were the marks of Tory victory were ratified by New Labour in the 1990s; changes to Labour's constitution that lessened union influence and strengthened the party centre at the expense of local activism implanted the consequences of defeat deep inside the party itself. New Labour's programme for educational change is built upon this defeat – as much material as ideological – of the old.

The position of other agencies of reform has likewise been changed. When Labour left office in 1979, teachers possessed statutory rights of bargaining over pay, and exerted a growing influence in negotiations over their conditions of work. They had a majority on the Schools Council, the government-established body that promoted curriculum reform; and their members were active in a host of associations, initiatives and networks that promoted a 'molecular', ground-level development of curriculum and pedagogy. Conservatism changed all this. The Schools Council was abolished, as were national negotiating rights; a strict regulatory regime – a national curriculum, and intensified school inspection – curtailed classroom autonomy. New Labour built on these foundations. From 1997, performance-related pay, stronger management regimes, and a system of 'professional development' linked closely to the priorities of national government, ensured that teachers would be limited to being only weak agents of change.

There have also been wider shifts. Post-war reformers envisaged mass education as involving not just institutional change but a cultural encounter between the formal curriculum of the school and the experience of working-class students. This envisaging took many forms, from theoretical to intuitive. It was sociologically present in the writings of Bernstein and Halsey on learning and social class (Bernstein 1971; Halsey et al 1972). It also formed the troubled background of official reports: the Newsom Report of 1963 begins with the reflections of a school-leaver on educational reconstruction: 'It could all be marble, sir, but it would still be a bloody school' (Newsom 1963: 2). In meditations like these there was expressed a kind of politics of recognition: it wasn't that the working class was an emancipatory force, nor the embodiment of a potential for higher things, but it was nevertheless a presence which neither policy nor practice could ignore. The ferocious disciplinary regimes of the secondary modern school, students' participation in strikes and walkouts, the mass truancy that accompanied the raising of the school leaving age in 1972, and the publication from the late 1950s onwards of texts that aimed to bring 'working-class experience' into the secondary classroom, were all in some sense aspects of this recognition; and these were indicators that in cultural as well as political terms there was a baseline to the project of mass education: it was about students who were understood as belonging to a particular class, who were shaped by that belonging, and whose agency the school had somehow to take into account.

Here too something has changed. The pre-1979 system was marked by low levels of certification, and by an encounter between the routines of the school and youth cultures that sometimes displayed overtly resistant elements. In contrast, the present population of the school is much more heavily certificated than its predecessors; it has experienced since the age of seven an almost annual battery of national tests and exams; its destination is not the youth labour market but some further form of education and training, followed by entry to a working population that is occupationally more diverse, and in large measure locked into further, post-school systems of lifelong learning. In these circumstances, 'recognition' is no longer central to the mentality of policy-makers or of significant numbers of teachers. More common is a can-do emphasis on 'individual empowerment' and the growth of a performance culture among school-students, underwritten by the increasing numbers entering and passing public examinations. In this context, public displays of identity are more likely to be centred upon the August celebrations of exam success than on spectacular forms of dissent; meanwhile the 'resistance' documented in the sociology of the 1970s (Willis 1977) comes to be seen as the pathological symptom of a dying social order, that of working-class masculinity.

'REVOLUTION'

These then are the forces and circumstances which have been politically sidelined or socially eclipsed, without whose passing the rise of New Labour would not have possible. What is replacing them?

Gramsci wrote of the 'revolutionary' element of 'passive revolution' thus:

> There is a passive revolution involved in the fact that – through the legislative intervention of the state – relatively far-reaching modifications are being introduced into the country's economic structure in order to accentuate the 'plan of production' element; in other words, that socialisation and co-operation in the sphere of production are being increased, without, however touching ... individual and group appropriation of profit (Gramsci: 119).

Substitute, here, 'education' for 'economic structure' and the comment applies to the topic of this chapter. For education is central to the 'plan of production' – the interventionist element – in New Labour. Blair's government has no intention in intervening strongly to shape either the production or the distribution of wealth. But Blair's famous listing of his priorities – 'Education, education, education' – gives some indication of where he thinks government can act to economic effect. As he argued in 1995:

Globalisation is changing the nature of the nation state as power becomes more diffuse and borders more porous. Technological change is reducing the capacity of government to control a domestic economy free from external influence. The role of government in this world of change is to represent a national interest, to create a competitive base of physical infrastructure and human skills. The challenge before our party is ... to educate and retrain for the next technologies, to prepare our country for new global competition, and to make our country a competitive base from which to produce the goods and services people want to buy (Blair 1995).

From this perspective, if government can create an effective education system – 'modernised' and 'world-class' in New Labour terminology – it can thereby, despite having withdrawn from core areas of economic life, contribute crucially to Britain's success in a more competitive global market-place. Education must be lifelong and it must be technologised, and if this is accomplished then Britain will be transformed not only into a country of 'innovative people' but also into the 'electronic capital of the world', capable of responding to the 'emergence of the new economy and its increased demands for skills and human capital' (Blair 1996; DfEE 2001).

This is New Labour's big idea – the transformation of education to serve a knowledge economy. It is a vision largely free both of the nostalgic cultural sentiments of Toryism, and of what are seen as the producer ideologies and impossible emancipatory expectations of Old Labour. It focuses insistently on international competitiveness. The school is repositioned: its spatial context is global and its performance is constantly measured in terms of international league tables of achievement (Lindblad 2001). Temporally, there is an insistence on short time-horizons and on the urgency of change. The emphasis on competition and speed of response produces a narrowing of educational focus: performativity in relation to 'hard' criteria of test and exam results, rather than the mixed and less precise objectives of earlier periods, becomes key. Performativity is managed by active national government, and by a system of educational governance that is more intensive and more extensive than under previous regimes. Here, the processes of 'socialisation and co-operation' to which Gramsci refers, and which I try to capture in the term 're-agenting', take new forms: passive revolution involves not only the sidelining of some political and social forces but also the calling into being of others.

ALLIANCES

Around the project of transformation, New Labour seeks to create new kinds of educational alliance, although 'alliance' is perhaps too politicised a term for the new networks by which education is governed and through which change is organised. There is no place in this system for the forces associated with earlier periods of reform, nor do the relationships through which it is constructed make much allowance for the negotiation of different pre-existing or potentially conflicting interests: the often tense and certainly unequal 'partnership' between unions, local authorities and national government that influenced educational change between 1944 and 1979 has not been restored. The rhetoric of parent power that accompanied the Conservative programme reform has likewise diminished: parents retain the formal right of school choice that they obtained through Conservative market-based reforms, but school 'accountability' is envisaged by New Labour more in terms of the meeting of government targets than in responding to parent demand or community need. Instead, 'partnership' has acquired a new meaning, which relates primarily to the operational accomplishment of strategies devised by a single, powerful agency – national government (Jones and Bird 2000). In this sense the field of education policy has been reworked, so that the development of policy through an explicitly political process of encounter between different social interests becomes less important than its elaboration through networks of agencies, local and national, whose origins and points of reference lie in the priorities of national government. Indeed, New Labour – with some assistance from its Conservative forebears – has itself brought into being some of the forces with which it now seeks to build 'partnerships'.

First among the partners are those operationally powerful but not strongly autonomous agencies that, through mechanisms of target-setting, resource allocation, programme specification, training, audit and inspection, penetrate deeply into the everyday procedures of educational institutions and the lifeworld of those who work and study in them. Taylor and her colleagues noted the emergence in the 1990s of a consensus, shaped in particular by the Organisation for Economic Co-operation and Development (OECD), around the idea of a 'performance-orientated' public sector, with a focus on 'results, efficiency and effectiveness', and with a bias towards a strengthening of the 'strategic capacities of the centre' at the expense of local units, 'which possess operational autonomy but only within firm national guidelines' (Taylor et al 1997: 81). Following this model, New Labour has retained the agencies of Conservative centralisation and added others of its own making: the school inspection agency OFSTED, the Teacher Training Agency, the Standards and Effectiveness Unit at the Department for Education and Skills, and the Qualifications and Curriculum Authority are complemented by major conjunctural initiatives – notably the Literacy and Numeracy Strategies – which are nationally directed and locally pervasive.

Via such bodies, New Labour has installed a regulatory system aimed to ensure high average levels of attainment within a pattern of schooling marked by increasing diversity of provision. In this climate schools have perforce developed management regimes that can achieve the targets required of them by government and its regulatory agencies. These regimes have produced some immediate successes: primary school leavers achieve ever-higher standards of literacy and numeracy, as measured by the national testing system; 16+ examination results continue to improve (DfEE 2001: 13). More widely, because they have been much more attentive to the detail of educational process than any previous government, they have transformed the lives of learners and teachers. They link the micro-world of classroom interactions to macro-level objectives of standards and achievement and in so doing create new roles for old 'partners' – not least for teachers.

Teachers are ambivalently placed in this process of change. They are operationally central but strategically marginal; they have become accustomed to innovation, and have acquired, through their participation in the drive to raise standards, new kinds of skill. Yet in terms of the management of the school they are thoroughly subordinate. Their involvement in change proceeds not along the classic avenues of teacher professionalism – representative pressure or classroom autonomy – but rather through a variety of organisations, projects and procedures which are designed to secure by means of directive and incentive their incorporation within a government framework of priorities. The National College for School Leadership is intended to create a cadre of heads and deputies capable of raising standards of performance and of promoting the new kinds of co-operation, and new practices of teaching and learning, that can make this possible. The General Teaching Council has been designed by government, in a style similar to inter-war Italian corporatism, to 'represent' the interests of teachers, and simultaneously to act as a transmission belt for the policies of government. At the same time, a nationally-directed programme of 'Continuing Professional Development' connects the in-service education of teachers to national priorities, while performance-related pay provides another link between the work of classrooms and the concerns of government; and a clutch of government and government-instigated initiatives – 'Best Practice Research Scholarships', 'Teacher of the Year' ceremonies – create new forms of recognition.

BUSINESS

A further strand that runs through these dense networks of change is constituted by private 'edubusiness'. In contrast to much of the post-1944 period, in which private sector involvement in education was mostly limited to the 'independent' sector, it is now extensively entwined with state schooling itself: the managerial-regulatory bloc which drives change comprises both 'public' and 'private' elements. Before 1997, public/private sector partnerships had already become a feature of the institutional landscape, as 'mixed economies' of welfare were created (Butcher 1995). New Labour took up and amplified these initiatives. Education Action Zones, launched in 1998, were presented as 'a new crusade uniting businesses, schools, local authorities and parents to modernise education in areas of social deprivation' (DfEE 1998). Transnational companies – Shell, for instance, and various ICT firms – were recruited, with some difficulty and no great effect, to support a cautious programme of locally-based innovation, within DfEE guidelines.

From 2000, this aspect of 'partnership' was less in evidence. Parts of the private sector had an interest in the development of e-learning, and the construction industry benefited from the Private Finance Initiative, which subsidised it to build schools and lease them back to local authorities (Whitfield 1999). But these issues apart, big business was not keen to become directly involved in state education, and later initiatives relied less on reluctant transnationals than on the small but growing edubusiness sector. Private educational companies won contracts to run failing LEAs, and New Labour sought business sponsorship for 'City Academies', in which the private sector would play a central managerial role. The government Green Paper of 2001 envisaged more extended private involvement: companies would be encouraged to take over failing – or even successful – schools (DfEE 2001). Hatcher (2002) calls this a process of 'exogenous marketization' – education-for-profit companies entering the school system. He notes that the Education Bill of 2002 takes the process further: it seeks to empower school governing bodies to invest in or themselves form companies that can provide services and facilities to other schools. This, Hatcher suggests, is a significant move towards a marketisation that is 'endogenous', driven by the entrepreneurial activity of schools themselves. As Stephen Ball noted of the reforms of the 1990s, the importance of these changes lies in the ethical as well as the economic privatisation which they effect (Ball 1998). Private companies inspect schools, broker the services of supply teachers, organise in-service training, and evaluate the success of government initiatives. At the same time, the spread of practices such as 'Best Value', in which the provision of local authority services is bench-marked against criteria of efficiency and value derived from private-sector practice, means that the public-private distinction is in important senses erased. New Labour argues that in this mixed economy the 'public interest' will be secured by government-specified protocols and outcome targets. But as we shall see this suggestion that the 'public interest' can be defined and guarded from a central point – rather than developed through a process in which local experiment, political and cultural diversity, and professional practice all have a part – creates important problems for the New Labour revolution.

HISTORIES AND FUTURES

Gramsci suggested that part of the impact of passive revolution lay in its ability to 'create a period of expectation and hope'. In this area,

where discursive productivity and the 'busyness' of policy are important in sustaining a sense of change, New Labour has been especially
active. Discursively, this is a copious government, ever-willing to
explain its own historical significance in relation to the failures of the
past and to celebrate the futures it is creating.

New Labour demarcates itself from its social-democratic predecessors along several fronts. The 2001 Green Paper begins with an
overview of the post-war period. For some historians, notably Eric
Hobsbawm (1994), these were the 'golden years' that post-1976 were
swept away. New Labour does not share this view. The governments of
Attlee and Wilson presided over a largely 'unskilled' working population that had possessed 'jobs for life' in local industries (2001:4). In the
supposedly static society of 1944-76 there was no strong demand for
certification and there was a 'general acceptance that only a minority
would reach the age of 16 with significant formal skills and qualifications' (ibid). Comprehensive reform had not done enough to challenge
this acceptance, and by setting 'social' as opposed to 'economic' goals
– emphasising inclusion at the expense of standards – it had contributed
to stasis. It had failed to differentiate among students, and to 'link
different provision to individual attitudes and abilities' (2001:5).

This is the 'organic' element, as it were, in Labour's explanation of
the problems of the past: an undynamic economy produces a school
system in its own image. But alongside it are accusations about a different kind of failure. New Labour sees the teaching force and the
educationalists who provided teachers with their pre-1979 rationale as
what could be termed an 'intellectual bloc', that shared a common
material position, and worked with a common understanding of the
educational talents and needs of the mass of the student population.
Again adapting Gramsci, and looking through New Labour eyes, we
could term this bloc a 'traditional' one: the post-war welfare state
created teachers in their hundreds of thousands, managed them only
lightly, allowed them to develop associational cultures both radical and
inertial, and set them to work in a system of low-level mass schooling.
The bloc's coherence was assured by a government disposition that
New Labour has caustically summarised as 'support without pressure':
schooling increased its share of national resources; teachers were seen
as the central source of educational change; government kept its
distance from the working of the system, and tolerated low levels of
attainment. Discursively, the bloc was shaped by two kinds of orientation: low expectations of students on the part of some teachers
co-existed with a world-view held by others in 'which schools made no
difference and were essentially agents of social control' (Barber 1998a).

New Labour tells a different story about Conservatism.
Conservatism lacked social concern and under-estimated the potential
of active government. But it still accomplished much necessary,
destructive work. The reforms of the 1980s obliterated the old educa-

tion system and 'dismantled collective power' – Blair refers appreciatively to this process as 'picking out weeds' (Blair 1996: 216). New Labour's first major legislation – the 1998 School Standards and Frameworks Act – took as its starting point the inviolability of much Conservative law-making: it retained testing, league tables, the national curriculum and local management of schools. Beyond these specific agreements, there are larger debts: New Labour's interests in differentiation and specialisation perpetuate Conservative themes; its attempts to remake the teaching force likewise have Conservative antecedents. It has also inherited an appreciation of the capacities of the private sector. In 1998, Labour's leading education adviser Michael Barber told educationalists that they should learn from the experience of 'successful companies' which were 'uniquely capable of managing change and innovation' (1998b). Since then New Labour has complemented its stress on the virtues of active government, freed from the entanglements and alliances of Labour's past, with a tendency to present 'business' as a source of creativity and renewal in education (DCMS/DfEE 1999).

But Conservatism, in this account, had one major failing: it did not 'plant new seeds' (Blair 1996: 217). Limited both by its own traditionalism and by the need to focus on immediate political conflicts, it could not establish a system responsive to the complexities of social, cultural and economic change. It relied too much on the market to promote dynamic leadership. It overlooked the importance of social inclusion. It failed to develop ways of connecting desirable policy outcomes to detailed, classroom-level processes of change. New Labour insists that it has, in contrast, met these challenges and in doing so has synthesised the right's programme of diversity with the left's aspirations to social justice. Its policy elite stresses the 'fusions' at the heart of its educational programme, that resolve the political conflicts and discursive polarisations which have afflicted educational change. Thus, for Michael Barber, 'pressure' on teachers can be fused with 'support', 'innovation' with organisational stability and, most important of all, 'equity' with 'diversity' (Barber and Phillips 2000); and if these 'apparent opposites' can be made to work in concert, then New Labour, reconciling the aspirations of left and right, will have rescued English education.

SHAPES AND TENSIONS

Gramsci writes that the remaking of societies and institutions that passive revolution effects is brought about by the 'cautious and moderate' work of government, and not by 'popular intervention' (105). Elaborating Gramsci, we might say that the reforms it creates always possess something of an exclusive character. Accomplished in the name of progress and the common good, they operate in practice to distribute agency and to achieve social outcomes in ways that favour only a limited range of social interests. In the process, they perpetuate old tensions and give rise to newer ones.

From this viewpoint, several features of New Labour schooling stand out. First, there is its highly differentiated character, in which the model of the inclusive comprehensive school has no part. What distinguishes the English secondary system from those of Wales, Scotland, Ireland and many countries in continental Europe is an institutionalised diversity of provision, around which differences in status, material resources and educational outcomes have solidified (Croxford 2001; Green 1990). Old Labour to some extent challenged this system, especially through comprehensive reform. But New Labour has created a new institutional settlement, and a symbolic order of schooling, in which 'ability', 'aptitude' and hierarchy are unchallenged principles. The elements of this settlement are many: the preservation of 'independent' schools and grammar schools; the status distinction between 'foundation' and 'community' schools; the strengthening of 'faith-based' education; and most recently the envisaged expansion of specialist secondary schools – which are able to select 10 per cent of their students on the basis of 'aptitude', and enjoy higher levels of funding (DfEE 2001). Within these separate institutions, government 'wants teachers to consider express sets, fast-tracking and more early entry to GCSE and advanced qualifications'. New Labour calls all this 'moving beyond old arguments to create a system appropriate for the 21st century ... built around the needs and aspirations of individual pupils and their families' (DfEE 2001: 5, 15); in Gramsci's terms, its mixing of energetic reform with a logic of divisiveness would exemplify a project of revolution-restoration which would leave egalitarian needs unsatisfied.

Second, there is the emphasis on 'inclusion', a term which counterbalances the system's divisive logic with a variety of programmes. In some of them, especially those connected with 'special needs', there is a strong and welcome emphasis on the human rights of pupils whom schools have traditionally excluded (Dyson and Slee 2001). 'Inclusion' in this case is motivated on grounds of equality – however much it may be inhibited by lack of resources or by market pressures that place a premium on schools admitting the academically 'able'. But 'inclusion' does not necessarily imply 'equality' (Levitas 1998). It is premised on an acceptance of the market as a basis for social organisation, and its intention is to reintegrate the market's casualties into productive and cohesive forms of social life. It is in this light that many New Labour initiatives, targeted at the inner cities, should be seen. They do not address the patterns of advantage and disadvantage that underlie educational failure; and they tend to identify the sources of failure in the cultures of the communities that are targetted by inclusion schemes (Whitty 2001). When Education Secretary Blunkett declared that 'we need parents who are prepared to take responsibility for supporting their children's education and we need a culture which values education and demands the best', he revealed much about the values of government (Blunkett, cited in Gewirtz 2001). His later call for migrants to observe 'norms of acceptability' indicated more precisely the conflict in which government was engaged with delinquent cultures – without giving any sense that this was a conflict government could win (Blunkett 2001).

The third tension lies in the system's unsustainable mix of managerialism and creativity. New Labour's system is self-consciously an innovative one, ever in search of new institutional forms and new curricula that can achieve its multiple aims – it is under Labour, after all, that 'creativity' has re-emerged as a educational principle (Buckingham & Jones 2001). But innovation is of both a pressured and a shadowed kind: pressured by New Labour's insistence that schooling has rapidly to create, with levels of spending still less in 1999 than the OECD average, a much higher level of human capital (OECD 2001); and shadowed by New Labour's anxiety that a system not tightly managed will see old problems – teacher influence, a more radical and unfocused climate of ideas – recur.

The new managerial emphasis discounts unofficial forms of school culture and knowledge as at best misguided, at worst obstructive. In an earlier period, 'culture' designated the space where the formal curriculum and procedures of the school encountered and to varying extents negotiated with the cultures of students; the work of teachers from this point of view had an essentially cultural character, and to a significant – albeit minority – extent drew from the knowledge and identities created by social movements. This has been replaced by an international set of norms that focuses on the improvement of organisational culture without reference to a wider perspective, or to the possibility of diversity. If 'creativity' is based on an emerging notion of the school as a space in which new social needs can be flexibly explored, and the gulf between social and economic life and education bridged over, then managerialism expresses a very different attitude to social change, based on a conception of the school as a force that through an act of will can repair a multi-faceted social crisis.

Finally, there is the question of pressure. For New Labour, each phase of education, from nurseries to adult reskilling, is seen in terms of learners' continuous redevelopment of themselves in terms of the 'knowledges, competences and motivation' required by technological and occupational change, and audited by a battery of tests, exams and personal portfolios. The home – through personal computers, electronic learning and the purchase on a massive scale of study guides and testing booklets – becomes itself a site of formal learning. For teachers, there exists a similar network of pressures – inspection, performance-related pay, the operationalisation of constant change – that has greatly decreased the space for classroom autonomy.

It is at this final point that the problems of the system are becoming most evident. Chronic problems of recruitment and retention are signs of a wider malaise in which questions of morale, fatigue, under-investment and lost autonomy are all present. As New Labour's policy-makers know, their 'modernisation' of schooling depends upon the commitment of teachers. The withholding of such commitment has not reached the spectacular heights attained at some points in the Conservative years, and teacher trade unionism is still weak, but the extent of teachers' involvement in reform is nonetheless limited. There is little support among teachers for central aspects of the government's programme – especially privatisation – and their participation in projects of change is heavily dependent upon the directives and incentives of an over-managed system. According to two New Labour advocates, 'sometimes it is necessary to ... consciously challenge the prevailing culture ... and to have the courage to sustain the challenge until beliefs shift ... The driving force at this critical juncture is leadership' (Barber and Phillips 2000). But as Gramsci knew, a project of leadership, pursued without regard either to a proportionate understanding of the depth of the problems it confronts, or to securing the consent of the governed, is fraught with difficulty. In this sense, the pressured, de-autonomised, under-resourced work of teachers expresses not just an occupational situation. A system that is both hierarchical and pressured develops many tensions, some of which display themselves at the level of politics, others as pathology. It seems reasonable to predict developing conflict at both levels – perhaps through action against a testing regime that is increasingly seen to contribute both to individual stress and to patterns of differentiation and inequality.

What is more difficult to discern is the articulation of such conflicts with the wider tensions of New Labour's education system. It is a divided system, which continues to make universal promises. It is a public system, but one that seeks justification in its ability to service what are ultimately private interests, and which is edging ever closer to full partnership with profit-orientated forces. In terms of pedagogy and curriculum it is less tolerant and encouraging of difference than some of the systems that have preceded it. Finally, it is not one system but four, and though New Labour has consistently presented a diagnosis of English problems as if it contained the key to the future of British schooling systems, these claims do not lessen the exposure of the English system to damaging comparisons with Edinburgh, Belfast and Cardiff, where hostility towards teachers and enthusiasms for formal processes of differentiation are much less in vogue. There are ample grounds in all of this for thinking that, despite all its drive and ingenuity, New Labour's programme will encounter the unyielding questions of social division that no project of passive revolution has yet been able to move away.

REFERENCES

Ball, S.J. (1997), 'Markets, Equity and Values in Education', in R. Pring and G. Walford (eds), *Affirming the Comprehensive Ideal*, London: Falmer.

Barber, M. (1998a), 'Dark Side of the Moon', in K. Myers and L. Stoll (eds), *No Quick Fixes*.

Barber, M. (1998b), *The Guardian* North of England Conference, 7 January.

Barber, M. & Phillips, V. (2000), 'How to Unleash Irreversible Change', Paper to conference of Directors of Education Action Zones, March.

Bernstein, B. (1971), *Class, Codes and Control: Volume 1*, London: Routledge and Kegan Paul.

Blair, T. (1995), *New Statesman*, 29 September.

Blunkett, D. (2001), 'Blunkett in Race Row over Culture tests', *The Guardian*, 10 December.

Buckingham. D., and Jones, K. (2001), 'New Labour's Cultural Turn', *Journal of Education Policy*, 16.1.

Butcher, T. (1995), *Delivering Welfare: the governance of the social services in the 1990s*, Buckingham: Open University Press.

Croxford, L. (2000), *Inequality in attainment at 16: a home international comparison*, Centre for Educational Sociology, University of Edinburgh.

Centre for Contemporary Cultural Studies (1981), *Unpopular Education*, London: Hutchinson.

Department for Culture, Media and Sport & Department for Education and Employment (1999), *All our Futures: report of the National Advisory Committee on Creative and Cultural Education*, London DCMS/DfEE.

'Newsom Report' (1963), *Half our Future: a report for the Central Advisory Council for Education (England)*, London: HMSO.

DfEE (1998), *Meet the Challenge: Education Action Zones*, London: DfEE.

DfEE (2001), *Schools Building on Success* (Green Paper), London: The Stationery Office.

Dyson, A. & Slee, R. (2001), 'Special Needs Education from Warnock to Salamanca: the triumph of liberalism?', in R. Phillips and J. Furlong (eds), *Education Reform and the State: twenty-five years of politics, policy and practice*, London: Routledge.

Gramsci, A. (1971), *Selections from the Prison Notebooks*, translated and edited by Q. Hoare and G. Nowell-Smith, London: Lawrence & Wishart.

Green, A. (1990), *Education and State Formation*, London: Hutchinson.

Hatcher, R. (2001), 'Getting Down to Business: schooling in the globalised economy', in *Education and Social Justice*, 3.2, pp39-50.

Hatcher, R. (2002), 'The Education Bill: a charter for marketisation', *Socialist Teacher 69*, April.

Hobsbawm, E. (1994), *Age of Extremes: the short twentieth century 1914-1991*, London: Michael Joseph.

Halsey, A. et al (1972), *Educational Priority: EPA problems and priorities* (Volume 1), London: HMSO.

Jones, K. (2002), *Education in Britain 1944 to the Present*, Cambridge: Polity Press.

Jones, K. and Bird, K. (2000), *Partnership as Strategy: public-private relations in education action zones,* British Educational Research Journal 24 (4), pp491-506.

Levitas, R. (1998), *The Inclusive Society? Social Exclusion and New Labour*, London: Macmillan.

Lindblad, S. (2001), 'Educating by Numbers: on international statistics and policy-making' (Paper for the Keele Conference on Travelling Policy/Local Spaces). www.keele.ac.uk/depts/ed/educat/cPaper/McKeown.pdf

OECD (2001), *Education at a Glance* Paris: OECD.

Simon, B. (1991), *Education and the Social Order*, London: Lawrence & Wishart.

Taylor, S., Rizvi, F., Lingard, B. and Henry, M. (1997), *Educational Policy and the Politics of Change*, London: Routledge.

Whitfield, D. (1999), 'Private Finance Initiative: the commodification and privatisation of education', *Education and Social Justice* 1.1 pp.2-13.

Willis, P. (1977), *Learning to Labour: how working-class kids get working-class jobs*, London: Saxon House.

2. Governing in the modern world?

John Clarke and Janet Newman

Modernity is a New Labour hallmark. Being modern both defines the New Labour project and is its shield against criticism. In its first term of office, modernity was a central thread of New Labour's approach to governing – it defined the project of realigning state and society in new ways in order to enable Britain to 'catch up' with modernity and to take its place in a new global order. Our aim here is to explore the ways in which New Labour has sought to realign the relationships between the state and society in pursuit of 'living in the modern world' (Miliband, 2000). The project of modernisation (or 'neo-modernisation', as Johnson and Steinberg argue, in chapter 15 of this volume) has aimed to create a system and process of government adapted to the demands and expectations of a modern society and a modern people:

> My passion is to continue the modernisation of Britain, in favour of hard-working families, so that all of our children, wherever they live, whatever their background, have an equal chance to benefit from the opportunities our country has to offer and to share in its wealth ... It is as if a glass ceiling has stopped us fulfilling our potential. In the 21st century, we have the opportunity to break through that glass ceiling because our historic strengths match the demands of the modern world (Tony Blair, in Labour Party, 2001, p3).

New Labour – and modernisation – has been both a political project and a process of electoral calculation. Both of these are dynamic, rather than static, so it is hardly surprising that the visibility, content and strategies of modernisation have shifted considerably. The fortunes of modernisation can be traced in a number of ways. For example, modernisation evolved from 'sticking to Conservative spending pledges' (1997) to 'invest and reform' in the NHS (2002). It is reflected in the shifting New Labour representations of public service staff (angels and heroes, or blockers and forces of conservatism). It is embodied in the recurring dependence (despite disappointments) on major IT initiatives and public-private partnerships as the motors of reform.

We view the project of modernisation as articulated around major fault lines in Labour's political project – a set of contradictions that the project aimed to manage and reconcile, but which nevertheless recurrently disrupts the process of reform. These fault lines have formed around the contradictions between Labour's ideal of building a consensual, inclusive society (addressing the divisions, conflicts and inequalities produced and deepened by the policies of Conservative governments) and its determination to continue the agenda of neo-liberal economic reform based on the presumed requirements of a global economy. Other, related, fault lines have surfaced in Labour's attempt to reform the state, its focus on reshaping the processes of governance, and its approach to transforming the social in the images of citizenship and community that informed its view of a 'modern' nation.

These issues have been explored in a number of studies of Labour's route to power and performance in government (e.g., Driver and Martell, 1998; Dwyer, 2000; Fairclough, 2000; Newman, 2001; Levitas, 1998; Lister, 1998, 2001). Here we treat modernisation as a practical project: producing a series of reforms of the economy, the state, public service organisation, welfare policy and practice, and of social/community relationships. We also view it as a narrative form that gives coherence to a profoundly uneven and often contradictory series of interventions and initiatives by Labour (see the fuller discussion in Epstein, Johnson and Steinberg, this volume). As a narrative, modernisation clothed the actions of government with a sense of movement, progress and purpose, overcoming the mistakes and outdated forms inherited from the past (Clarke and Newman, 1997). It has also provided a legitimating framework for specific changes. To be 'un-modern' is an uncomfortable place to be: critics have been dismissed as 'old thinking' or the 'forces of conservatism'. Modernisation has defined a specific politico-cultural project, concerned not only with reforming the state, but with installing a modern society through remaking state-society relationships and inculcating new modes of citizenship. New Labour's political project has articulated new forms of governing with an imagery of modernity that has identified the combination of globalisation, work and consumerism as the elementary forms of a 'modern' nation.

MODERN GOVERNANCE: REMAKING THE STATE

New Labour's programme has aimed to remake the relationships and processes of governance in the image of a 'modern' state (Cabinet Office, 1999a). Devolution in Scotland, Wales and Northern Ireland (albeit in very different constitutional forms), experiments in regional governance, and attempts to remake local government (such as directly elected mayors), all suggest a significant shift in architecture, powers and processes of the nation state. New Labour has pursued a commitment to reduce or dissolve the boundaries between public and private sectors (most notably through public-private partnerships), disentangling

Labour from its historic association with statism and collectivism. At the same time, their emphasis on public service reform has been under-pinned by a marked increase in the centralisation of power, enacted through the plethora of goals, targets and standards, coupled with an unprecedented expansion of audit and inspection regimes. The relation-ship between state and people was to be revived through a commitment to public consultation and participation. The style of policy-making has also been reformed – albeit only at the margins – around the imperatives to become joined up, holistic, problem solving and inclusive (Cabinet Office, 1999b). Above all, the reforms have been underpinned by an intensely managerial style and form of governance – one based on quasi-scientific pragmatism, legitimated by a philosophy of 'what counts is what works' (Davies, Nutley and Smith, eds, 2000). The belief that it is possible to discover, once and for all, 'what works' in public policy has marked a new height in the valorisation of scientific rationalism as the basis for public decision-making. It has also registered the manageriali-sation of politics itself (Clarke, Gewirtz and McLaughlin, eds, 2000; Muncie, 2002; Newman 2001a).

This claimed pragmatism has masked deep contradictions in Labour's approach to governance. Modernisation is not a coherent, unified project. It has deployed conflicting models of governance, overlaid on each other in complex configurations. Some have empha-sised a tightening of top down control, others a more collaborative, consensual style of governance. Some have reflected a focus on confor-mity to externally specified standards; others have stressed the need for innovation and entrepreneurship. Some have been based on a rational, managerial form of knowledge and power, others on a partial move towards participative democracy. Each model of governance rests on a distinctive set of assumptions about power and authority, a view of the 'proper' relationship between government and the governed, and a set of images of how change can best be brought about. Each also estab-lishes different claims to legitimacy. For example, there have been lines of tension between Labour's goals of modernising mainstream services – especially hospitals and schools – and those relating to the desirabil-ity of 'joining up' government to co-ordinate long term policy approaches to issues such as social exclusion, child poverty, ill health. The overlaying of different models has produced deep contradictions within the modernisation programme that impact on practitioners charged with delivering Labour's agenda (Newman, 2001, 2002).

The project of modernising the state and public services has tried to reconcile conflicting pressures. One tension emerged where Labour's commitment to devolution and the decentralisation of power ran up against its dependency on highly centralising forms of political management. This has been visible in New Labour's ambivalent approach to running the party, the government and the public services (see also Tincknell, this volume). A second has been produced by the disjuncture between Labour's emphasis on consensual governance and social inclusion on the one hand, and the sharpening of conflicts around who is to be included as citizens and the intensification of social divisions on the other. The focus on citizen involvement through new technologies of participation has been accompanied by new strategies for regulating citizens, policing non-citizens and new apparatuses for managing the distinction between the two groups. The presentation of modern politics as post-ideological and pragmatic has been central to New Labour's attempt to build a new political settlement, but it has been regularly interrupted by social, cultural and, more occasionally, political challenges to New Labour's vision of a consensual unity.

There is an ambivalent relationship between the project of modernising governance and New Labour's conception of a modern society. New Labour has represented the modernisation of governance as bringing the institutions, relationships and processes of governing into alignment with a society that is already 'modern'. This society has undergone changes (for example, in working patterns, gender roles and the experience of consumerism) that have required government to 'catch up'. This pressure for change has been embodied in the figure of the 'sceptical citizen-consumer' who expects an 'active, enabling welfare state' (Department of Social Security, 1998). However, the New Labour project has extended beyond the modernisation of the apparatuses of government to the production of a particular version of social modernity. Modernisation has also meant an attempt to enforce a (relatively) coherent direction in the face of the diverse forces, trends and trajectories that create divergent possibilities of being modern.

This relationship between state and society has been one of the most important and difficult issues for contemporary social and political analysis. Many approaches to new forms of governance have addressed the withdrawal, rolling back or hollowing out of the state as processes of governing and co-ordinating spread beyond the institutional confines of the state into (civil) society (see, for example, Kooiman, 1993; Pierre, 2000; Pierre and Peters, 2000; Rhodes, 1997). Alternatively, Foucauldian-based approaches to changing governmentalities have emphasised the new forms of subjection that have been developed in post-welfarist, neo-liberal governing strategies (see, for example, Dean, 1999; Rose, 1999; and Kingfisher, forthcoming, for a comparative analysis for neo-liberal approaches to welfare 'reform'). Our analysis here differs from these two views. We want to emphasise rather more the particular complexity of political formations and strategies, and we want to see the reforms of governance as attempts to remake the state-society boundaries and the relations of power that flow across them. Elsewhere, we have argued that it may be better to view state power as being dispersed through new relationships within civil society, rather than being diminished or surrendered (Clarke and Newman, 1997; Newman, 2001). In the process, new social agents are sutured into positions of power, effectivity and dependency.

A MODERN SOCIETY: REMAKING COMMUNITIES

New Labour's political success has owed much to its promised difference from the period of neo-liberal Conservative rule. A core
difference has been the perception that there is, after all, such a 'thing
as society' and that the 'public' is a meaningful term to use in thinking
about how social life might be organised and ordered. To be sure, these
have been very limited claims – no return to an 'older' socialism or even
social democracy was ever intended (indeed, Blair once famously
inserted a careful hyphen into the word 'social-ism' to indicate New
Labour's philosophical grip on the existence of social interrelation-
ships). Nevertheless, this encounter with the social/public has
recognised residual and emergent cultural and political commitments
to the social as a site of struggle, contestation and possibility.

New Labour may have consistently tried to manage expectations
downwards, but the social/public has remained a persistent focus for
social and cultural forces engaged in attempts to redress inequalities,
assert identities, demand recognition and redress. These concerns have
ranged from lesbian and gay challenges to institutional discrimination,
through disability activism to demands for an expansively multi-cultural
view of the social, alongside the pressure to reduce the inequalities generated by neo-liberalism. These claims on the social (and in the name of the
social) have formed a vital part of the political landscape that New Labour
has had to negotiate (see also Clarke, 1999, 2001; Clarke and Newman,
1997, 1998; see also Epstein, Johnson and Steinberg, this volume).

New Labour's response to this rich variety of claims has been a
commitment to social inclusion in the conception of a nation of
'communities' of place and identity arranged in a non-antagonistic and
consensual social order (Byrne, 1999; Levitas, 1998). New Labour's
commitment to a modern society that is inclusive has produced a new,
and complex, architecture of exclusions. These have not been articulated as simple social categories – rather they have been coded as
elements of a *moral* order. Given that New Labour had created the
conditions of inclusions, those who have remained outside in some
way are, by definition, there either by choice or as a result of their own
failings – they are 'irresponsible' in some sense. A gallery of 'self-
excluding' groups has been constructed – dysfunctional families,
'persistently delinquent' children, school truants, work-avoiders and
welfare cheats, bad neighbours, aggressive beggars and so on (see also
Mac an Ghaill and Haywood, this volume, on 'absent fathers'). What
these groups have in common is their wilful failure to take up the
opportunity to join in as members of a decent and civilised society.
They have failed the 'responsibility' test, preferring to be disorderly
and disruptive – when they could be like the rest of 'us'. Gail Lewis
(2000) has written of how the unequal patterns of school exclusion
affecting young black people were transmuted into the results of
moral/cultural deficits and failings in black communities. Equivalent

moral codings have been put to work around asylum and migration, where, as Solomos and Schuster (this volume) argue, the business of government is to test for 'genuineness'. Those lucky enough to be stamped as authentic may eventually enter the ranks of the Included. This distinction (viewed as independent of racial and ethnic character- isation) has sustained the government's consistent refusal to see any connections between racism and the exclusionary policies, practices and rhetorics directed at asylum-seekers and migrants. What is striking about the distinctions between the included and excluded is how these moral codings found their way into government policies and appara- tuses for managing the social order. For example, the 'New Deal' and its requirements for the unemployed; curfews; parental responsibility orders and 'contracts'; school evaluations of parental 'quality'; the calculation of health risks and 'worth'; and the constantly innovative approaches to regulating migration and asylum have all been sites where such moral categorisation has been put into practice.

Much of New Labour's modern-ness has been founded on the assumption that neo-liberal globalisation defines the conditions of possi- bility. This has generated the conceptions of change and adaptation at the heart of its modernisations. The national economy had been transformed by its relationship to a global economy, and citizens are being trans- formed by their relationships to working in this new context. Most of New Labour's language about change has expressed the thrill of trans- formation and has equated change with progress (for example, in changed gender roles, or overcoming 'outdated' attitudes that disadvan- taged some groups unfairly). At critical points, however, the language of change has been supplanted by the language of strain – progressive modernisation is displaced by a conservative anxiety about morality, authority and their erosion (Clarke and Newman, 1998). The critical site of this concern has been the troubled world of the Family. New Labour has remained strangely nostalgic for the communitarian mythology of autonomous (and hard-working) families, producing moral order and bound together in self-regulating communities. Concern that the Family is not what it used to be has linked a range of strategies and policies – from the employment policy (directed at 'hard working families') to social inclusion (trying to ensure that families are 'hard working'). This articulation of work and the family in New Labour has also enabled 'social' policy to be increasingly integrated with 'economic' policy (and governed through the Treasury). The tax system (for example, in work- ing family tax credits) has become as important as the benefit system for New Labour's construction of a modern society centred on the 'hard working family' (Levitas, 2001; Lister, 2001).

New Labour has known there are social and political risks involved in 'doing morality'. As a consequence, it has attempted to reconcile its enthusiasm for The Family with a grudging tolerance for other forms of household (see also Weeks and Epstein, Johnson and Steinberg, this volume). The effort to avoid 'moralising' has meant an increasing use of the 'what counts is what works' formula for policy-making and presentation – and what works, of course, is the (normal) Family. In the context of education policy, Sharon Gewirtz (2001) has described the view of parents as educational consumers as a process of 'cloning the Blairs'. As with many other aspects of being modern, it appears that this 'works' so well as a way of life, it is difficult to imagine anyone choosing to live differently. What New Labour has championed is a conception of modern society marked by a 'thin' multi-culturalism – where differences may be tolerated, or even celebrated, so long as they are differences that *don't* make a difference.

Nevertheless, New Labour's quest for a modern society has been consistently interrupted by challenges about who the 'we' of the nation are and who we might become. This reflects the consistently 'unsettled' character of the social settlement in Britain (Clarke and Newman, 1997; Clarke, 1999; Hughes and Lewis, 1998), in which contending identities are evoked by divergent trends in the composition of Britain and its changing contexts. The possible identities of Britain, and British-ness, are traversed by a range of trajectories, including:

- changing political formations and identifications in the context of devolution
- the shifting attachments to Europe and the 'special relationship' with the US
- changing gender roles, behaviours, attitudes and identities with unstable relationships to shifting practices of household and family formation
- unsettled borders and boundaries, themselves subject to differential relaxation and intensification in an increasingly migratory world
- shifting and highly charged conceptions of the intersection of Nation and Race, where racialised formations of Englishness/Britishness-as-Whiteness continue to resist attempts to construct the modern as multi-cultural.

In this context, it is not surprising that 'citizenship' has emerged as one of the defining sites of social and political conflict for New Labour.

A MODERN NATION: REMAKING CITIZENSHIP
Citizenship has been at the centre of this attempted realignment of state and society – it is the status that articulates the relationships between nation/people, the state and welfare. New Labour has consistently tried to remake the figure of the citizen – emphasising more active, consumerist, modes of relationship to public services; promoting a more independent (family centred) approach to self-provisioning; and emphasising 'responsibilities, not rights' as the keystone of a civil society. Two particular aspects of this remaking of citizenship stand out in New Labour discourse, policy and practice: one is the valorisation of Work; the other is the problematic of nationality and citizenship.

As many commentators have argued New Labour has celebrated Work as the central social, political, economic and personal task (see, inter alia, Levitas, 1998 and 2001; Lister, 1998, 2001 and 2002). It is (waged) work that 'inserts' people into the social; that attaches them to citizenship rights; that reduces public spending; that gives their lives a sense of value and purpose; that provides their children with role models; and, not least, ensures the happy congruence of the national and global economy. The 2001 Manifesto reasserted this view of work's transformative powers: 'Employment's not just the foundation of an affordable welfare state, it is the best anti-poverty, anti-crime and pro-family policy yet invented' (Labour Party, 2001: 24). Work has been the central link between economic and social policies in both New Labour governments – from taxation to social security; whether addressing concerns about lone mothers or laddish louts. Its real centrality was registered in the growing role played by the Treasury (and the tax system) in 'incentivising' desirable behaviour (being employed). But it was symbolically announced in the renaming of the Department of Social Security as the Department of Work and Pensions.

This modern conception of work has been a resolutely 'equal opportunity' view, accepting (and reinforcing) patterns of gender change that have undercut the older equivalence between male bread-winning and waged work. New Labour has enthusiastically endorsed the critiques of the white, male, able-bodied imagery of the Worker, insisting that everyone should be entitled to work. Indeed, they have insisted that everyone who can should, and possibly must, work. At this point, it becomes possible to see how other possibilities are consistently excluded and repressed. Not-working (and the 'dependency' it is believed to create) is a stigmatised condition, not to be encouraged by government action, agencies or benefits (Williams, 2001). In the process, the whole repertoire of ways in which people might not be engaged in waged work (including voluntary activity, caring labour as well as the effects of forms of exclusion and discrimination) are continually wished away.

This 'opening up' of the right to work (and the responsibility to work) has fit with New Labour's 'modern' view of gender (and disability). But it has also left unchallenged the distinction between public and private realms – where only paid work in the public realm was valorised. In the process, the apparently infinite flexibility of women's capacity for labour has been subjected to new demands, as pressures to be 'economically active' have mounted while leaving the distribution and volume of domestic responsibilities untouched. As we have argued elsewhere the reduction of public provision and public funding for a range of welfare benefits and services during the 1980s and 1990s transferred financial and labour costs to the (uncalculated) private realm (Clarke and Newman, 1997, chapter 7). From reduced benefit values to substitute labour in relation to heath care and education, the private realm (and mainly female work within it) 'bridged the gap' left by public withdrawal. Women's position on this shifting public-private boundary was compounded by their changing patterns of work (waged and unwaged) in public services and the voluntary sector. Work intensification has been common to both sectors, while declining public sector employment (and worsening conditions of service) has affected many female dominated occupations (teaching, nursing and care work, for example).

At the same time, the pursuit of work as the point of connection between families and the national and global economies has produced a view of work centred on the 'flexibilities' of adaptation to employer demands. Borrowing from the US, 'welfare to work' overshadowed the changing relationships between state and citizen (Deacon, 2002; Peck, 2001). The 'New Deal' for the unemployed has been continuously extended (to new categories) and strengthened (in terms of the conditions and disciplines that can be brought to bear). The commitment to work was intensified in the proposals of StepUP (announced in April 2002, requiring 'job seekers' who passed through the New Deal without finding work to accept subsidised minimum wage jobs). In an echo of New Labour's pragmatic 'what counts is what works', we might suggest that for defining citizenship, 'who counts is who works' (Dwyer, 1998, 2000; Lister, 1998).

New Labour embarked on a systematic programme of realigning state-society relationships around the figure of the citizen. As we suggested above, a key element of this has been to reconstruct the character and conditions of citizenship – making the citizen independent, responsible and morally upright. But New Labour has also attempted to redraw access to citizenship and the relationships between citizenship, national membership and national identity. These efforts have been centrally addressed to processes of migration and asylum–seeking, but they have also given renewed salience to longer standing issues about 'modern societies' being multi-ethnic and multicultural (Hesse, 2001; Parekh, 2001; see also Solomos and Schuster, this volume). New Labour's position has shifted from a profound hostility to migrants and asylum seekers (who were viewed as reinforcing Britain's wisdom of keeping separate and strong border controls within the EU). A more differentiated view has developed which recognises the 'economic case' for useful and productive migrants in a global economy, but has sought to intensify the defences against the illegal, the non-genuine, the criminal and the fraudulent. The 2002 White Paper ('Secure Borders, Safe Haven') acknowledged economic virtue:

> Migrants bring new experiences and talents that can widen and enrich the knowledge base of the economy. Human skills and ambitions have become the building blocks of successful economies and the self-selection of migrants means that they are likely to bring valuable ideas, entrepreneurship, ambition and energy (Home Office, 2002: 11).

At the same time, it has argued for strengthened borders and for the more actively supported (enforced?) integration of 'new citizens' into the social and political culture:

> In an increasingly diverse world, it is vital that we strengthen both our sense of community belonging and the civic and political dimensions of British citizenship ... [Language teaching, education and examination for citizenship] ... will strengthen the ability of new citizens to participate in society and engage actively in our democracy. This will help people understand both their rights and their obligations as citizens of the UK, and strengthen the bonds of mutual understanding between people of diverse cultural backgrounds (Home Office, 2002: 11).

Despite the continual challenges from many groups and organisations, New Labour has always insisted that these were are issues of 'race'. They have refused the perception that the processes of immigration control and asylum are racialised and racialising or that they are connected with racialised differences, antagonisms and inequalities within Britain. The system of moral codings that we discussed above has been central to this understanding. Processes of border control have been about sifting the good migrant from the bad (the criminal, the irresponsible, the immoral, the feckless, the 'benefit tourist' and the non-genuine), and such categories are supposed to transcend racial/ethnic distinctions. This conception of 'well-managed' entry control and integrative processes for those allowed in echoed the classic British governmental formula for creating 'good race relations': controlled entry (not 'flooding' or 'swamping') is combined with a positive view of assimilation/integration (Hesse, 2001). Nevertheless, the conjunction of internal and external dynamics has continually reasserted the citizenship/multi-culturalism nexus as a critical one for politics and policy.

MODERNITY: MAKING THE BEST OF A BAD JOB, OR BETTER LATE THAN NEVER?

Modern society and modernised governance have implicated one another in New Labour's efforts to install a new political settlement. Modernised governance needs a modern society as a reference point for its legitimacy. A modern society, in turn, must have a modernised apparatus of governing to manage the contradictions and conflicts of alternative routes to becoming modern. The modernisation of governance has aimed to construct a new Public, with new roles, rights and responsibilities, and has engaged in new (consultative, participatory and legitimately active) relationships with the State. The modernisation of society has evoked a new People, at home in their hard-working families, attached to and active in their various (but non-antagonistic) communities, happy to work and consume enthusiastically – and preferably not too much trouble to government.[1]

New Labour's approach has been shaped by the problem of negotiating other conceptions of the modern that it has sought to repress or contain. The modern society so avidly sought by New Labour has encountered other imaginaries, other possibilities, other trajectories jostling for a place in the future. In particular, we would point to other possible ways of being 'European', 'global' and 'internationalist' that have had to be repressed or contained in New Labour's alignment of a modern Britain with the dominant US, neo-liberal tendency (see also Johnson, this volume). Equally, possibilities for pursuing a new equalities agenda with a commitment to a diverse society and reducing inequalities have been co-opted to a much shallower concern with social inclusion, centred on the imagery of a nation of hard working families. Even the modernisation of governance has avoided the transformative possibilities of a citizen-empowering Chartist republicanism in favour of a much more limited horizon. New Labour's attempt to make one modernity come true in practice has struggled to contain its own internal contradictions (not least its combinations of economic modernisation with social traditionalism). But it also has had to refute, repress or incorporate other potential modernities.

Nevertheless, the wish to transcend political and ideological conflict through a pragmatic, unifying and coherent commitment to modernisation has had limitations as a strategy. The modernised approach to delivering public services based on a 'what works' philosophy has claimed to move beyond old, outdated debates about whether public or private sector is best. But it could not resolve the need to take political decisions or to make judgements that would inevitably satisfy some 'stakeholders' more than others. New Labour's vision has been persistently interrupted by groups and issues that challenged the post-ideological imagery of governance based on rational, managerial forms of knowledge and power.

Modernisation, then, can be viewed as an attempt to close off possible alternative forms of 'being modern'. New Labour has attempted to enforce one configuration as the sole imaginable and desirable way of 'living in the modern world' (what Steinberg and Johnson, this volume, argue is the 'one-wayism' of the Third Way). But Labour's governance practices – its policies, relationships and institutional forms – have struggled with the problem of how to install and secure this one vision. Gramsci talked about viewing 'the life of the state as a series of unstable equilibria'. New Labour's modernisation project has attempted to establish a new settlement, a new equilibrium, in which we will become reconciled to living in this version of a modern world. Not surprisingly, this new equilibrium has proved both elusive and unstable. In particular, New Labour's efforts to treat differential inequalities and the struggles over them as settled – allowing a view of equalised opportunities tempered by pockets of social exclusion – has been less wholly successful. The difficult question is whether the various co-opted, repressed, excluded social possibilities can become active and effective political forces.

NOTE

1. See also Epstein, Johnson and Steinberg, this volume, for discussions of the distinctive antagonism of the hegemonic tendency of Blairism/New Labour towards popular dissent and resistant forms of activism.

REFERENCES

Byrne, D. (1999) *Social Exclusion*. Buckingham, Open University Press.

Cabinet Office (1999a) *Modernising Government* (Cmnd. 4310. London, The Stationery Office.

Cabinet Office (1999b) *Professional Policy Making in the 21st Century*, London, The Stationery Office.

Clarke, J. (1999) 'Unfinished Business? Struggles over the social in social welfare', in P. Gilroy, L. Grossberg and A. McRobbie, eds, *Without Guarantees: in Honour of Stuart Hall'*. London, Verso.

Clarke, J. (2001) 'Unstable states: the transformation of welfare systems.' Paper presented to American Anthropological Association annual conference, Washington D.C., November.

Clarke, J., Gewirtz, S. and McLaughlin, E., eds (2000) *New Mangerialism, New Welfare?* London, Sage/The Open University.

Clarke, J. and Newman, J. (1997) *The Managerial State: Power, Politics and Ideology in the Remaking of Social Welfare*, London, Sage.

Clarke, J. and Newman, J. (1998) 'A Modern British People? New Labour and the reconstruction of social welfare'. Paper presented to the *Discourse Analysis and Social Research Conference*, Copenhagen Business School, September.

Davies, H., Nutley, S. and Smith, P., eds (2000) *What Works? Evidence-based policy and practice in public services*. Bristol, The Policy Press.

Deacon, A. (2002) *Perspectives on Welfare*. Buckingham, The Open University Press.

Dean, M. (1999) *Governmentality: Power and Rule in Modern Society*, London, Sage.

Department of Health (1997) *The New NHS: Modern – Dependable* (Cmnd 3807). London, The Stationery Office.

Department of the Environment, Transport and the Regions (1998) *Modern Local Government: In Touch with the People*. London, The Stationery Office.

Department of Social Security (1998) *New ambitions for our country: A new contract for welfare*. London, The Stationery Office.

Driver, S. and Martell, L. (1998) New *Labour: Politics After Thatcher*. Cambridge, Polity Press.

Dwyer, P. (1998) 'Conditional Citizens? Welfare Rights and responsibilities in the Late 1990s'. *Critical Social Policy*, 18 (4), pp.493–518.

Dwyer, P. (2000) *Welfare Rights and Responsibilities: Contesting Social Citizenship*. Bristol, The Policy Press.

Fairclough, N. (2000) *New Labour, New Language*. London, Routledge.

Gewirtz, S. (2001) 'Cloning the Blairs: New Labour's programme for the resocialization of working-class parents'. *Journal of Education Policy*, vol 16 (4), pp. 365-378.

Hesse, B. (2001b) 'Introduction: Un/settled Multiculturalisms.' In B. Hesse (ed.) *Un/Settled Multiculturalisms: Diasporas, Entanglements and Transruptions.* London, Zed Books.

Home Office (2001) *Secure Borders, Safe Haven: Integration with Diversity in Modern Britain.* Norwich, The Stationery Office (Cm 5387).

Hughes, G. and Lewis, G. eds. (1998) *Unsettling welfare: the Reconstruction of Social Policy.* London, Routledge.

Kingfisher, C, ed. (forthcoming) *Globalisation, Neo-Liberalism and Welfare Reform.* Basingstoke, Palgrave.

Kooiman, J. ed. (1993) *Modern Governance: Government-Society Interactions.* London, Sage.

Labour Party (2001) *Ambitions for Britain: Labour's Manifesto 2001.* London, The Labour Party.

Levitas, R. (1998) *The Inclusive Society?* Basingstoke, Macmillan.

Levitas, R. (2001) 'Against Work: A utopian incursion into social policy.' *Critical Social Policy*, Vol 21 (4), pp. 449-466.

Lewis, G. (2000) 'Discursive Histories, the Pursuit of Multi-culturalism in Social Policy', in G. Lewis, S., Gewirtz and J. Clarke, eds, *Rethinking Social Policy*, London, Sage/Open University.

Lister, R. (1998) 'From equality to social inclusion: New Labour and the welfare state.' *Critical Social Policy*, Vol. 18 (2), pp.215-25.

Lister, R. (2001) 'New Labour: A study in ambiguity from a position of ambivalence.' *Critical Social Policy*, Vol. 21(4), pp. 425-448.

Lister, R. (2002) 'Towards a New Welfare Settlement?' in C. Hay (ed.) *British Politics Today.* Cambridge, Polity Press.

Miliband, D. (2000) 'Living in the Modern World.' *Fabian Review*, 111 (4), Winter.

Muncie, J. (2002) 'Policy Transfers and 'What Works': Some Reflections on Comparative Youth Justice.' *Youth Justice*, vol. 1(3), pp.27-35.

Newman, J. (2001) *Modernising Governance: New Labour, Policy and Society.* London, Sage.

Newman, J. (2002) 'Cutting Edges or Blunt Instruments? Practitioner narratives of modernisation in UK public services'. Paper presented to Fifth International Conference on Organizational Discourse, London, July.

Parekh, B. (2000) *The Future of Multi-Ethnic Britain.* London, Profile Books (The Parekh Report from the Runnymede Trust Commission on the Future of Multi-Ethnic Britain).

Peck, J. (2001) *Workfare States.* New York, The Guilford Press.

Pierre, J. ed. (2000) *Debating Governance: Authority, Steering and Democracy.* Oxford, Oxford University Press.

Pierre, J. and Peters, G. (2000) *Governance, Politics and the State.* Basingstoke, Macmillan.

Rhodes, R. (1997) *Understanding Governance.* Buckingham, Open University Press.

Richards, S. et al (1999) *Cross Cutting Issues in Public Policy.* London, DETR.

Rose, N. (1999) *Powers of Freedom: Reframing Political Thought.* Cambridge, Cambridge University Press.

Williams, F. (2001) 'In and beyond New Labour: Towards a new political ethics of care.' *Critical Social Policy*, Vol. 21(4), pp.467-93.

3. Labour's loves lost? The legacies of moral conservatism and sex reform

Jeffrey Weeks

INTRODUCTION

One of the piquant pleasures of the second Labour landslide victory of June 2001 was the unexpected tribute to Labour achievements in catching the moral zeitgeist from leading Conservatives. One of the former 'big beasts' of the Tory jungle, Michael Heseltine, offered a vivid perception of Labour's perceived success:

> While the Conservative Party has looked backwards, Labour has adopted the vocabulary of the future. Britain has moved on – whether for good or ill scarcely matters. Marital breakdown, single-parent families, partners, gay rights, a multi-ethnic population are all parts of modern life ... (Heseltine 2001: 13).

In the same edition of the *Evening Standard* in which this encomium appeared, its editor, Max Hastings – former editor of the arch-Tory *Daily Telegraph*, a former military correspondent, an enthusiastic fox hunter, and a High Tory by inclination and history – made a similar comment:

> ... it does not matter a thing whether we like or dislike the world of working women, unmarried mothers, ethnic minorities, football fans, animal rights, drug takers, gays, cosmetic surgery, Princess Diana self-fulfilment, women in the army, bunny-hugging and explicit sex at the movies – this is modern Britain. Any political party that seeks to deny its reality, as the Tories have done implicitly or explicitly for years, is unlikely again to win power (Hastings 2001: 5).

Without any obvious herald, in the context of a government which had cautiously played down its liberalism with regard to sexual values, and which had indeed been derided by some for being out of touch with the country's growing tolerance of diverse life styles, sexuality erupted into the subsequent campaign for the Conservative leadership. It became a marker of the divide between traditional moral authoritarianism and a new social liberalism, which advocated greater toleration of different lifestyles, and was espoused by younger Conservatives, led by Michael Portillo. Despite Portillo's own hard right career as a Thatcherite minister, his new liberalism fired his subsequent bid for the Tory leadership (even though ultimately, as it happened, it also destroyed his chances). And the Blair Labour Party was hailed as being in tune with the way we live today – whether people liked that way or not.

Here we have a perplexing paradox. The Blair government in its first term was often assailed by self-declared progressives for its conservatism on the 'moral agenda', particularly with regard to drugs, the administration of justice and its attitude to crime, but also on issues relating to the family and sexuality. Since 1997 the philosopher John Gray (2001: 21) has been commenting that Britain is amongst the most liberal countries in Europe. Yet the new Labour government elected in that year has often seemed scared of its own shadow in relationship to many of these matters. Terrified in particular of the tabloid media in pursuing a liberal, let alone a radically progressive agenda, its liberalism seemed at best to follow the path of stealth, whilst its conservatism was allowed to spin.

There are two obvious examples of Labour's ambivalent liberalism in the first term, illustrating its Janus-like character. First of all there were the dogged, though ultimately fruitless, efforts to repeal 'Section 28' of the 1988 Local Government Act. This had prohibited the promotion of homosexuality as a 'pretended family relationship' by local authorities, and had been rushed into law by the Thatcher government in response to a well orchestrated panic about gay propaganda being directed at school children (Weeks 1991; Moran 2001). In practice, it had never been used, but it had become a symbol of state homophobia for the lesbian and gay community. During the first Blair administration, after a fierce struggle, repeal was implemented in Scotland by the new devolved government. In England and Wales, however, despite the efforts of the Labour government, repeal was ultimately blocked in the House of Lords during the first term. Moral conservatives, including some Labour peers, were able to conjure up sufficient support to stymie repeal for the major part of the UK, and the Blair government seemed at a loss about how to overcome the opposition. Here was a thwarted liberalism.

A more conservative, or at least contradictory, approach was offered by the government's family policy. On the one hand, it fully acknowledged, even exposed, a diversity of family forms in a discussion paper on families (Ministerial Group on the Family 1998). But on the other it extolled marriage and the two-parent family as the ideal arena for bringing up children. It wished to recognise a plurality of intimate patterns, but wanted to accompany this, apparently, by advocating an ideal form. In doing this it pleased neither its radical constituency nor

its would-be friends in the conservative media. It got the worst of all
worlds.

Contradictions and ambivalences certainly litter the Blair government's moral agenda. But the deeper question is whether it is possible
in the complex, diverse pluralistic society Britain has become to please
anyone when a government delicately sets out on reforming the moral
agenda. Michael Heseltine, at the very least, clearly believed in 2001
that the Blair strategy was more effective in addressing the value
complexity of contemporary Britain than his Conservative opponents.
But is a more radical strategy possible or feasible?

This article sets out to understand the intricacies and complexities of
the Blair moral agenda by exploring three lines of enquiry. The first is
into the Labour legacy itself. With the exception of a brief flowering of
the permissive moment under Roy Jenkins in the 1960s, and the well-
meant gesture politics of the socialisms in one borough of the 1980s,
the history of Labour administrations, I argue, is one of moral conservatism. The Blair government shines like a progressive beacon in
comparison with these. What therefore are the cultural and institutional roots of such a contradictory legacy? Secondly, I want to explore
the unfinished sexual revolution of the recent past. There have been
real transformations in many people's lives over the past two generations, a revolution of every day life, which is acknowledged but not
fully understood. It has led to new freedoms but also new uncertain-
ties. It is the resulting ambiguities, ambivalence and moral confusions,
I suggest, that are the real background to the contemporary paradoxes
of moral politics, which affect all political parties. Might the limitations
of the Blair agenda be simply a cautious wish to ride and prod, rather
than lead a grass roots transformation? This might not be heroic, but
could it be the most sensible approach? Thirdly, in the context of very
real changes, I will argue that we have seen the emergence of quite new
discourses of equality in relationship to intimate life and around sexual
choice, which have yet to play themselves out fully. These emergent
discourses may reflect more aspiration than reality, but they are affecting the terms of moral discourse. How do you balance rights and
responsibilities, personal autonomy and mutual involvement? The
Blair government grapples with these questions in a variety of seem-
ingly contradictory ways, here nodding to communitarian principles
(Etzioni 1995), there offering a pragmatic adaptation to growing individualism. But what is surely interesting is not so much the
government's timidity as its careful renegotiating of the boundaries
between the normal and abnormal, the acceptable and unacceptable.

THE LABOUR LEGACY
One of Blair's first biographers, John Rentoul (1996: 287), wrote that
Labour 'has always been seen as a liberal party'. But how liberal is
liberal? Whatever its progressive pretensions, the Labour Party has

rarely been in the vanguard of sexual reform throughout its hundred-year history. Since its formation at the beginning of the twentieth century the Labour Party has always been an uneasy amalgam of the progressive intelligentsia and a largely morally conservative working class, especially as represented through the trade union movement. The post-1918 Labour Party, committed as it was to a socialist agenda of a sort, concentrated on utopian ends in theory and better public administration in practice. But beneath this notional over-arching ideological unity, the party always had a plethora of pragmatic policies – few of which addressed directly the diversities of family or intimate life. By the mid-century the party was an awkward amalgam of a fairly basic moral conservatism, reflecting its working-class constituency and the weakness of its voters from the modernising middle class (on which it nevertheless depended to win elections once in a generation), and an often bohemian leadership (at least in private). Ramsay MacDonald, its first prime minister, had after all begun his political career in the undergrowth of socialist organisations of the 1880s and 1890s, where concerns with the rights of women and 'homogenic love' (that is, homosexuality) had been significant; but by the 1920s, and the time of his first premiership, a new sobriety dominated (Rowbotham and Weeks 1977). Subsequent leaders may have had fairly exotic private relationships, but the party's outward face was highly respectable. Labour's most successful prime minister to date, now universally hailed as a model prime minister, Clement Attlee, was the acme of moral conservatism and social respectability: laconic, pipe-smoking, deeply traditional, with his public school tie, his passion for cricket and *The Times* crossword. The hindsight of history bathes the Attlee government in a glow of ideological clarity and socialist commitment. We tend to forget that that government was riven by personality conflicts (very similar to those of the Blair administrations), constant back-bench unease, battles for economic survival, conservatism towards crime, and a commitment to a welfare system that was deeply gendered, embodying a notion of citizenship that was implicitly familial and heterosexual (Weeks 1998). No libertarian reforms marked or marred that government. In fact, it was the very greyness of the administration – however much it may have been justified by its battles to reconstruct the economy after the war, and to lay the foundations of the welfare state – that inspired the revisionism of the 1950s to put a new emphasis on personal freedoms.

In the blood of socialists, as Anthony Crosland – the most influential of social democratic revisionists in the 1960s – famously suggested in his *The Future of Socialism* (Crosland 1964: 355), 'there should always run a trace of the anarchist and the libertarian, and not too much of the prig and the prude'. The implication was clear: the party had adhered to a rather dour Labour/Fabian tradition, which was no longer relevant to the new world of post-war affluence. Instead

Crosland looked forward, as society became more social democratic, to 'the cultivation of leisure, beauty, grace, gaiety, excitement and all of the proper pursuits, whether elevated, vulgar, or eccentric, which contribute to the varied fabric of full private and family life' (Crosland 1964: 353). The apotheosis of this modernising hope could be said to have arrived in the second half of the 1960s, presided over by the liberal and reforming Labour Home Secretary, Roy Jenkins, a close friend, and enduring rival, of Crosland's. The wave of reforms that were introduced, ostensibly on the initiative of backbench MPs and peers, but largely with government support, constituted the most important body of reforms regarding personal morality for a hundred years. Male homosexuality was partially decriminalised. Abortion law reform ended the scourge of the back-street abortionists. The obscenity laws were reformed. Divorce was made slightly easier. Stage censorship was abolished (Weeks 1981). For the opponents of these reforms, this was where the moral rot began. For the rest of population new, if limited, freedoms were opened up, and we are still living with the framework in which they took place.

'The permissive moment' was brief, and in retrospect it can be seen as a promising but limited flowering. Already by 1968 the new Home Secretary, James Callaghan, confidently signalled the end of permissiveness, and the return of moral conservatism. The strongest marker of this was the refusal to contemplate any reform of the laws relating to drugs, and many of the problems related to prohibition of recreational drugs that we live with today can be traced back to that symbolic moment (Weeks 1981). James Callaghan proudly represented the social and moral conservatism of the base of the Labour Party, not only in issues related to private freedoms but more broadly in relationship to the social policies of the Labour government.

Harold Wilson, the prime minister who presided over both the reforming and the conservative moments of the 1960s, displayed little interest either way. Ben Pimlott's (1992) massive biography of Wilson, which details all the ins and outs of court politics and economic and international crises, makes few references to the debate over private life. And however important the reforms were in the 1960s, the most interesting factor in retrospect is not the way in which the reforms removed restraints but the modest shift had actually took place in the modes of regulation of social and especially sexual behaviour. The so-called 'Wolfenden strategy' that lay behind most of the reforms relied on a distinction between private behaviour (which was regarded as a domain of choice between consenting adults) and public behaviour (which was the legitimate realm of regulation and control). So partial decriminalisation of male homosexual behaviour in private was balanced by (at least in intention) more effective policing of public behaviour. The legalisation of abortion in certain circumstances was accompanied by a shift in the locus of regulation from the law to medicine. The point that has to be underlined is that none of the reforms relied on a qualitative reassessment of the practices concerned. There was no positive affirmation of homosexuality, no espousal of the woman's right to choose, no explicit adoption of divorce by consent. The reforms were largely concerned with redrawing the balance between consent and control (Weeks 1981; Weeks 1991).

The long mainstream tradition of cautious conservatism in relationship to sexuality continued throughout the 1970s and 1980s. When the Greater London Council, led by Ken Livingstone, attempted to let a hundred flowers bloom at County Hall in the 1980s in pursuit of a new majority of minorities, including sexual minorities, the response from the Labour Party establishment varied from the sceptical to the horrified. Perhaps in the end this was not surprising, as the whole experiment in progressive municipal socialism in the 1980s with regard to sexuality ended in the debacle of the imposition of Section 28 (Weeks: 1991). Again, leading party spokesmen showed a deep ambivalence in their opposition to it (see Cooper 1994).

The controversy aroused by the Blair government's attempt to repeal Section 28 some twelve years later revealed why there was such caution in the party's high command. The furore in Scotland against the attempt to repeal the Section, led by the old Labour supporting Roman Catholic primate Cardinal Winning, drew on a deep conservatism in Scottish culture. This in turn echoed the conservatism of a large part of the core constituency of Labour in England and Wales, and underlined the difficulties of keeping that uneasy coalition between metropolitan progressivism and working-class conservatism together (Yates 2001: 9). The new Labour leadership – often Christian Socialist in its roots – never quite found the language of radical toleration it needed to combat the Cardinal's absolutism. And yet, of course, on this occasion the opposition of the conservative elements in the Labour coalition did not stop the government pursuing its plans for reform. Something had changed.

In part this reflected the impact that both feminism and lesbian and gay politics from the 1970s had had in changing a large part of the climate in the Labour Party. It reflected the large, and by and large more liberal membership of the Labour majority in the Commons. It also reflected a commitment on the part of Blair and his immediate allies in the party's leadership to adopt a more liberal policy with regard to homosexuality and other sexual issues. That policy sat somewhat uneasily with the government's familial rhetoric, and Blair's own personal lifestyle. But the fact that for the first time a Labour government directly committed itself in its own bill to an equal age of consent, and to repeal of Section 28, did signal a significant shift. This shift in turn reflected a dawning awareness of the way British society itself had been transformed since the 1960s.

THE LONG, UNFINISHED REVOLUTION

The Blair government came to power in 1997 in the midst of a profound transformation of intimate life, sexuality, and of patterns of domestic life. Many of the changes in Britain are global in their extent, based on the widespread process of de-traditionalisation and individualisation (Giddens 1991, 1992). But Britain seems to have adopted a particular take on these long-term trends. For example, despite the various efforts of successive governments to valorise marriage, Britain has the highest divorce rate in the European Union, and one of the highest rates of babies born outside marriage (Duckworth 2001: 6). In Britain by 2001, 39 per cent of births were outside marriage, compared with the EU average of 26 per cent, and only about 27 per cent in Britain ten years earlier. Such trends are symptomatic of radical shifts in behaviour and attitudes. The delay of marriage, the rise of co-habitation, which has now become the norm before, and frequently an alternative to, marriage, the rapid rise of single households, the emergence of new patterns of intimacy, such as lesbian and gay 'families of choice', are indices of real change (McRae 1999; Weeks, Heaphy and Donovan 2001). We can rightly make a series of necessary qualifications about these bald developments. National surveys still tell us that on the whole the British population is more conservative than many people think (Wellings et al 1994; but see Johnson et al 2001; Frean and Peak 2001: 10). Most people still marry and then re-marry. The average number of partners is relatively low. Serial monogamy is the norm. Cohabitation before marriage may now be routine, but most offspring of such unions are still registered by both parents. Homosexual relations may be more tolerated, but there is widespread resistance to the recognition of same sex partnerships, and the legal situation remains generally inequitable. Similarly, despite the 'transformation of intimacy' that Anthony Giddens (1992) has proclaimed, there are still great inequities in the relationship between men and women (Jamieson 1998).

But at the same time there is no doubt that by and large the British population, especially in the younger age group, has become more tolerant in its attitudes towards sexual diversity. The media generally is not only more explicit in its representations of sexuality, but also more liberal in its representations of diversity. There is plentiful evidence that the old taboos against homosexuality are beginning to fade away. And whatever the difficulties, and continuing patterns of inequality, violence and struggle, and the continuing inequities between men and women, new patterns of life, and new values, are emerging. It is no longer possible, if indeed it ever was, to see Britain as a homogenous society, with a single moral standard. It is well on the way to becoming a pluralistic society, not simply in cultural and ethnic terms, but also in attitudes to the family and sexuality (Frearn 2002).

These new patterns can be seen as examples of a new or accentuated individualism in most Western culture. The 1990s demonstrated that, whatever the social authoritarian efforts of conservative politicians like Reagan in the United States and Thatcher in the UK, the triumph of economic liberalism has tended to undermine traditional patterns of life and to elevate individual choice, in personal as well as economic matters. This new individualism has aroused extreme anxieties amongst moral conservatives (Phillips 2000). It has left, more generally, an underlying sense of unease, which is manifest in recurrent 'moral panics' around sexual issues. The widespread anxieties about rampant child sex abuse underlie not only a long-overdue recognition of a genuine problem but also a sense that boundaries, especially between adults and children, are in danger of dissolving, with unknown consequences (Weeks 2001).

Yet whatever the undercurrent of uncertainty (Weeks 1995), most people, perforce, have to negotiate the rapids of change. Today, John Gray (2001: 21) has argued, people's identities and beliefs are more varied than ever before: 'Families and sexual relationships are improvised and fluid. Fulfilment is found in the private world, and individual self-realisation is the central object in life.'

People are not particularly interested in politics generally, or the politics of family and sexuality in particular. They do not have grand visions of new ways of living, even as at an everyday level they do engage in 'everyday experiments in living' (Giddens 1992; Weeks, Heaphy and Donovan 2001). There is both a pragmatism in the adaptation to changes in every day life, and a new contingency as people have, in a real sense, to create values for themselves. Their liberalism may well be limited to a form of live and let live morality. There is little positive endorsement of different ways of life. Yet there are very few households in Britain that are not touched by the transformations of everyday life. Most people know single parents. Most people know a member of their family who may be lesbian or gay. Many households have experienced divorce, re-marriage cohabitation, broken families, reconstituted families. These broad, shared experiences explain why attempts during the 1980s and 1990s to return to Victorian, or 'basic' values, were dismal failures. We are in the midst of a long revolution. The revolution is unfinished, partial, uneven in its impact. But we all now have to live with the consequences and implications. And the evidence surely is that most people adapt extremely well.

NEW DISCOURSES OF EQUALITY?

In many ways the policies of the first Blair administration towards intimate life can be seen to reflect the ambiguities of the population as a whole. There can be no doubt that leading members of the government, including Tony Blair, Jack Straw as Home Secretary, and David Blunkett as Education Secretary, adhered to traditional views of the centrality of the family (despite the fact that Straw and Blunkett themselves are divorced). Even in this leading trio, however, we can see differences, with Blair and Straw broadly associating their commitment to the family with socially liberal policies towards homosexuality, while Blunkett is seen as resolutely conservative, and was an opponent of an equal age of consent for homosexuality and heterosexuality (Waites 2001). Balancing this, the financial and welfare policies of the government, dominated by the Chancellor of the Exchequer Gordon Brown, concentrated on children rather than families as such, developing a taxation policy that is neutral between the merits of married and unmarried parenting (Lewis 2001). Furthermore, Blair's cabinet between 1997-2001 was the first in British history to have openly gay members (Chris Smith, Nick Brown, Peter Mandelson), as well as openly lesbian or gay junior members of the government and MPs. There is no doubt that the government was highly sensitive to many of the major changes that had taken place in patterns of life. The awkward problem it faced was how to balance this recognition of sexual pluralism with its leading members' commitment to marriage and family life.

Recognition of the mutual responsibilities involved in family life was an important aspect of the communitarian philosophy which had influenced leading members of the Labour Party prior to the election of 1997. The family was seen as an arena in which rights and responsibilities were mutually negotiated, and which provided the appropriate forum for bringing up children. The government continued the policy of its predecessor Conservative government by emphasising, particularly, parental responsibilities, and the responsibilities of the father, and the Child Support Agency was reformed by the Labour government to aid this (Lewis 2001).

Liberal fears about the government devotion to the traditional family had, of course, been aroused early on in the term by its attitude to single parents. The early cuts to lone parent benefits were justified on the grounds of maintaining strict government expenditure limits, and simply followed the Conservative budgetary policies. But they were widely seen at the time as an obeisance to the family lobby. They aroused intense backbench hostility, and the cuts were quietly restored in the next budget (Lewis 2001: 495; Toynbee and Walker 2001: 18-19). Subsequently, the New Deal, and the budgetary emphasis on children's needs rather than family forms, did improve the financial situation of lone parents. This was accompanied by a new emphasis in attitudes to lone parenting: an emphasis on the importance of single parents being able to work. This was quite different from the punitive attitudes of the Conservative government towards single parenting, and undoubtedly benefited many single parents. The problem, however, as Lewis (2001), has pointed out, was that the approach tended to ignore wider questions of care, and care of children in particular. It was particularly insensitive to what Duncan and Edwards (1999) have described as the 'gendered moral rationalities' which differentially shape the responses of particular communities about the appropriate balance between single parents' responsibilities for children and their desire to work.

There can be no doubt then that key members of the government, including Tony Blair and Jack Straw themselves, were at one with the Conservatives about the implication of family change, particularly with regard to the instability faced by children. The government committed itself to teaching the value of marriage to children, and this was linked as a quid pro quo in the attempt to abolish Section 28 (Moran 2001). On the other hand, the Labour government was sharply attacked by defenders of the family for its refusal to be prescriptive about family by providing incentives to marriage (Phillips 1999). Gordon Brown, for example, followed the logic of previous Conservative budgetary policy by abolishing the married couples' tax allowance in April 2000. The use of the term 'families' rather than 'family' in its consultation document signalled some recognition by the government that there was now a diversity of family forms (Ministerial Group on the Family 1998). But on this, as on many other things, the government was not prepared to go too far. There was no hint in the document of the existence of lesbian or gay families, or of the contemporary 'gayby' boom (Weeks, Heaphy and Donovan 2001). The overwhelming impression was that on this, as in other policy matters, the government was steering a cautious third way between traditional values and the new more diverse constituencies it had to address.

One of these constituencies, to which both explicit and implicit promises had been made in the run up to the 1997 election, was the non-heterosexual population. The Labour Party had adopted in the 1980s a raft of pious aspirations. Blair himself, as Home Affairs spokesperson before 1994, had committed himself to what was a radically new commitment to equality in his advocacy of a common age of consent for homosexuals and heterosexuals (Rentoul 1996: 288; see also Epstein, Johnson and Steinberg 2000).

In retrospect this commitment can be seen as a significant break from the Wolfenden strategy which had governed national and indeed party policy since the 1960s, though it was not articulated as such. The Wolfenden Committee's recommendations on homosexual law reform in 1957, and subsequently passed during the period of office of the 1964-1970 Labour government, had never made a clear commitment to the equal worth of homosexuals. The 1967 Act, which partially decriminalised male homosexuality, had clearly continued to see homosexuality as an inferior form. What was significant about Blair's declaration in the context of attempts in the early 1990s to reduce the age of homosexual consent was the notion that there were no rational grounds for denying an equal age of consent for homosexuals and heterosexuals. And despite the criticisms that came from gay activists during the period of the first Blair administration, there were in fact substantial attempts to enact a greater degree of equality. For example, partners of lesbian or gay citizens were allowed to migrate into the country on the same terms as unmarried heterosexual partners. After some hesitation, the government also ensured that openly gay men and lesbians could serve in the armed forces on the same terms as heterosexuals. The occasion for this was a finding in the European Court of Human Rights in favour of a group of gay men and women who had been sacked once their homosexuality was revealed. It remained illegal for any form of sexual activity to take place between any serving men and women, but this applied whether the individuals involved were gay or straight (Toynbee and Walker 2001: 176).

The same application of common principles can be seen in the debate over the age of consent. In its initial attempts to equalise the age of consent at 16, the government conceded a new offence of abuse of trust, where predatory teachers or care workers or others in a position of power might pressure those under 18, but this was an offence that applied across the heterosexual/homosexual divide. And this legislative endeavour had another significant feature. Unlike the passage of the 1967 Act, which was ostensibly on the initiative of backbench MPs, efforts to equalise the age of consent were sponsored by government bills. And when the third attempt to get it through was again blocked in the House of Lords in 1999, the government then invoked the Parliament Act, which allowed them to override the Lords' veto, to push it through. This was the first time that any government had so clearly endorsed gay equality in this way (see Waites 2001).

Hubbard (2001: 59), following Cooper (1998), has seen these significant but ambivalent efforts at reform during the first term as a failure on the part of the Labour government to commit itself to full citizenship for marginal sexual subjects. There can be no doubt that the government seemed reluctant to set out a coherent programme of reform that would signal a radical policy towards full sexual citizenship (Donovan, Heaphy and Weeks 1999). Its uneasy attempt to combine a commitment to the family as the best focus for bringing up children with a recognition of diversity did not suggest it was willing explicitly to challenge the more conservative social forces within its own constituency, let alone to allow the more rabidly socially conservative forces represented by the *Daily Mail* to disrupt its popularity with the largest possible group of the British population. Yet, it had already brought about significant change in its first four years of office, and achieved the most significant shifts in the regulation of non-traditional forms of sexuality since the 1960s. The coming into force of the Human Rights legislation at the end of the first term opened a possibility of yet more significant shifts in the second term (see Weeks, Heaphy and Donovan 2001: chapter 8). Discourses of human rights have in fact emerged strongly for the first time in Britain. The emergent discourses may reflect more aspiration than reality, but they are likely to affect the terms of moral debate way into the future.

An early signal of this in the second term was the government's acceptance of a decision in the European Court of Human Rights in July 2002 which ruled that UK law breached the human rights of transsexuals by refusing them revised birth certificates marking their new gender identities. In December 2002, the government announced its intention to legislate to 'enable transsexual people confidently to take up those rights which have been denied to them in society, including the right to marry in their acquired gender' (Ford 2002a: 12). This was just one of several initiatives which committed the government to an equality agenda. During 2002 the government legislated to allow lesbians and gays to adopt on the same terms as non-married heterosexual couples; published a White Paper, *Protecting the Public*, which promised changes to the rape laws, better child protection, and the repeal of a number of anti-gay laws dating back to Victorian times; and outlined plans to introduce civil partnerships for same sex couples (Richardson 2002: 20; Ford 2002b: 4; Waugh 2002: 1; Dyer 2002: 11). It also finally succeeded in repealing Section 28. All this suggested that the government had at last decided that the tide of public opinion was in favour of further reform. Following the 2001 election the government had set up a Cabinet Office study of 'civil partnerships', to include same sex and unmarried heterosexual couples, and some commentators had suggested that this would allow the government to kick a touchy subject into the long grass (Charter 2002). In fact the opposite seemed to be the case. During 2004 new legislation to approve same sex unions began to progress through the House of Lords, with full government support. A new sexual offences act (2004) additionally removed the distinction between homosexual and heterosexual offences (Bainham and Brooks-Gordon 2004). Hand in hand with a growing liberalisation of public attitudes, the government seemed prepared, finally, to endorse the case for sexual justice and equal citizenship.

SOME CONCLUSIONS

The lines of enquiry pursued in this paper suggest three tentative conclusions. First, this is a much more radical government on sexual and relationship issues than any previous Labour government. This may not be saying a great deal given the history outlined above, but it can still be seen as a brave nod in the direction of greater sexual equality in the light of an ambiguous public opinion. This is the second point: the confusions and ambiguities of the Blair government can be seen as a reflection of wider cultural confusions. As Lewis (2001: 496) has observed, this is an area of policy making about which people have very particular notions as to what is appropriate or inappropriate, and these may differ deeply between generations, classes, ethnic groups and regions. She cites an Observer/ICM Poll in late 1998, which suggested that a majority of people believe the government should steer clear of telling them how to conduct their private lives. While attitudes tended towards being non-judgemental they were not necessarily permissive. 47 per cent agreed that divorce should be made more difficult, as opposed to 44 per cent who disagree. A similar ambivalence was evidenced in all the opinion polling with regard to recognition of homosexuality. While people by and large were willing to have homosexuals as their neighbours, they still tended to be very cautious about allowing lesbian or gays to parent children. In such a sensitive area, where ambiguities of the population at large reach into the cabinet room itself, it is difficult to see how any government would be willing to run too far ahead of public opinion. It was precisely when there was evidence of significant shifts in public attitudes that the government chose to act (for example, see Gray 2002: 9; Frearn 2002: 9). But the third point surely is that this puts the onus not on governments themselves to leap too far ahead of public opinion, but on those who desire change to ensure that the case is made from the grassroots upwards. The lesson of the past generation indeed is that the changes with regard to family and sexual life have not been led by the political elite but by grass-roots shifts which are subject to a whole variety of long term social trends.

The 'long revolution' has been a revolution in everyday life. Whilst we may wish reforming governments to be a little more explicitly enthusiastic in endorsing these changes, the public mood generally seems to be: 'let well alone' unless some spectacular abuses or contradictions come to light. Clearly, the Blair government has shown itself unwilling to race too far ahead of public opinion. But at least it is riding the tide, and, as Heseltine (2001) suggested, it may well be reading the public mood more accurately than many of its critics care to believe or accept.

REFERENCES

Bainham, Andrew, and Brooks-Gordon, Belinda (2004) 'Reforming the Law on Sexual Offences', in Belinda Brooks-Gordon, Loraine Gelsthorpe, Martin Johnson, and Andrew Bainham (eds), *Sexuality Repositioned: Diversity and the Law* Oxford: Hart Publishing: 261-296.

Charter, David (2002) 'Adoption Bill held back over row over unmarried couples', *The Times*, 16 March.

Cooper, Davina (1994) *Sexing the City: Lesbian and Gay Politics within the Activist State*, London: Rivers Oram Press.

Cooper, Davina (1998) 'Regard between Strangers: Diversity, Equality, and the Reconstruction of Public Space', *Critical Social Policy*, Volume 18 (3): 465-492.

Crosland, C.A.R. (1964) *The Future of Socialism*, London: Jonathan Cape.

Donovan, Catherine, Heaphy, Brian, Weeks, Jeffrey (1999), 'Citizenship and Same-Sex Relationships', *Journal of Social Policy* 28(4): 689-709.

Duckworth, Lorna (2001) 'Divorce Rate falls but UK still tops European Lead', *The Independent*, 13 June.

Duncan, Simon, and Edwards, Rosalind (1999), *Lone Mothers, Paid Work and Gendered Moral Rationalities*, Basingstoke and London: Macmillan.

Dyer, Clare (2002) 'New Legal Rights for Gay Couples', *The Guardian*, 7 December.

Epstein, Debbie, Johnson, Richard, Steinberg, Deborah Lynn, (2000) 'Twice Told Tales: Transformation, Recuperation and Emergence in the Age of Consent Debates 1998', *Sexualities*, Volume 3(1): 5-30.

Etzioni, Amatai (1995), *The Spirit of Community: Rights, Responsibilities and the Communitarian Agenda*, London: Fontana Press.

Ford, Richard (2002a) 'Transsexuals to get new birth certificates', *The Times*, 14 December.

Ford, Richard (2002b) 'Blunkett sweeps away Victorian anti-gay laws', *The Times*, 20 November.

Frean, Alexander, and Peek, Laura (2001) 'Women warm to more partners', *The Times*, 30 November.

Frearn, Alexandra (2002) 'More Britons choose a childless, single life', *The Times*, 18 December.

Giddens, Anthony (1991), *Modernity and Self Identity*, Cambridge: Polity Press.

Giddens, Anthony (1992), *The Transformation of Intimacy: Sexuality, Love and Eroticism in Modern Societies*, Cambridge: Polity Press.

Gray, Chris (2002) 'Four in every 10 babies now born to unmarried parents', *The Independent*, 13 December.

Gray, John (2001) 'The Little Party', *The Guardian* 4 June.

Hastings, Max (2001) 'The Tories Need Not Just a Leader, but to join the 21st Century', *Evening Standard*, 8 June.

Heseltine, Michael (2001) 'A Disaster for the Tories – A Personal Tragedy for William', *Evening Standard*, 8 June.

Hubbard, Phil, 'Sex Zones: Intimacy, Citizenship and Public Space', *Sexualities*, Volume 4 (1): 51-71.

Jamieson, Lynn (1998) *Intimacy: Personal Relationships in Modern Society*, Cambridge: Polity Press.

Johnson, Anne M., Mercer, Catherine H., Erens, Bob, Copas, Andrew J., McManus, Sally, Wellings, Kay, Fenton, Kevin A., Korovessis, Christos, Macdowall, Wendy, Nanchahal, Kiran, Purdon, Susan, and Field, Julia (2001), 'Sexual behaviour in Britain: partnerships, practices, and HIV risk behaviours', *The Lancet*, 358 (9296), 1 December: 1835-1842.

Lewis, Jane (2001) 'Women, Men and the Family', in Anthony Seldon (ed.) *The Blair Effect: The Blair Government 1997-2001*, London: Little, Brown and Company.

McRae, Susan (1999) *Changing Britain: Families and Households in the 1990s*, Oxford: Oxford University Press.

Ministerial Group on the Family (1998) *Supporting Families: A Consultation Document*, London: HMSO.

Moran, Joe (2001) 'Childhood Sexuality and Education: The case of Section 28', *Sexualities*, Volume 4(1): 73-89.

Phillips, Melanie (1999), *The Sex-Change Society: Feminized Britain and Neutered Male*, London: The Social Market Foundation.

Pimlott, Ben (1992), *Harold Wilson*, London: Harper Collins.

Rentoul, John (1996), *Tony Blair*, London: Warner Books.

Richardson, Colin (2002) 'Quite glad to be gay', *The Guardian*, 27 December.

Rowbotham, Sheila, and Weeks, Jeffrey (1977) *Socialism and the New Life*, London: Pluto Press.

Toynbee, Polly and Walker, David (2001) *'Did Things Get Better? An Audit of*

Labour's Successes and Failures London: Penguin.

Waites, Matthew (2001), 'Regulation of Sexuality: Age of Consent, Section 28 and Sex Education', *Parliamentary Affairs*, Volume 54: 495-508.

Waugh, Paul (2002) 'Gays to win same rights as married couples', *The Independent*, 6 December.

Weeks, J. (1981) *Sex, Politics and Society: The Regulation of Sexuality since 1800*, Harlow: Longman.

Weeks, J. (1991) *Against Nature: Essays on History, Sexuality and Identity*, London: Rivers Oram Press.

Weeks, J. (1995) *Invented Moralities: Sexual Values in an Age of Uncertainty*, Cambridge: Polity Press.

Weeks, J. (1998) 'The Sexual Citizen', *Theory, Culture and Society* 15 (3-4): 35-52.

Weeks, J. (2000) *Making Sexual History*, Cambridge: Polity Press.

Weeks, J. (2001) 'Live and Let Love? Reflections on the Unfinished Sexual Revolution of our Times', in Rosalind Edwards and Judith Glover (eds.), *Risk and Citizenship: Key Issues in Welfare*, London: Routledge.

Weeks, Jeffrey, Heaphy, Brian, and Donovan, Catherine (2001), *Same Sex Intimacies: Families of Choice and Other Life Experiments*, London and New York: Routledge.

Wellings, K., Field, J., Johnson, A.M. and Wadsworth, J. (1994) *Sexual Behaviour in Britain: The National Survey of Sexual Attitudes and Lifestyles*, London: Penguin.

Yates, Charles (2001) 'Leader of Scotland's Roman Catholics dies at 76', *The Independent*, 18 June.

4. New directions, or 'the same old story'? New Labour's policies on race relations, immigration and asylum

Liza Schuster and John Solomos

It is appropriate in assessing the impact of New Labour in power that we look at shifts in its policies around race relations and immigration. This is a particularly important policy arena to explore, since questions about race and immigration represent policy issues on which it was assumed in 1997 that there was 'clear blue water' between the Conservatives and New Labour. Certainly, on the basis of the proliferation of legislation in these areas and developments in migration policy in particular, these assumptions would appear to be well-founded.

In what follows, however, we question the extent to which these interventions represent a break with the experience of the Conservative governments from 1979 to 1997, or of previous Labour administrations. We argue that, while New Labour has continued to employ the discourse of inclusion it developed in opposition, and has opened up to certain forms of migration, its actual policy in relation to both ethnic minorities and migrants, particularly undocumented migrants and asylum-seekers, has been marked by a continuing preoccupation with exclusion and control. Underpinning the rhetoric of inclusion, cohesion and belonging remains the belief that strict immigration controls are necessary for 'good race relations', and that it is legitimate and necessary to select from among would-be entrants those most likely to fit into and to benefit British society (Blair speech to CBI 27.04.04). This is in spite of recent developments that demonstrate the extent to which references to control – of entry and of ethnic minorities – are embedded in a discourse that legitimates the fear of the other, whether that other is a Roma asylum-seeker or a British-Bengali Muslim.

The period since the election of the Labour government in 1997 has seen some important developments in policies towards race relations, immigration and asylum. Perhaps the most important of these relating to race has been the publication of the Macpherson Report[1] into the murder of Stephen Lawrence,[2] which led to the reform of the 1976 Race Relations Act and a public commitment to the development of new initiatives to tackle racial discrimination within the public sector.

In terms of migration, Labour quickly introduced the 1999 Asylum and Immigration Act, to be followed by the 2002 Nationality, Immigration and Asylum Act; it has also for the first time since the immediate post-war period declared that Britain needs migrants and has opened legal channels for entry. We will argue that the 2002 Act marks an interesting convergence between two policy areas – race and migration – that have traditionally been treated as linked but separate. This convergence was hastened by both the 2001 unrest in Britain's northern cities and the events of 11 September.[3]

NEW LABOUR, RACE AND IMMIGRATION

In opposition, New Labour worked closely with representatives of minority communities and groups campaigning on a range of issues, from black deaths in custody to asylum and immigration. Shadow Cabinet Ministers such as Jack Straw had become closely associated with, for example, the Stephen Lawrence campaign and the demands for a public enquiry. Labour members had also taken part in public meetings and protests around the 1993 and 1996 Asylum and Immigration Acts. However, while New Labour in opposition seemed comfortable with its multicultural and anti-racist positions, different positions were discernible within the party in relation to migration. During the debates following the readings of the 1993 and 1996 Bills, it was noticeable that senior figures in the party did not contradict some of the fundamental tenets of the Conservative government's arguments, preferring instead to focus on the letter of the law, wary of being seen as soft on migration. Though critical of the use of the term 'bogus', New Labour nonetheless accepted that the majority of claimants were not 'genuine'. It was left to Old Labour backbenchers to unambiguously point out the racist nature of the proposed legislation (*Hansard*, 2 November 1992, Col. 65). In opposition, the leadership of New Labour seemed more concerned with addressing its electoral 'vulnerability' on immigration, and avoiding accusations of being 'soft'.

When New Labour came to power in 1997 and Jack Straw took over at the Home Office, he was known as someone who was 'good on race relations'. Together with Tony Blair he had been critical of the 1993 and 1996 Acts introduced by the Conservative government. So when, on becoming Home Secretary, his first acts were the launch of a public enquiry into the murder of Stephen Lawrence, the introduction of racially aggravated offences in the 1998 Crime and Disorder Act and a review of the entire immigration and asylum system, expectations that in terms of race and immigration this would be a radically different government seemed to have been confirmed.

REDEFINING RACIAL EQUALITY AND SOCIAL JUSTICE

In terms of racial equality, it did seem that at least in this area there was a clear difference of approach between New Labour and the

Conservative Party. While both parties had introduced restrictive migration legislation, the Race Relations Acts of 1965, 1968 and 1976 had all been brought in by Labour governments (for historical context see Schuster & Solomos 2004). In opposition, New Labour had developed close links with ethnic minority and anti-racist organisations such as the National Assembly Against Racism, the Joint Council for the Welfare of Immigrants, the 1990 Trust and a number of other community and campaigning organisations. And New Labour had more black and Asian MPs than the Conservatives and Liberals put together. All of these factors raised hopes and expectations, and two major initiatives since 1997 indicated New Labour's commitment on these issues: the publication of the Macpherson Report into the death of Stephen Lawrence and the passage of the 2000 Race Relations (Amendment) Act.

The Macpherson Report

The publication in February 1999 of the Macpherson Report into the murder of Stephen Lawrence could be seen as a *symbolic* turning point in New Labour's policy agenda on race and racial inequality (Macpherson, 1999). The amount of media coverage given to the Report, as well as the widespread support (including from the right-wing tabloid *Daily Mail*) for the campaign organised by Stephen Lawrence's family to uncover the full facts surrounding his murder, seemed to be a sign that his death was not merely another episode in the tragic litany of racist murders and 'deaths in custody'.

Yet in many ways the Report can be said to contain little that is new, either in conceptual analysis or in policy agenda setting. As we have argued elsewhere (Solomos, 1999), the definition of institutional racism was borrowed from American debates in the 1970s, reflected the discussions of institutional racism contained in the Scarman Report, and relied on definitions already contained in the 1976 Race Relations Act. Most recommendations (66 out of 70) focused on the police and criminal justice system, though those recommendations relating to the recruitment and retention of ethnic minority staff and racial awareness training informed provisions in the Race Relations Amendment Act 2000. The Report seemed to carry a great deal of weight, judged by the public attention it received on publication and in the period that followed. An important element of its influence was that its recommendations seemed to go further than the actual events surrounding the murder of Stephen Lawrence and the police response to the murder. The recommendations on racism, education and social policy were in some ways part of its strength, but they also provided a hostage to fortune, a high standard by which progress should be measured. The treatment of Stephen Lawrence's family and of his friend Duwayne Brooks by the police highlighted the everyday processes that shape the experience of minority groups at the hands of institutions such as the police, and yet the list of black British men killed in custody and of their treatment by the police continues unabated, as does the ongoing abuse and discrimination experienced by black and Asian people in almost every facet of their lives.

The full impact of the Macpherson Report in terms of practical policy change in the longer term remains to be assessed, but the experience of the Scarman Report in 1981 and New Labour's response to the anger of young Asian men in Burnley and Oldham twenty years later (see footnote 3) should warn us against making any facile predictions about the nature of the improvements that we are likely to see (Scarman, 1981). If anything, the experience of the past two decades teaches us that the ways in which policy recommendations are translated into practice remains fundamentally uncertain, particularly as the nature of policy change depends on broader political agendas, and on sudden and highly publicised events such as the confrontation between the state and non-white youth (Solomos 1991).

It would be far too simplistic to dismiss the Report's key policy recommendations or to say that it is bound to be ignored. However, it would be in line with trends over the past two decades to point to the limited nature of reform and policy change in this field. Even in the aftermath of the major outbreaks of urban unrest in 1980/81 and 1985, the promise of reform and new agendas was replaced after a time by a degree of complacency and inactivity (Benyon and Solomos, 1987). As Stuart Hall remarked in the aftermath of the 1985 riots: 'I have a reluctance about entering once again into what seems to me a terribly familiar and recurring cycle. The cycle goes something like this. There is a problem that is followed by a conference; the conference is followed by research; the research reinforces what we already know, but in elegant and scholarly language. Then nothing happens' (Hall, 1987: 45).

The preliminary evidence since 1999 indicated that at least some key elements of the Macpherson Report would be implemented, particularly as the government sought to show that it was taking the question of 'institutional racism' seriously within its own institutions, such as the police and the civil service. In terms of public agenda-setting it seemed likely that the public debate about race and public policy would be shaped in part by symbolic and substantive responses to the Report, such as the 2000 Race Relations (Amendment) Act.

2000 Race Relations (Amendment) Act

During the long period of Conservative domination from 1979 to 1997 there had been numerous calls for the strengthening of the 1976 Race Relations Act. These calls were backed up by detailed submissions from the Commission for Racial Equality (CRE) and by research that highlighted the limitations of the 1976 Act, limitations that had become pronounced as early as the 1980s. Despite these calls the Conservative Party did little to strengthen the legislation, and it was New Labour that took up the question while in opposition. It came as no surprise therefore, particularly in the context of public debates about this issue, that when New Labour came to power it signalled its intention to pass a new Act to remedy past weaknesses and set the agenda for the future.

The 2000 Race Relations (Amendment) Act was the product of this commitment to social justice and an attempt to respond to the Macpherson Report, which called upon 'every institution ... to guard against disadvantaging any section of our communities'. It is the main initiative that New Labour has put on the statute books that addresses questions of race directly, though the issue of race relations features indirectly in New Labour's immigration legislation, as we will discuss below.[4] The main innovation is that it extends the 1996 Race Relations Act further, to apply to public authorities. As a result the Act enforces on public authorities a new general statutory duty to promote racial equality and end discrimination and gives the Commission for Racial Equality extra powers to enforce the new regime (Home Office, 2001). The expectation embodied in the act is that public authorities will take action to prevent acts of race discrimination before they occur, and to ensure that in performing their public functions they should 'have due regard to the need to eliminate unlawful racial discrimination, and promote equality of opportunity and good relations between persons of different racial groups'.

These duties apply to local authorities, central government departments, schools, colleges and universities, the police, prison, fire and probation services, criminal justice agencies, NHS trusts and non-departmental public bodies, such the Arts Council (Home Office 1999). The Act outlines both general and specific duties, which came into force in April 2001 and December 2001 respectively, although the CRE's powers to enforce these duties only came into effect from 31 May 2002.

While many departments within the public sector already had policies on equal opportunities in place, there had been little progress in actually achieving racial equality in either recruitment or retention (Appelt and Jarosch, 2000; Bhavnani, 2001). Previous legislation had focused on preventing discrimination, though with very little success. The new Act shifts the focus to racial equality. However, according to a report by the Audit Commission (2002), 40 per cent of councils have not even reached the first of five levels of good practice on race equality, as laid down by the CRE in 1995.

The 2000 Act was generally welcomed as a step in the right direction by those working on questions of racial discrimination and exclusion. There was, however, some disappointment that the Act did not take up all of the recommendations made by the Commission for Racial Equality for strengthening the 1976 Race Relations Act. Furthermore, the Act did not extend to cover the role of public authorities in relation to immigration and asylum and refuge. Section 19 explicitly states that the Act does not apply to laws or persons in relation to immigration or nationality. To some extent this is an inevitable aspect of any immigration policy, since, as Anne Dummett points out: 'All immigration laws are of necessity discriminatory on grounds of nationality, since they must distinguish between nationals of the legislating state and non-nationals' (Dummett, 2001: 1). It is also symptomatic, however, of the way in which New Labour has been wary of any attempt to radically rethink the logic of policies on immigration and asylum.

ECONOMIC MIGRANTS, ASYLUM-SEEKERS AND SYMBOLIC POLITICS

The number of Acts and measures relating to migration introduced by New Labour is breath-taking. In terms of primary legislation alone, there has been so far three Acts of Parliament, in 1999, 2002 and 2004. But there have also been a number of secondary measures relating to entry. It is interesting that these measures and migration policy as a whole are apparently marked by an extraordinary duality (Flynn 2003). On the one hand, the government seems to be opening the borders wide to citizens of the new EU member states, third country nationals that can fill Britain's skills gaps, and students – who pay very high fees and may also become skilled workers. David Blunkett remarked that he saw no obvious need to limit the number of migrants coming, provided there were jobs for them to do. At the same time, the treatment of asylum-seekers by this same government has been extraordinarily harsh. They have been removed from the benefits system, dispersed, detained and deported in unprecedented numbers and most recently rendered deliberately destitute as a means of exerting pressure to leave the country on those whose claims have failed. This treatment has also been extended to their children.

These contradictions were apparent early on. Shortly after taking power, the White List introduced by the previous Conservative administration was abolished, and the percentage of applications for asylum that were accepted increased.[5] The Home Secretary also granted leave to remain to approximately 70,000 long-standing applicants. While the granting of limited leave to remain brought relief to many thousands of asylum-seekers in Britain, from the government's perspective it also served to reduce in some small measure the pressure from an increasingly unmanageable backlog of applications.

The Labour Party in opposition had been extremely critical of the White List, which had seemed to mark a departure from the principle that every individual had the right to have his or her case examined individually; so the abolition of the White List was welcome, though not a surprise. However, in 2002 a White List was reintroduced – though absence of persecution is a less important criterion for regarding countries as safe than issues of strategic interests and deterrence. Other signs of continuity, both with the previous government and with

Labour's historical record on immigration, were provided by the new government's response to the Chahal decision, and to the arrival of around eight hundred Roma from Slovakia and the Czech Republic.

Just before the 1997 General Election, in November 1996, the European Court of Human Rights found against the Home Secretary in the case of Karamjit Singh Chahal.[6] A consequence of this decision was that the ability of the government of the day to deport a person on national security grounds was severely curtailed. In order to address this difficulty, just after the election the New Labour government brought the Special Immigration Commission Bill before the House. The interesting point here is the tone of the discussions across the floor of the House, in which Conservative members accepted and approved the new Home Secretary's response to the decision of the ECHR, and during which it was quite clear that the Commission was created not to protect the rights of those facing deportation, but so that the government could once again proceed to deport.

In relation to the arrival of relatively small groups of Roma, the new government's response was even more rapid. In direct response to widespread and hostile media coverage of these arrivals, in October 1997 Jack Straw announced that, where officials believe that a claim is manifestly unfounded, an asylum-seeker would have only five days to appeal, instead of twenty-eight days, confirming media and public perceptions of the Roma as 'bogus' asylum-seekers. These cases are not likely to have significant impact on the numbers of people allowed to remain in Britain, but they do serve to illustrate New Labour's concern with being, and being seen to be, tough on immigration, and protective of the powers of the executive.

All of the above developments occurred in the first year of New Labour's term of office. In the summer of 1998 the results of the migration review were published as the White Paper *Fairer, Faster, Firmer: A Modern Approach to Immigration and Asylum* (Home Office, 1998). Those carrying out the review of the immigration and asylum system were charged with 'thinking the unthinkable', giving rise to expectations that policy in this area might move in new, and perhaps more progressive, directions. It was accepted that the immigration system, and asylum in particular, was in a shambles, and that 'something' would have to be done. Although there was acknowledgement in the White Paper that migration was good for Britain, the result was an Act embodying a degree of harshness towards would-be migrants, asylum-seekers and members of ethnic minority communities in Britain that was extraordinary, though unsurprising in view of Labour's historic record.

The Act withdrew new asylum-seekers from the welfare system, and introduced vouchers to be exchanged for goods in shops (including charity shops) and supermarkets. It also instituted a dispersal scheme (which, as its early critics had warned, led to a massive increase in racist attacks (IRR 2000)). In addition its provisions enabled a sharp increase in detentions and deportations, and a reduction in the number of appeals. The only progressive element of this Act was the introduction of an automatic right to bail hearings, which, however, never came into force and was abolished in the 2002 Nationality, Immigration and Asylum Act. The Labour Party's massive majority of 174 meant that the government was able to force through these draconian measures, in spite of a prolonged campaign by many who had opposed the previous Conservative legislation. The effects of the 1999 Act were quickly felt by its targets.

The voucher scheme for destitute asylum-seekers with additional difficulties (destitution alone brings with it no entitlement) met strong opposition from Liberal Democrats, Labour backbenchers such as Diane Abbott, Jeremy Corbyn and Neil Gerard, as well as many of the charities operating the charity shops; they predicted – accurately as it transpired – that this would lead to the stigmatisation and humiliation of asylum-seekers, marking them out clearly as 'different' and 'dependent', and making them targets for hostility. Pressure from a wide range of groups, including those just mentioned, and importantly, Bill Morris of the TGWU, together with reporting of the difficulties faced by individuals and families trying to use the vouchers, led to a review of the system, and its subsequent abolition.

Dispersal was a second key element of what became the 1999 Immigration and Asylum Act. It was designed to relieve the pressure that had been building on local authorities, in particular in London and parts of the south-east, especially parts of Kent. Once again, NGOs and concerned others warned that dispersal was a recipe for increasing racism and racist violence, and that it would leave people with limited language skills and little or no support in areas of Britain that were largely homogeneous, as well as socially deprived (Bloch and Schuster 2002, IRR 2000). Those who warned that this would mean dumping asylum-seekers in sink estates were proved correct. There have been a number of reports – from Liverpool about the Landmark hostel, from Glasgow about the Sighthill estate, which witnessed the first murder of an asylum-seeker (Firsat Dag), and from the National Audit Commission (Audit Commission 2000) – warning that the conditions in which asylum-seekers were being housed were unsafe, and unfit for human habitation in some cases, and that they expose them to attacks.

As a result of the Act, there was also a massive increase in the number of places for detention, especially in prisons (of almost 2,000 detainees, about 75 per cent were held in prisons, a practice criticised by UNHCR). That this practice is in contravention of the UK's human rights obligations was confirmed by a decision in September 2001, in which the judge found in favour of four Kurds, arguing that there was no evidence that they would abscond, and ordered the government to pay compensation. The Home Secretary appealed successfully against this decision, but promised that asylum-seekers would no longer be held in prisons, and the construction of purpose-built detention centres continued apace. The first dedicated detention centre for families was opened at Oakington in Cambridge in March 2000, since then being joined by another at Harmondsworth outside Heathrow, and one at Yarl's Wood in Bedfordshire (partially destroyed by a fire in February 2002). It is worth noting here that the policy of detaining asylum-seekers on arrival was originally proposed by Anne Widdicombe, and was at first ridiculed by the Labour Party. Subsequently, a fire at Yarl's Wood and unrest following the suicide of a detainee at Harmondsworth in 2004 led to large number of detainees being transferred again to prisons.

At the beginning of 2001, while still Home Secretary, Jack Straw proposed a significant new direction in asylum policy. He attacked the Geneva Convention, arguing that it was no longer fitted to today's world. As the 2001 General Election approached, he also spoke with approval of the attempts to find a harmonised definition of 'refugee' at EU level. In pursuit of a far less liberal policy, Straw argued that 'there is a limit on the number of applicants, *however genuine*, that you can take' (*Observer*, 20.5.01 – our emphasis), and that a cap or quota would have to be introduced. He went on to explain that the limit is dependent on 'the ability of the country to take people and public acceptability'. He did not refer to the role that government can and does play in creating public tolerance and acceptance.[7]

The 1999 Act amounted to 'bad law'. Aside from its incoherence legally, it also misdiagnosed the challenges posed by asylum-seekers and migrants. Like the previous two Acts, it defined the 'problem' facing the state as one of control, of the state's inability to control the numbers of people entering the country. These numbers were perceived to be a problem because it was assumed they would exacerbate 'racial' tensions, and because of the perceived costs to an overstretched welfare system. However, the 1999 Act must, like its predecessors, be judged a failure even in its own terms, because it did not reassert the state's control over its borders and it did not create a system that was either fair or fast. More importantly, however, it is a 'bad law' because it increased the misery and humiliation of very many asylum-seekers, and, in validating the fears and prejudices of those hostile to migrants in general and asylum-seekers in particular, it contributed to the growth in violence and hostility towards those groups. According to a report produced by ECRI in 2001:

> Problems of xenophobia, racism and discrimination ... persist and are particularly acute *vis-à-vis* asylum-seekers and refugees. This is reflected in the xenophobic and intolerant coverage of these groups of persons in the media, but also in the tone of the discourse resorted to by politicians in support of the adoption and reinforcement of increasingly restrictive asylum immigration laws.

Inevitably, dissatisfied with the clear failure to reduce the numbers coming, the government commissioned yet more research, and produced another White Paper – this time one that explicitly links race relations and migration. Once again the emphasis is on control and the national interest, and on pre-entry selection, but there is also a demand that those allowed in develop a 'shared sense of belonging and identity' (Home Office, 2002: 1; Sales 2002).

THE 2002 NATIONALITY, IMMIGRATION AND ASYLUM ACT: RACE AND MIGRATION

New Labour's first term in office saw the introduction of legislation that sought to include into British society citizens who had been excluded by discrimination and racism, as well as legislation that attempted to exclude asylum-seekers. Importantly, however, it also saw the beginnings of a shift in relation to 'economic' migration. In September 2000 Barbara Roche, then immigration minister, argued that Britain was suffering a skills shortage and needed migration. A government report was published emphasising the positive contributions that migrants can make, and arguing that ultimately migration is good for the country and the economy (Glover *et al* 2001). At one level this marked a significant (but not unprecedented) shift in migration policy, and one that has maintained its momentum (see Blair's speech to CBI 27.04.04).[8] Once again, nevertheless, the bulk of the 2002 Act that was brought in by Straw's successor at the Home Office, David Blunkett, focused on asylum-seekers, and marked a shift towards assimilation and away from concerns with discrimination and racism. In part, this was due to events at home and abroad in 2001.

On his second day in office (after the General Election of June 2001, David Blunkett had announced another shake-up of the immigration and asylum system, including the opening of legal migration channels to fill the skills shortage and a crackdown on 'illegal migration'. He had also set up a Ministerial Group on Public Order and Community Cohesion, in response to the urban unrest in the Northern towns, whose brief was 'to examine and consider how national policies might be used to promote better community cohesion, based upon shared values and a celebration of diversity' (Cantle 2001: 1). Then, in 2002, Blunkett published the White Paper, *Secure Borders, Safe Haven: Integration with Diversity in Modern Britain*, which in turn has led to the 2002 Nationality, Immigration and Asylum Act.

Most of the 2002 Nationality, Immigration and Asylum Act, the major piece of legislation in this field that New Labour has introduced during its second term, is devoted to measures designed to reduce the number of asylum-seekers entering Britain and to facilitate the removal of those deemed to have no right to remain. The key provisions of the Act (Home Office 2002c) aim to:

1. Establish an end-to-end asylum process, with a system of induction, accommodation and removal centres.
2. Speed up the asylum process, improve contact management and reduce opportunities for abuse of the system.
3. Strengthen borders by ensuring that immigration controls are sufficiently robust to exclude those who are an immigration or security risk, but to be efficient, flexible and responsive so as to speed the entry of the many people who are coming here legitimately.
4. Tackle illegal working, people trafficking and fraud.
5. Update nationality law and enhance the importance of citizenship.

The implementation of these provisions has not been particularly smooth for the government. By July 2003, only one induction centre, at Dover, had been opened, and, owing to objections from local people in the areas where they were to be sited, no accommodation centres. There is an increased tracking and monitoring, especially of new applicants, facilitated by greater reporting restrictions that require people to sign in at police stations regularly. Of the provisions that have come into effect, the most devastating for asylum-seekers has been Section 55, which denies support to those who do not apply for asylum immediately on arrival and gives effect to plans first introduced by the Conservatives in 1996. As a result of this decision and the lack of an entitlement to a work permit, many asylum-seekers are now without any form of support (see Schuster & Solomos 2004).

At the same time, the numbers of work permits issued have increased significantly, indicating that the Home Office accepted not just that Britain needs workers, but also that the the absence of legal channels of entry was responsible for a growth in undocumented migration and the 'abuse' of the asylum system. The Highly Skilled Workers (HSWP), Seasonal Agricultural Workers (SAW) and other low-skilled Sector Based Workers (SWB) are channels permitting the entry of certain workers required by particular sectors of the economy – in particular IT, agriculture, construction, catering and food processing. Highly skilled migrants have always been able to get work permits, but the HSWP allows workers meeting strict criteria to enter for the purposes of seeking work. The creation of entry channels for unskilled workers is an echo of the European Voluntary Workers scheme: the SAW and SWB schemes imposed strict conditions for entry and stay on such workers, including age limits (18-25 and 18-30 respectively). Furthermore, these schemes have been introduced at a time when new arrivals from the ten new EU member states are expected to ease labour market shortages.

New Labour's acceptance that migration is needed for the efficient running of the economy does mark a shift from the Conservatives' long-standing perception of migration as marginal to the economy – something to be tolerated rather than welcomed. But it is highly selective and continues to be colour-coded; Blair reportedly argued that quotas would have to be introduced for applicants from 'New' (Black and Asian) Commonwealth countries under the Working Holidaymakers Scheme (*Sunday Telegraph* 6.6.04) following a 'dramatic' increase in applications from India, Pakistan, Nigeria and Ghana. In other words, while there have been shifts and progress in migration policy under Labour, these continue to be intimately linked with issues of race and racism, and the liberalisation of 'economic' migration channels has been accompanied by harsh and restrictive measures towards undocumented migrants and asylum-seekers.

CONCLUSION

The picture that emerges from this analysis is mixed. On the one hand, the government seems to have followed through on its commitment to address the racism that afflicts British society, and has introduced legal channels for, and a positive discourse on, migration. On the other hand, initial indications from the CRE and the Audit Commission (though not from the Home Office) are that progress is painfully slow in the area of race relations and the positive moves in relation to migration remain defensive – as reflected for example by the government's introduction of a registration scheme for migrants from the new EU member states just before expansion, in response to tabloid hysteria, and the dispersal, detention and enforced destitution of asylum-seekers.

New Labour's commitment to racial equality, social justice and inclusion is inherently limited by its concern to be seen to be 'tough on immigration' and to be in tune with what it sees as the core values of the society as a whole. In this context it seems incapable of producing radical changes either to racial equality strategies or to asylum policies, since it needs to present itself as in tune with the concerns of popular opinion. It is significant in this context that David Blunkett has sought to justify the government's tough stance on asylum by adopting the language of the tabloids, in warning of the need to avoid the 'swamping' of schools and social services by migrants and refugees (*Guardian*, 25.4.02), and of the need to prevent the arrival of 'hordes' of 'illegal migrants' (*Radio 5 Live*, 30.5.02). At the same time another government minister, Peter Hain, felt moved to warn of the dangers of Muslim communities becoming more isolationist and helping to feed 'both rightwing politics and their own extremists' (*Guardian*, 13.5.02). Such pronouncements should not be read in isolation, since they are products of a specific political environment, but they are perhaps a signal that New Labour's 'third way' on race relations and immigration will lead us towards a race relations strategy based on 'integration' understood as assimilation, rather than on 'multiculturalism', and on a migration strategy more firmly based on selection and national interest rather than rights or protection. It has become evident that rather than questioning and challenging some of the moral panics around this question, New Labour has, if anything, added to them. One of the saddest aspects of what has happened is that New Labour's agenda has helped to sustain a climate of fear about refugees and asylum-seekers, and has increased the fear and racist violence suffered by these groups themselves.

Labour's return to power after eighteen years may come to be seen as a tragic missed opportunity for all sections of British society, including established minority communities and new arrivals. It could have shifted the terms of the debate in this and in other areas. In practice, however, New Labour's policies on migration and on race relations have displayed marked continuities with previous Labour and Conservative governments. This is because the same flawed logic underpins all of the legislation on migration and on race relations, namely that good race relations depend on strict immigration controls.

The Race Relations Amendment Act (2000) may make some difference in the medium term, particularly in tackling forms of institutional racism in the labour market within the public sector. Yet both the 1999 Immigration and Asylum Act and the 2002 Immigration, Asylum and Nationality Bill can be seen as doing little to address the limits of previous policies on immigration and nationality. Rather, the rhetoric and the substance of these policies can be seen as moving New Labour towards a policy agenda that is underpinned by the contradictory strategies of punitive controls on new groups of migrants and asylum-seekers and measures to encourage the integration of established migrant communities. In a context of growing racism and continuing public concerns about immigration, the rationale of governmental policies seems to be to appease popular opinion rather than set out a new policy agenda that challenges both existing racial inequalities and the emerging patterns of exclusion aimed at new migrants.

In writing this paper we have benefited from the helpful advice and support of various colleagues and friends, most notably Claire Alexander, Les Back, Chetan Bhatt, Alice Bloch and Michael Keith. We are grateful too to Deborah Lynn Steinberg for her comments and patience.

NOTES

1. In 2000, a second significant report was published by the Commission on the Future of Multi-Ethnic Britain, chaired by Bhikhu Parekh. This was not officially sponsored by the Government but it included detailed analysis of policy agendas on race relations legislation and immigration (Parekh 2000). The Parekh Report did attract some lively debate when it was published, but it was not translated into a clear agenda that would shape public policy in practice (see Schuster & Solomos 2004).
2. Stephen Lawrence was a black student, murdered in south London in

April 1993. Following a long campaign led by his parents, the new Labour government announced a public enquiry. The results of the inquiry, led by Judge William Macpherson, were published as a report that concluded that the Metropolitan Police were institutionally racist. In response, the Labour government passed the 2000 Race Relations (Amendment) Act.

3. The 2001 urban unrest was concentrated in Oldham, Burnley and Bradford. In May 2002, less than a year later, three British National Party candidates were elected to the local council in Burnley.

4. For the Home Office's self-evaluation, see *Race Equality: The Home Secretary's Employment Targets. The Second Annual Report on Progress* July 2001.

5. The white list was a list of countries in which it was presumed that there was no risk of persecution. Applications from nationals of these countries were dealt with in fast-track procedures.

6. The Court accepted that Mr Chahal, a Sikh separatist, was at serious risk of torture (Art.3) if he was returned to India. The court found that because there was no effective domestic remedy to review the Home Secretary's decision (Art.13) to deport on the grounds of national security, Mr Chahal's rights had been violated.

7. This new toughness was also reflected in the 'New Vision for Refugees' proposed in 2003 by Blair and Blunkett, which included plans to export asylum-seekers to Transit Processing Camps in countries just outside the EU and to establish Regional Protection Zones.

8. There is extensive literature on the use of migrants (including refugees) to fill labour shortages (e.g Joshi & Carter 1984, Schuster 2003b).

REFERENCES

Appelt, E. and Jarosch, M. (2000) (eds) *Combating Racial Discrimination: Affirmative Action as Model for Europe* Oxford: Berg.

Audit Commission (2002) *Equality and Diversity* London: Audit Commission.

—— (2000) *Another Country: Implementing Dispersal under the Immigration and Asylum Act 1999* London: Audit Commission.

Benyon, J. and Solomos, J. (eds) (1987) *The Roots of Urban Unrest* Oxford: Pergamon.

Bhavnani, R. (2001) *Rethinking Interventions to Combat Racism* Stoke on Trent: Commission for Racial Equality with Trentham Books.

Bloch, A. (2000) 'A New Era or More of the Same? Asylum Policy in the UK' *Journal of Refugee Studies* 13, 1: 29-42.

Bloch, A. and Schuster, L. (2002) 'Asylum and Welfare: Contemporary Debates' *Critical Social Policy* 22, 3: 393-412.

Cantle, T. (2001) *Community Cohesion: A Report of the Independent Review Team* London: Home Office.

ECRI (2001) *Second Report on the United Kingdom* Strasbourg: European Commission Against Racism and Xenophobia.

Dummett, A. (2001) *Ministerial Statements – the Immigration Exception in the Race Relations (Amendment) Act 2000* Immigration Law Practitioners' Association.

Glover, S. *et al* (2001) *Migration: An Economic and Social Analysis* London: Home Office.

Hall, S. (1987) 'Urban Unrest in Britain' in J. Benyon and J. Solomos (eds) *The Roots of Urban Unrest* Oxford: Pergamon.

Home Office (2002) *Nationality, Immigration and Asylum Bill* London: The Stationery Office.

—— (2002) *Secure Borders, Safe Haven: Integration with Diversity in Modern Britain* London: The Stationery Office.

—— (2001) *Race Relations (Amendment) 2000: New Laws for a Successful Multi-Racial Britain* London: Home Office.

—— (1999) *Race Equality: The Home Secretary's Employment Targets* London: Home Office.

—— (1998) *Fairer, Faster and Firmer – A Modern Approach to Immigration and Asylum* London: The Stationery Office.

IRR (2002) *The Dispersal of Xenophobia: A Special Report on the UK and Ireland* European Race Bulletin, London: Institute of Race Relations.

Joshi, S. & Carter, B. (1984) 'The Role of Labour in the Creation of a Racist Britain' *Race & Class* 25, 3: 53-70

Macpherson, Sir William, Chairman (1999) *The Stephen Lawrence Inquiry* London: the Stationery Office.

Parekh, B. (2000) *The Future of Multi-Ethnic Britain: Report of the Commission on Multi-Ethnic Britain* London: Profile Books

Sales, R. (2002) 'The Deserving and the Undeserving: Refugees, Asylum Seekers and Welfare in Britain' *Critical Social Policy* 22, 3: 456-78.

Scarman, Lord (1981) *The Brixton Disorders 10-12 April 1981* London: HMSO 1981.

Scarman, Lord (1985); 'Brixton and After', in J. Roach and J. Thomaneck (eds) *Police and Public Order in Europe* London: Croom Helm.

Schuster, L. (2003a) 'Asylum Seekers: Sangatte and the Tunnel' *Parliamentary Affairs* Special Issue on Crisis Management 56, 3: 506-522.

Schuster, L. (2003b) *The Use and Abuse of Political Asylum in Britain and Germany* London: Frank Cass.

Schuster, L. & Solomos, J. (2004) 'Race, Immigration and Asylum: New Labour's Agenda and its Consequences' (with John Solomos) *Ethnicities* 4, 2: 267-300

Schuster, L. and Solomos, J. (2002) 'Rights and Wrongs across European Borders: Migrants, Minorities and Citizenship' *Citizenship Studies* 6(1) 37-54.

Solomos, J. (1991) *Black Youth, Racism and the State: The Politics of Ideology and Policy* Cambridge: Cambridge University Press.

Solomos, J. (1993) *Race and Racism in Britain* 2nd Edition Basingstoke: Macmillan.

Solomos, J. (1999) 'Social Research and the Stephen Lawrence Inquiry' *Sociological Research Online,* 4(1). http://www.socresonline.org.uk/socresonline/4/lawrence/solomos.html

5. Thrice told tales: modernising sexualities in the age of consent

Debbie Epstein, Richard Johnson and
Deborah Lynn Steinberg

The issue ... is not at what age we wish young people to have sex. It is whether the criminal law should discriminate between heterosexual and homosexual sex. It is therefore an issue not of age, but of equality (Tony Blair, *Hansard* 21.2.94).

On 30 November 2000, in the first Parliament of the New Labour government – and on the third attempt to change the law (the first of which occurred under the last Parliament of the Conservatives) – the Sexual Offences (Amendment) Act was passed. This Act made three legislative changes. First, it reduced the age of consent to sexual activity for gay men from 18 to 16,[1] thus equalising it with the age of consent for heterosexual people.[2] Second, it ended the criminalisation of sexual activity between and by gay young men under the age of sixteen.[3] Third, the Act introduced a new offence relating to 'abuse of trust'. This applies to people over the age of 18 having a sexual relationship with an under 18 year old while occupying a position of trust (e.g. teacher, counsellor, etc). This third provision applies to all sexual relationships, whether gay or straight.

The landslide election of New Labour in May 1997, after eighteen years of Tory rule, had engendered and was the result of considerable hopes for change across a range of social policies. There was, it seemed, an unequivocal yearning for a new, more tolerant and gentle society, a new order of government and of social life. This yearning was made manifest and articulated in very explicit terms in the extraordinary levels and manner of public mourning that took place following the death of Princess Diana in August 1997.[4] The move by New Labour, only a year after coming into office, to equalise the Age of Consent for gay men with that of heterosexuals represented an iconic moment in which that promised shift seemed to be actualised, not only in terms of sexual politics, but indeed in the political landscape itself. As evidenced in the quote above, Blairism seemed to hold out the promise of a new era, this time defined by inclusivity, equality and plurality.

In this chapter we are interested in the narratives and discursive frameworks that were deployed in the second Age of Consent debate in the House of Commons. We have chosen to focus on this interim debate because it is here that we see both one of the first strikes by New Labour against the previous Conservative hegemony in Parliament, and some of the iconic rhetorics and story-forms that have come to characterise the Blairite project. In our account, we pull out three main themes. First is the overall shift from a conservative and moral traditionalist hegemony to *a broad liberal alliance* on sexual matters in the Commons – a shift in which grand narratives of progress, modernisation, rationality are central. Second are the *diverse* political and discursive components that are combined *within* New Labour. Third, we consider the *limits* of the dominant tendency within this alliance, which we term 'social liberal'. Perhaps our most important arguments concern the ambiguities of the Blairite stress on 'inclusivity' and citizenship, in which a radical rhetoric is often accompanied by characteristic containments, by the conditional assimilation of some groups and the creation of new exclusions for instance.

MATTERS OF METHOD: NARRATIVES AND DISCURSIVE STRATEGIES

We approach our analysis of the 1998 Commons debate through a combination of narrative and discursive analysis.[5] In doing so, we trace the highly charged and performative deployment of narrative as a vector through which law is made. Simultaneously, we explore the strategic combinations of discourses (for example, medico-moral, religious, human rights) that fuel and inform particular story lines.

As we shall see, the narrative practices of parliamentary debate operate at a number of levels. There are 'little' narratives about particular persons or episodes. Characters are named and acquire exemplary status: for example 'paedophiles' in 'positions of trust', or young gay men forced to take their own lives or 'go on the game'. Stories of a medium level tell of typical legal consequences: for example, failing to reform the law or failing to draw 'a line in the moral sand' (Bell, Labour, col. 796) will destabilise society, or increase inequality, or make us uncompetitive in the global economy. Such stories, in turn, anchor and draw meanings from narratives that are truly grand. These third level stories typically take the state and history of the nation as their object and explore dystopian or utopian futures and pasts. Here change or stasis in the law serve competing definitions of the decline of civilisation or of social progress.

At the same time, debates in Parliament are pervaded by a concern for the nature and consequences of legislative decisions and entitlements. Hence our own reading starts from what we call 'the narrativisation of consequences'. We can analyse the debates as a series of competing narrations which centre on outcomes that are feared or preferred. A common form of debate is: if A, then B, where B is a host of hopes or horrors. The specifically evaluative functions of narrative – which narrative theorists variously name as moral 'point of view', 'evaluative function' or 'so-whatness' (Labov, 1972; Genette, 1980) – connect also with law-making, especially when it is seen as having a 'declarative' function. It is through such narrations that moral values – and the individual and collective subjects or communities anchored in them – are affirmed or attacked.

WHAT IS THIS HOUSE? SEXUAL STORIES AND THE WORD OF LAW

The House of Commons can be understood as a distinctive discursive/narrational space in at least three ways. First, even a cursory examination of parliamentary debate reveals a complex conglomeration of speech rituals – labyrinthine to the point of absurdity at times. Second, story-telling is an important dimension of the culture of the House and of the jurisprudential process of law-making. It is in this context that the narrativisation of consequences has particular currency. Arguments for and against particular changes in law are substantively conducted through rival stories which are more or less realist or apocryphal in character. Realist, or 'grounded' narratives make an ostensible claim to an empirical or lived experience. For example, MPs might claim that a number of their constituents have written to them to tell of experiences of homophobic harassment in school. Apocryphal narratives, in contrast, would seem to take more poetic license, often involving extravagant, even fantastical, claims that are delivered as if proved.

Third, not only is Parliament (notwithstanding the arrival of more women MPs in 1997) inhabited overwhelmingly by a particular class of men (white, business/professional, middle-class, upper-middle-class or even aristocratic); it is also characterised by a competing set of privileged masculinities, which are themselves constituted through the history of British and English imperial relations with their Others.[6] These relations are articulated, in part, through modes of discourse. Terminologies of 'maiden speeches' and 'bloodying', for example, are graphic heterosexual metaphors that (pre)figure the parliamentary space as one of masculine imperative and conquest. Furthermore, the traditional conduct of Members through formalistic rituals of bullying, heckling, jeering and jockeying constitute parliamentary dialogue as a symbolic blood sport. This has consequences for the forms and tellability of particular stories.[7]

THE GOOD, THE BAD AND THE LATENT: SEXUAL TEXTS AND SUBTEXTS

Of the many story-clusters that constituted the textual economies of the Age of Consent debates, three in particular interest us here. The first one is the contestation of the Conservative and New Labour repertoires that were mobilised around a particular, diversionary, amendment to the main proposal of equality of consent for gay men. This proposal concerned the dangers of the 'abuse of trust' by professionals dealing with young people. The second group was those relating to counter-narratives about the age at which sexual identity/preference becomes 'fixed'. In this arena of contestation, key New Labour themes emerged, particularly those concerning citizenship and 'evidence based policy'. Thirdly there was the 'good gays/bad gays' stories, which, while drawing on Conservative discourse, were nonetheless central to Blairite versions of liberal reform and 'liberal (in)tolerance' (Smith, 1994; Epstein and Steinberg, 1998: 10ff).

Latent predations: ghosts of conservatism past

In the early stages of debate, Joe Ashton, a Labour MP, proposed an amendment to the Bill which supported the equalisation of the age of consent, 'except when one party is in a position of authority, influence or trust in relation to the other, in which case both parties must have attained the age of 18' (*Hansard*, 1998, cols 755-6). This amendment applied equally to heterosexual and gay sex. Thus, at one level, it seemed entirely congruent with the equality discourse that underpinned the Bill. However, because it drew explicitly on a conservative protectionist discourse about 'innocence' and 'childhood', it opened a space for opponents of equality (largely Conservative MPs) to take over. The 'abuse of trust' issue (as it became referred to) allowed the introduction of three diversions into the discussion of gay men's age of consent: girls, displaced children and the heterosexual 'paedophile'. An inordinate amount of parliamentary time (and huge swathes of the *Hansard* transcript) are devoted to preoccupations about the special vulnerabilities or, in the latter case, dangerous proclivities of these figures.

This in turn had a number of striking consequences. On the one hand, the discussion of girls effectively sidelined gay men.[8] At the same time, the references to children from all manner of 'broken' homes (for example, children in boarding school, foster homes, children's homes and step-families)[9] returned gay men to the debate but only allusively and in a negative light. Haunting the putatively exhaustive list of displaced child victims of unstable or otherwise illegitimate families was Section 28's 'pretended', quintessentially gay, family.[10] It is notable that the heterosexual nuclear family, a pervasive site of child abuse, is missing from the list. Moreover, throughout the debate, and despite its obvious contradictions, the juxtaposition of an amendment for gay equality with protracted discussion focused on heterosexual 'paedophiles' had the effect that a deviant *heterosexual* masculinity could symbolically stand in for gay men (with their putatively predatory natures) and *vice versa*.

While Ashton himself disavowed anti-gay intent, his motion

nonetheless provided abundant discursive resources for a moral tradi-tionalist narrativisation of consequences. This can be seen at many levels in the following narrative, a Conservative appropriation of some of the key themes raised by the Ashton Amendment:

> The hon. Lady [Ann Keen who moved Clause 1] spoke of her back-ground and of her experience as a nurse; she spoke with feeling and with great knowledge. Before I entered the House 28 years ago, I was, for 10 years, a schoolmaster and I want to refer to that period in my life for a moment or two. During that period, I came across some extremely unhappy young men who had been preyed upon by older men, and whose whole manner and way of life had been changed and distorted as a result. Many of those young men were 15, 16 or 17 years old. I speak as the father of two sons who are now well over that age and I do not believe that a 16-year-old boy is indeed a fully mature adult. It is impor-tant that we take that into account in our deliberations this evening (Cormack, Conservative, cols 762-3).

The 'little' narrative here draws on the conventions of 'public' boys' boarding school auto/biographies concerning 'paedophilic' schoolmas-ters and the more or less ritualised abuse of younger boys by older boys. Here, of course, Cormack's personal identification as schoolmaster and reference to 'older men' would seem to disavow key parts of that story-line. As a middle level story, we have an edifying tale of the long-term personal consequences of such predations for young men. Presupposed is the grander moral traditionalist (predominantly Conservative) narra-tive of the 'corruption of morals' and its multiple instances, often invoked precisely in the face of proposed liberalisations of law around sexuality. Versions of this story-line (which weave through the whole debate) condense to yield a horrific list that amounts to a wholesale state of moral decline: lowering the age of consent to 16 would fail to protect and succour the vulnerable (Cormack, Conservative, col. 762); allow male rape (ibid, col. 764); licence pimps of young people (Bermingham, Conservative, col. 766); threaten to reduce the age of consent to 14 or be the first step in abolishing it entirely (Lewis, Conservative, col. 772); discourage trainee actors from returning to heterosexuality (Brazier, Conservative, col. 779); generalise the 'rum, sodomy and the lash' (or at least the sodomy) ascribed to Her Majesty's navy (Cormack, col. 763); encourage the spread of AIDS (Winterton, Conservative, col. 769); permit the 'buggery' of sixteen year old girls as well as boys (Butterfill, Conservative, col. 759); take the first step towards recognising the pension and marriage rights of homosexual couples (Bell, Labour, col. 796).

Both discursively and narratively, then, Joe Ashton's motion ensured that many elements of the Conservative repertoire were restored, *sub rosa*, to the debate; it was clearly not possible to refuse the notion that the House has a duty to protect boys and girls from child abuse. The most that supporters of equality could do, and they did it repeatedly, was to acknowledge the validity of this issue and then attempt to point out that it was a separate question. More resourcefully, they proposed a counter-narrative that featured discriminatory law itself as the child abuser, and especially law that criminalised young men for having gay relationships. Neither of these strategies was successful in curtailing the digression. Yet at the same time, moral traditionalists were forced to take up improbably liberal positions: as defenders of the rights, for example, not just the 'innocence', of young people. Thus, while a Conservative repertoire could be reasserted, overt homophobia could no longer be assumed to be normative or to occupy the moral high ground. A final complexity here is the promise, in the very moment of liberalisation, to create a new margin and new forms of regulation. This *combination* of granting 'equality' and pursuing closer regulation is typical of the dynamics of Blairism more generally. Indeed, the eventual adoption of Joe Ashton's amendment into the final form of the law suggests that New Labour's alliance could accommodate its own forms of social conservatism – some, as noted by Jeffrey Weeks in this volume, inherited from older Labour.

Stories of the age of fixation

> The [British Medical Association] report ... makes it clear that all the reputable research evidence shows that adult sexual orientation is usually established before the age of puberty in boys and girls (Keen, col. 760).

> I am content to accept that some may be born with a genetic predisposition to homosexuality – I am not medically knowledgeable enough to pass comment. I am convinced, however, that many people are not born homosexual – it is for them that we must have a special regard. Would anyone seriously suggest that every sailor who followed a homosexual way of life was born homosexual? ... I do not believe that every young man who followed that way of life was born to it (Cormack, col. 763).

As in the earlier debate, a matter of considerable concern on both sides was the age at which homosexual identity could be said to be fully achieved and 'fixed'. In 1994, supporters of equality told developmental stories (drawing on medical and psychological discourses) of homosexuality as 'fixed' at birth, an innate and immutable (perverse) characteristic. In 1998, this developmental narrative was reasserted, although in modified form: homosexuality, while not innate, was nonetheless held to be 'fixed' by the age of 16, at the latest. In both 1994 and 1998, the anti-equality faction largely constructed homosexuality through a social determinist story of wilful (perverse) choice or seduction/corruption. However, this account was modified in some cases, as evidenced in Cormack's concession that, well, *some* gays might have been born that way.

These stories also carry implicit contestations about the status of 16-year-olds: were they citizens or children? fixed or unfinished? mature or vulnerable? rational agents or confused victims? Interestingly, whatever the precise age at which fixation was accepted to have occurred and whatever the construction of 16-year-olds, the logical conclusion of both arguments associated homosexuality with maturity, however unintentionally. The argument that permission to take part in homosexual acts inevitably threatens the stability of heterosexual identities not only imputes a greater attractiveness to homosexuality, but also a relative immaturity to those young men who assume themselves to be heterosexual, as compared to those who have 'chosen' to be gay. Ironically, then, whatever the age of fixation (even if later than 16), homosexual identity emerged as a signifier of maturity achieved and of rational identity. For supporters of inequality the uncertainty and unfinishedness of heterosexual identity did not, however, signal a disqualification from the right to have heterosexual sex.

Questions about the legal status of 16 year olds ran parallel to questions about their narrational status: were they heroes or anti-heroes, victims or criminals, subjects or objects? Moreover, we can read four modalities of developmental narrative in the age of fixation debates: a medical story about physical growth and emotional maturity, which is linked to a psychological story about child development measured in ages, stages and eventual fixity of identity; a legal story about competence in law and entitlement to citizenship; and a rationalist pedagogical story about the consequences of the provision or denial of health and sex education. As we have seen in the quotes above, the first three narratives can be conscripted for either Conservative or New Labour standpoints. The fourth both requires and produces a 'social liberal agenda' which is typical of New Labour:

> Fearful of being branded criminals, many young gay men are unable to seek health advice and sex education. In the past 10 years we have learned much about reducing sexual health risks. We know that personal health depends on good self-esteem, accurate health information, access to advice and support. All these essentials are undermined by our unequal age of consent (Keen, col. 759).

Despite Conservative contestations, a utilitarian/empiricist[11] mode of narration (medical and/or pedagogical) dominated the age of fixation stories. Indeed, these debates both illustrated and inscribed the emergent many-versioned liberal hegemony of a House dominated by New Labour. The age of fixation stories can be read, then, as a dialogic space in which it was possible to reclaim the authorial voice of the Labour majority from the powerful latent conservatism that hijacked much of the discussion.

Finally, embedded in the age of fixation stories are competing meta-narratives of childhood. In the first, often specifically Christian, moral traditionalist narrative, childhood is a battle of innocence against guilt or corruption: children, always objects rather than subjects, are to be protected from the corrupting influences of immoral adults (or from their own confused and perverse potentialities). Salvation is offered in the form of legislated inequality: childhood becomes a shifting characterisation – an age of fixation that is not fixed. In the second, an alternative story of innocence, and one central to the New Labour repertoire of citizenship more generally, childhood becomes a time of struggle out of ignorance into knowledge.[12] Equality before the law signposts the road to enlightenment and rational citizenship. Innocence, as ignorance, becomes the looming threat, the harbinger of the spread of HIV, intolerance and death. The implication of this is that the transformation of sexual politics necessarily involves a recasting of the politics of childhood, but only within certain limits. Within New Labour's rationalist construction of childhood, those below the age of 16 are still not seen as legitimate social agents, nor are their versions of the real, as against adult rationality, to be much attended to.

Good gays, bad gays

Eve Sedgwick (1994) has pointed out that a distinction between 'good gays' and 'bad gays' is central to a broader cultural and narrative repertoire of homophobia. The stress on sexuality as a private matter functions both as a defence (against homophobia) but also as a limitation on open debate and action around sexual inequalities and ways of living. Conventionally, constructions of the 'good homosexual' have focused on a quiet life on the margins with as much conformity to, and as little disturbance of, the central categories as is possible. Homosexual rights within this construct are subject to that condition. By contrast, the 'bad homosexual' is politically active and culturally assertive.[13]

The 1998 debate rehashed this old opposition, but also strikingly rewrote it:

> I have every respect for some of the pressure groups that have been acting on behalf of homosexual people – Stonewall, for example, is measured and reasoned in its campaigns – but with respect I have no sympathy whatsoever for militant groups such as OutRage! that want to publicise the cause of homosexuals at all costs ... Once [equality before the criminal law] has been achieved, there is no reason for the fuss that is often made to go on. Let all the publicity-seeking pressure groups accept that equality will have been achieved and let them leave the rest of society in peace (Laing, Con., col. 772).

It is, of course, not surprising to witness a Conservative invoking the good gay/bad gay distinction. What is striking is that Laing, a Conservative who *supported* equalisation (on liberal individualist grounds), also argued for the good gay activist. Stonewall can, by no means, be construed as quiet, or privatised, or as making no challenge to heterosexist law or wider cultural homophobias. Nevertheless, they are a group committed to the formal institutions of law (using the courts, and particularly the European Court of Human Rights), to party political structures (with particular loyalties to New Labour), and to an assimilationist agenda of social liberal reform (for example, gay marriage). Threaded throughout the debates, Stonewall was constructed as the New (Labour) version of the acceptable gay and was counterposed to OutRage! which continued to stand for the gay-beyond-the-pale.

This rewriting of the 'good gay' reflected in part the waning hegemony of the previous Conservative project to refuse the language of citizenship and rights with respect to gays. A concern for the consequences of social exclusion, both for the excluded and for the legitimacy and function of Britain as a 'modern state', is at the heart of the New Labour repertoire – as evidenced by its creation of the Social Exclusion Unit within the Cabinet Office. At the same time, the version of inclusive citizenship on offer, with its concomitant 'rights and responsibilities', is clearly assimilationist in mode. It is the margin that is invited to the centre (so long as they change themselves), the 'good' Other whose claim for membership is validated (so long as they adopt the values of the club).

In this context, a sexual ontology in which sexual difference is seen as natural and 'fixed' by the age of 16 corresponds to the splitting of gay from straight as separate communities. With sexualities divided in this way, it is possible for social liberal speakers to disavow discrimination and to preach tolerance, yet still hold lesbian and gay experiences at a distance, as nothing to do with 'us'. Curiously, it is the Conservative homophobe who works with a more fluid account of sexual identity, who better grasps the interdependence of sexual categories, the mixed and deeply relational character of 'gay' and 'straight'. Finally, as so often in the limited repertoire of narratives of the House of Commons, only part of the story is articulated here. The key absent figure for both Labour and Conservative, the wolf at the door (or worse, in the House), is the militant gay demanding not merely equality but 'illegitimate privilege'.[14] In this story, the predator, encamped outside and lying in wait, turns his rapacious eye to the very edifices of society and social stability. He will of course, having first gorged himself on innocents, blow the House down.

UN/CIVIL SOCIETIES: BRITAIN IN A POST-CLOSET WORLD

This House has the opportunity to end discrimination and we have to make a choice. We can take from the past those values of respect for others that are most enduring and translate them into the modern world, or we can simply cling to those old prejudices that have been most damaging and have forced generations of lesbians and gay men to live as second-class citizens (Keen, col. 762).

As this extract suggests, the 1998 debate was intimately intertwined with a project of New Nation. Contestations over imagined futures, imagined pasts and imagined communities crystallised into specific narratives and counter-narratives embedding Britishness in competing notions of equality, modernity and progress.

Ration(alis)ing equality
One of the markers of a shifted terrain of debate in 1998, and a new liberal hegemony, was the defining narrational prominence of equality discourses, deployed by *both* opponents *and* supporters of the amendment. Yet equality discourses could be deployed to very different ends, through the narration of different sets of imagined negative consequences, all of them harnessing notional in/equalities, to the question of abuse. Ann Keen, in the quote above, signals a particular take-up of the question of the abuse of young people that so preoccupied the digressive tendencies within the larger debate. Implicit in her concern with discrimination against, and criminalisation of, young gay men is a story about the ways in which inequalities under the law promote abuse and themselves constitute an abuse. This story was taken up by all who supported equalisation. Harms enumerated included: robbing gay men of their teenage years; promoting fear of coming out; promoting secrecy in the event of sexual abuse (since the law criminalised the victim, if under the age of consent, as well as the perpetrator); promoting homophobic bullying; promoting alienation from the family; and preventing young men from seeking sexual health advice, thus interfering with a social and educational agenda to reduce sexual health risks more generally. This social liberal narrativisation of consequences can be seen to be in direct contestation with Conservative narrations about the 'corruption of morals' that would follow from lowering the age of consent. At the same time, Conservative contributions were forced to take note of the liberal stories: 'I urge hon. Members to consider the consequences of their actions before they vote. If, like me, they consider that there is a case for homosexuality to be tolerated as equally as possible, but balanced by regard for the consequences, they will support my amendment' (Blunt. Con., col. 795).[15]

As with Blunt's statement, most of the Conservative stories were prefaced with an expression of general support for the idea that *some* kind of equality for lesbian and gay people was a legitimate concern. This would have been virtually unthinkable in 1994, when opponents of equalisation clearly did not feel compelled to frame their advocacy of discrimination within a discourse of equality. Clearly, the speech space of the Commons had shifted, such that unmitigated bigotry could no longer be spoken freely. Perhaps the most interesting version of mitigated advocacy of in/equality was that forwarded by Eleanor Laing:

> I have three main reasons for supporting the new clause. First, I believe in equality. Having said that, I do not believe that all people are equal. They are not; every person is different in some way from every other person. The equality that the new clause addresses is equality before the law, and I believe that everyone should be equal before the criminal law. I stress that I am referring specifically and precisely to the criminal law. If new clause 1 becomes part of the Bill, there is no automatic or necessary implication for the treatment of gay people under the civil law with regard to marriage, pension rights or any other such rights. That is not what we are discussing, it is not the matter before us, and it has no relevance to this debate; we are talking about equality before the criminal law (Laing, Con., col. 770).

Laing's clear rejection of civil equality while supporting the principle of equity before the criminal law represents a version of rationed equality. Though one is a neo-liberal and the other a moral traditionalist, both Laing and Blunt propose versions of limited tolerance. This is a very different stance from that of the Conservative Commons majorities of the Thatcher/Major years, but one that falls considerably short of full citizenship.

New histories: modernising sexualities

Unsurprisingly, given New Labour's overarching investment in 'modernising' itself and 'modernising' Britain, a discourse of modernity pervaded the 1998 debate. This articulated to concerns about democracy and Europeanisation, and was narrated through what might be read as competing histories of progress. The more familiar and conventional version emerged in homophobic interjections into Eleanor Laing's (qualified) support for equalisation. In this context, Julian Lewis' intervention encapsulated the position:

> The purpose of an age of consent is not to criminalise the children who have sex when they have not reached that age of consent; it is to protect the children below that age by criminalising the adults who have sex with them. Does she [Eleanor Laing] not recognise that the history of the age of consent for heterosexual sex has been that as society has evolved and become more civilised, the age ... has risen (Lewis Con., col. 771-2).

Lewis invokes a rather inaccurate progress narrative of the teleology of Age of Consent legislation. As Walkowitz (1980) has noted, Age of Consent legislation has not evolved in a linear trajectory but rather has followed the vagaries of shifting moral climates, and indeed moral panics. Moreover, if a rising age of consent serves as an index of civilisation, perhaps 50 would be more civilised than 16, 18 or even 21.

Keen, although also located within an evolutionary narrative of civilisation, nonetheless offers a significantly revised march towards progress:

> The House has the opportunity to end discrimination and we have to make a choice. We can take from the past those values of respect for others that are most enduring and translate them into the modern world, or we can simply cling to those old prejudices that have been most damaging and have forced generations of lesbians and gay men to live as second-class citizens. We have an opportunity to welcome all those men and women as equal members of our society and, this time, we must take it (Keen, Lab., col. 762).

In this story, the index of civilisation is one of increasing tolerance, equality and democracy, and of progressive anti-racism, anti-sexism and sexual tolerance. Keen, in line with dominant New Labour rhetoric, proposes the possibility of a refigured British as well as sexual history, one which can be measured by its progressive trajectory towards the eradication of discrimination. At the same time, both Keen's and Lewis's versions of history invoke imagined communities that shore up rather than challenge a notional Britishness. Indeed, Britishness throughout the debate was (re)constituted through narratives of progress, located in part through its approach to or distance from 'Europe' and 'democracy':

> The uneasy compromise of 1994 has already been challenged in the European Court of Human Rights. In the case brought by Ewan Sutherland and Chris Morris, who was 16 and still criminalised by our law, the European Commission of Human Rights condemned our unequal age of consent. Such an inequality is a violation of article 8 of the convention – the right to privacy – and of article 14, which provides that the rights set out in the convention are to be enjoyed by all citizens without discrimination (Keen, Lab., col. 757).

In this context Europe, the European Court, and other European countries (col. 760; col. 785) were invoked as synonyms for justice, rights and democratic processes of law. This is in stark contrast to the representation of Europe normally invoked by Euro-sceptics, as a bureaucratic dictatorship. However, nowhere was this counter-invocation to be found in the Age of Consent debate, even where Euro-scepticism was offered a direct opening. Perhaps most importantly, in the new history of progress (newly dominant), and the imagined future it provoked, lesbians and gays were expressly conscripted into imagined communities of Britishness, albeit a Britishness with a marked European debt, and one that was internationalist (and therefore progressive) in orientation. Keen went on to argue that Britain should follow South Africa in finding 'a way of including all its citizens in a new nation where the rights of all minorities are protected' (Keen, Lab., col. 760).

THRICE-TOLD TALES

The Age of Consent debate marked a distinct shift both in the immediate discursive field of sexual politics and in the wider political terrain. The Sexual Offences (Amendment) Act 2000 was not simply a minor reform. It recognises as legitimate the civil and citizenship claims of gays, lesbians and 'queers'. In so doing, it destabilises a whole gamut of legislated inequality and discriminatory policy (from Section 28 to pension, inheritance and immigration policies). Thus, notwithstanding Eleanor Laing's insistence that equality under criminal law should not impinge on civil law, the logic of the change does precisely that.

A second shift was the uncoupling of the homophobic standpoint from both moral high ground and claims of consensus. Clearly evidenced in the 1998 debates was the attenuation of conservative sexual repertoires and the rise – politically and discursively – of a broadly based liberal hegemony. In this context, Conservative moralism was cut off from its grander narratives: the state as theocratic, the nation as really Christian, law as declarative of 'the normal and the natural'. In the speech community of the Commons itself, neo-Conservative and Christian speakers had to state their principles as personal confessions, as declarations of interest, rather than as claims to self evident truth or collective common sense: 'I speak, quite unashamedly, for the traditional, orthodox, Christian point of view' (Cormack, col. 762); 'the views that I put [are] ... as a Second Church Estates Commissioner' (Bell, col. 775); 'I shall briefly give my personal view' (Fowler, Conservative, col. 780). Against the distinctly grounded and rationalist tone of equalisation supporters, such declarations carried a hint of lunacy, an 'out-of-touchness' with the New Zeitgeist both within and beyond the Commons (though not, of course, in the House of Lords). More typical was Fowler's obeisance to the collective gay presence: 'I hope I shall be acquitted of the charge of being antagonistic to the homosexual community' (ibid.).

Related to this, and signalling a third shift, was the ascendancy of the versions of inclusivity, equality discourse and reworked narratives of modernity and progressive nation that have become iconic in the repertoires of New Labour. It is important, however, not to overestimate these transformations. Embedded in the seductive possibilities for social/sexual reform are residual, and often reworked, conservative themes: Joe Ashton's amendment was retained; there was a heterogeneous alliance under the umbrella of a discourse of equality that could be held out for everyone but simultaneously rationed; and the new law would be accompanied by the abandonment of efforts to repeal Section 28, and the creation of new policies reaffirming governmental commitments to highly conventional and normative family forms.[16] Thus the social liberalism of New Labour could both force Conservatives on to the defensive, and yet accommodate some of their deepest concerns.

In a larger context, this episode is suggestive of two related aspects of New Labour politics more generally: its internal diversity and the conservatism of its liberalism.

New Labour's liberal spectrum

As can be traced through the Age of Consent debates, three distinct (and often contestatory) liberalisms constitute the New Labour spectrum: a *neo-liberal* stress (shared with some Conservatives) on individual freedoms, privacy and equality before the law; a *radical-liberal* view of 'rights' (e.g. the human rights discourse associated with the European Court and often shared with Liberal Democrats); and what we have termed a *social liberal* focus on collective interests whether they pertain to the nation as a whole or to particular communities. These social-liberal interests, distinctively New Labour, are typically grasped as indices or standards of progress, factual and measurable. The standards themselves are anchored in moral absolutes that are not much discussed, but are more typically invoked, for example by grand narratives of modernisation and progress. One interesting feature of the Age of Consent debates is the way in which the insistent economic criteria of modernity elsewhere prominent in Blairite discourse (and in the wider New Labour agenda), usually linked to the globalisation of capital and labour, here give way to broader civilisational or 'way-of-life' definitions. This is a further reason why the sexual sphere is of such great importance politically – notwithstanding the tendency, as we have seen in this context, to narrow the sexual agenda and render it as technical as possible (for instance by prioritising questions of health or biology, rather than questions of identity, active citizenship and pleasure).

Furthermore, while there is great emphasis on inclusivity in this social-liberal discourse, it is a rigidly conditional inclusion: 'minorities' are split off as 'separate communities' to whom tolerance should be extended; and equality is purchased at the price of assimilation to privileged 'ways of life' and 'values' (the heteronormative family) that must remain undisturbed. As Blairism acquires its distinctive policies, this version of equality as conditional inclusion comes to be generalised within the broader modernising agenda of New Labour. (Schuster and Solomos in this volume, for example, trace this tendency in the context of race politics and asylum policies.)

At the same time, it is clear that other, emergent, more (optimistically) disruptive, tendencies were also in play in these debates. Keen showed a knowledgeable appreciation of gay activism, community self-organisation and leadership, and invoked 'diverse metropolitan communities', defined by 'welcoming and celebrating the cosmopolitan lifestyle that diversity brings' (col. 761). She also insisted (and this was shared by many other speakers) that 'it is about time that families were all equal' (col. 762). This not only challenges the more typical liberal splits and their attendant hierarchies, but also suggests a competing project of modernisation – one that departs from the patriarchal moral conservatism that defined old Labour as well as (social authoritarian) Conservatism.

As we revise this essay the future of New Labour policies in the sexual domain is not clear. (The record since 1998 is more fully reviewed in Chapter 3.) The analysis in this chapter suggests that New Labour is a heterogeneous political formation – even excluding older-Labour elements. However it also shows some consistent features – many foreshadowed in 1998. This step forward was not the result of political campaigning, or of a party that set out to change the terms of debate. It followed, rather, from a longer cultural preparation in which everyday life changes and cultural representations ran ahead of the law and of political opinion. 1998 was not New Labour's sexual revolution; rather, New Labour was the (appropriating) *beneficiary* of a 'long revolution' in sexual mores.

New Labour's role in sexuality politics therefore conforms to the model of 'passive revolution' which is explored through this volume. New Labour makes instrumental use of the parliamentary process to change the law and set up new forms of governmentality, and it is through these – not some popular mobilisation – that it intervenes in social identities and ways of living. Its intellectual activity is mainly at the level of ways and means, facts and evidence; its ways of thinking about issues are relatively fixed. It does not risk, on the whole, a broader cultural politics in which its own goals and the social identifications which ground them are (willingly) open to question.

NOTES

1. The reduction was from 18 to 17 in Northern Ireland, which has a higher age of consent for heterosexuals.
2. The age of consent for lesbians effectively was already on a par with heterosexuals. However, this was largely a product of the general history of legal invisibility for lesbians.
3. Previously, gay male partners both under 18 and over 18 were criminalised by the law, whereas in heterosexual sex, only the person over the age of consent would have been regarded in law as committing the offence of unlawful sex (statutory rape).
4. See for example, Kear and Steinberg (1999) and Walter (1999) for extended discussion of the ways in which this specific yearning was consistently reiterated by mourners themselves.
5. For a detailed discussion of this method, see Epstein, Johnson and Steinberg, 2000.

6. See for example Hall, 1992. We have in mind here not only relations with previously colonised parts of the world, but also the internal relations of the British Isles between England, Scotland, Wales and Ireland.

7. See Plummer (1995) for an extended discussion of contextual possibilities of story-telling.

8. See also Heywood and Mac An Ghaill, and Weeks, this volume, for the ways in which New Labour discourses of equality and social inclusion have heralded (at least a partial) reconstitution of the gay 'paedophile' figure as emblematic of dangerous/pathological masculinity.

9. 'In this country, 200,000 children live away from home; 110,000 are in boarding schools, and 50,000 live at any one time with foster parents; 2,600 15 and 16-year-olds are in prison on remand; many others are in hospital, private children's homes or local authority homes. Many of them have parents overseas to whom they cannot turn; many of them are abused. The list of abuses is horrendous – even stepfathers are sometimes abusers' (Ashton Labour, col. 764).

10. The notorious Section 28 of the Local Government Act 1988 stated that:
    (1) a local authority shall not:
        (a) promote homosexuality or publish material for the promotion of homosexuality
        (b) promote the teaching in any maintained school of the acceptability of homosexuality as a pretended family relationship by the publication of such material or otherwise;
        (c) give financial or other assistance to any person for either of the above purposes referred to in paragraphs (a) and (b) above.
    (2) Nothing in subsection (1) above shall be taken to prohibit the doing of anything for the purpose of treating or preventing the spread of disease. (Section 28 Local Government Act 1988)

11. This is a utilitarian story because it judges legislation by social results. It is empiricist because, unawares perhaps, it defines 'results' in quite an obvious but also narrow way, according to 'health risks'. It appeals to a 'we' defined somewhere between health practitioners, sex educators and social researchers. This was the story form that most helped the Labour majority to regain the main authorial voice in this debate. It also helped form the New Labour mainstream which we have termed 'social liberal'. While opposed to inequality before the law (in this domain at least), 'social liberalism' looks beyond the negative freedoms of individuals ('freedom from') for its social utopias, in this case to 'rational' health policies in which government can take a lead. The limits of this stance, as a sexual politics, are related to the 'obviousness' of the predominant association of sexuality with 'health': this leaves aside many aspects of sexuality that deeply concern young people – sexuality as personal identity, for example, or as pleasure, or as an element in 'relationships'.

12. The centrality of this repertoire to New Labour is evidenced by the Government's introduction of a citizenship curriculum into the required teaching of all state schools.

13. For full discussion of the constitution of 'good gays' and 'bad gays' in the 1994 debate see Epstein and Johnson (1998).

14. See also Stacey (1991) for the ways in which the 'illegitimate privilege' construction permeated contestations surrounding Section 28.

15. Blunt's proposed amendment (which was not in the end voted on) was similar in intent to Ashton's but stipulated that where one partner was over 21, the other must be over 18.
16. The Government 'Guidelines on Sex and Relationship Education' (2000), for example, stipulate that homophobia must be combated but that children must be taught about the importance of marriage.

REFERENCES

Bakhtin, Mikhail (1981) *The Dialogic Imagination*. Austin Texas: University of Texas Press.

Barker, Martin (1981) *The New Racism: Conservatives and the Ideology of the Tribe*. London: Junction Books.

Barthes, R. (1993) *Mythologies*. London: Vintage. Translated by Annette Lavers.

Bland, Lucy (1995) *Banishing the Beast: English Feminism and Sexual Morality, 1885-1914*. London: Penguin.

Brown, Phillip and Sparks, Richard (eds.) (1989) *Beyond Thatcherism: Social Policy, Politics and Society*. Buckingham: Open University Press.

Butler, Judith (1993) *Bodies that Matter: On the Discursive Limits of 'Sex'*. New York: Routledge.

Cohen, Philip and Bains, Harwant S. (eds) (1988) *Multi-racist Britain*. Basingstoke: Macmillan Education.

Cooper, Davina (1994) *Sexing the City: Lesbian and Gay Politics Within the Activist State*. London: Rivers Oram Press.

Department for Education and Employment (DfEE) (2000) 'Guidelines on Sex and Relationship Education'. London. HMSO.

Epstein, Debbie (1993) *Changing Classroom Cultures: Anti-racism, Politics and Schools*. Stoke-on-Trent: Trentham Books.

Epstein, Debbie and Johnson, Richard (1998) *Schooling Sexualities*. Buckingham: Open University Press.

Epstein, Debbie, Johnson, Richard and Steinberg, Deborah Lynn (2000) 'Twice Told Tales: Transformation, Recuperation and Emergence in the Age of Consent Debates 1998' *Sexualities* 3(1): 5-30.

Epstein Debbie and Steinberg, Deborah Lynn (1998) 'American Dreamin': Discoursing Liberally on the *Oprah Winfrey Show*'. Women's Studies International Forum. 21: 77-94.

Evans, David (1993) *Sexual Citizenship: The Material Construction of Sexualities*. London: Routledge.

Genette, Gérard (1980) *Narrative Discourse: an Essay on Method* Ithaca, NY. Cornell University Press. (trans. Jane E. Lewin).

Gilroy, Paul (1987) *There Ain't no Black in the Union Jack*. London: Routledge.

Hall, Catherine (1992) *White, Male and Middle Class: Explorations in Feminism and History*. London: Verso.

Johnson, Richard (1996) 'Sexual Dissonances: or the "impossibility of sexuality education"'. *Curriculum Studies: Special Issue: The Sexual Politics of Education* 4: 163-190.

Kramer, Heinrich and James Sprenger (1971) *The Malleus Maleficarum*. (translated with an introduction, bibliography and notes by the Reverend Montague Summers). NY. Dover Publications.

Labov, William (1972) *Language in the Inner City*. Philadelphia: University of Pennsylvania Press.

Mort, Frank (1987) *Dangerous Sexualities: Medico-Moral Politics in England since 1830*. London: Routledge & Kegan Paul.

Plummer, K. (1995) *Telling Sexual Stories: Power, Change and Social Worlds*. London: Routledge.

Redman, Peter (1999) *Boys in Love: Narrative Identity and the Cultural Production of Heterosexual Masculinities*, unpublished PhD Thesis, University of Birmingham).

Szasz, T. (1970) *The manufacture of madness a comparative study of the inquisition and the mental health movement*. Syracuse, N.Y.: Syracuse University Press.

Sedgwick, Eve Kosofsky (1990) *Epistemology of the Closet*. Berkeley: University of California Press.

Sedgwick, Eve Kosofsky (1994) *Tendencies*, London: Routledge (first published in 1993 by Duke University Press).

Smith, Anna Marie (1994) *New Right Discourse on Race and Sexuality: Britain 1968-1990*. Oxford: Blackwell.

Solomos, John (1989) *Race and Racism in Contemporary Britain*. Basingstoke: Macmillan.

Sontag, Susan (1991/1977) *Illness as Metaphor / AIDS and Its Metaphors*. Harmondsworth: Penguin.

Stacey, Jackie. (1991) 'Promoting Normality: Section 28 and the Regulation of Sexuality', in Franklin, Sarah, Celia Lury and Jackie Stacey (eds.) *Off-Centre: Feminism and Cultural Studies*. London. Harper Collins.

Walkowitz, Judith (1980) *Prostitution and Victorian Society: Women, Class, and the State*. Cambridge: Cambridge University Press.

Weeks, Jeffrey (1985) *Sexuality and Its Discontents*. London: Routledge.

Weeks, Jeffrey (1986) *Sexuality*. London: Tavistock.

Williams, Raymond (1977) *Marxism and Literature*. Oxford: Oxford University Press.

6. Transformations under pressure: reworking class and gender identities under New Labour

Richard Johnson and Valerie Walkerdine

INTRODUCTION

> I know these strategies put pressure on you. They put pressure on all of us – not least David Blunkett and me, with our commitments to ambitious national targets. And rightly so, for a key modernising principle of this government is that we are all accountable (Tony Blair to National Association of Head Teachers, 2 June 1999).

During the period of the Blair governments a distinctive social politics has emerged. This politics emphasises ways of life and forms of identity: it 'puts pressure' to change the attitudes and behaviour of citizens, more technically our 'subjectivities'. This is the distinctiveness of New Labour: different from Thatcherism (though with strong neo-liberal continuities); different from old Labour (or any kind of socialism); different from a radical Liberalism or a politics focused on 'rights'; different finally from the New Left and from the radical social movements of the 1960s and 1970s which sought popular empowerment. Instead, New Labour contains and limits popular aspirations by promising a shiny modern future without social exclusions. It is a form of 'passive revolution'.

At the centre of this politics is the construction of new, flexible and self-invented subjects, 'freed' from ties of community or collective solidarity in order to take part in new 'opportunities'. It is a well-established argument now that neo-liberalism, in conjunction with the new global capitalist labour markets, demands a particular kind of psychological subject (Sennett, 1997; Giddens, 1991; Rose, 1999): flexible, autonomous, not expecting a job for life, and working less in manufacturing and more in service, communications, and new technologically based businesses. As Nikolas Rose puts it:

> However apparently external and implacable may be the constraints, obstacles and limitations that are encountered, each individual must

render his or her own life meaningful, as if it were the outcome of individual choices made in furtherance of a biographical project of self-realisation (1992: 12).

New Labour politics takes this process further than the market emphasis of Thatcherite Conservatism. Thatcherism 'released' individuals to enjoy 'freedom' from state interference. It weakened possible agencies for collective working-class identity, like trade unionism. New Labour, however, uses government to work directly on the subjectivity of citizens, in order to produce subjects capable, in Rose's words, of 'bearing the serious burdens of liberty'. It incorporates an ideal subject into its forms of administration. It translates and subverts older (socialist) ideas, like 'equality' and 'social justice', to fit this project. New Labour politics is the *cultural* and *social elaboration* of neo-liberalism, centred on the subjectivities of citizens. As Blair says, it 'put[s] pressure on you; put[s] pressure on all of us'. It sets 'standards', 'targets' and tests, with consequences for failure that go far beyond market disciplines.

In this process unequal relationship of class and gender do not disappear.[1] Rather, inequalities are re-worked and deepened, while their discursive disappearance makes talking about them more difficult. However, bright and shiny the New Labour project may appear, however much a progressive re-invention of Britain, it remains quite as moralising or normative as the traditionalism of Thatcher and Reagan and their neo-conservative successors. It depends upon a concept of a normal subject, the model for which is white and middle-class and gendered in particular ways. As a corrective to New Labour's easy social celebrations, we stress, in this chapter, the difficulties and losses that are involved, and especially what Sennett and Cobb have called 'the hidden injuries of class' (1993) – the frequently devastating consequences for those whose conditions of life do not fit the dominant norms.

New Labour's politics of gender differ from Thatcherism in that its rational, autonomous, hard-working subjects are often figured as female. Like the self-invented subject of the classic makeover of women's magazines, these are subjects who must constantly remake themselves, consuming themselves into being, by 'looking the part'. This is a necessary condition for that short-term contract or that (often devalued) professional opportunity. Women and girls, tutored by media directed towards them since the 1950s, are often experts at personal re-invention. Through an extension of these practices, through changes in occupational patterns, and through girls' successes in the education system, the classic liberal subject has become the professional woman, whose 'emotional intelligence' bolsters a humanist version of a sharing democracy, which denies any regulative function.

We explore these specifically gendered processes in two main ways: first, by critically reviewing the female future set out by the New

Labour think-tank Demos in 1997; second, by using examples from an in-depth longitudinal qualitative study of the lives of young women in Britain born in 1972/3 (Tizard and Hughes, 1984; Walkerdine and Lucey, 1989; Walkerdine, Lucey, Melody, 2001). Our use of this extensive study of 'growing up girl' is necessarily selective, but our examples are true to its findings.

'TOMORROW'S WOMEN'

> As male jobs disappear, women's importance in society is set to rise, as is their confidence. Forty per cent of women believe that women are naturally superior to men. Women will soon make up the majority of the workforce and Britain is becoming increasingly shaped by feminine values. Values such as empathy, care, community and environmentalism, are now central to British society ... Work has become more important for women, and nearly all groups of women have become relatively less committed to the family over the last ten years (Demos, 1997: 8).

In the manner of the life-style profiles of market researchers and advertisers, *Tomorrow's Women* uses five main categories to describe women now and in the future: 'Networking Naomi', 'New Age Angela', 'Mannish Mel', 'Back to Basics Barbara' and 'Frustrated Fran'. The first four categories attempt to map routes for women to enter the labour market for professional and business jobs via formal educational qualifications. Only one 'kind' of woman is singled out as creating a problem for the rosy female future – Frustrated Fran (though all of Demos' categories, like 'Mannish Mel', could certainly bear critical inspection). Fran is described as under 35, in the census groups C1, C2 and D:

> Many are also single parents. Their jobs are typically unskilled, part-time and on fixed term contracts, and they give little in the way of either fulfilment or actual reward ... Among this group, many are mothers with young children who feel hemmed in by the lack of state support, the absence of affordable childcare and the unhelpful attitudes of their male partners ... Fran feels cut out of the action, and lacks confidence in herself (Demos, 1997: 142-43).

Very similar social fictions have informed New Labour's policies towards single mothers and 'social exclusion' more generally. The forms of 'support' for working-class women like 'Fran' have centred on returning them to employment, in effect to the unskilled, part-time and often casual jobs from which pregnancy and having a child may have provided a temporary refuge.

It is no coincidence that Demos' model of self-invention is couched in the language of consumer life-styles. But these are not only crude images. These are also 'fictions that function in truth' in Michel Foucault's phrase (1979). They are embedded in the actual policies and practices of New Labour – in the regulation of education, work, social order and social inclusion. Like all such fictions they involve a forgetting, a forgetting of the Other, in this case the suppressed Other of Old Labour – including those experiencing economic and work-based inequalities, which can also be termed 'class'.

To move beyond Demos' stereotypes, and also beyond Old Labour's stress on class formations as 'objective' and male, we draw attention to the cultural and subjective aspects of classed femininity which both discourses elide. Class differences are more than life-style choices, or low-paid single mothers with psychological problems. They are linked to exclusions that arise precisely from the life-style constructions which Demos uncritically recycles, and from the pressure for continuous self-invention (e.g. 'lifelong learning') which new forms of regulation prescribe.

UNEQUAL OPPORTUNITIES

It has been argued that the feminisation thesis presented by Demos and others ignores the major structural changes which are re-ordering gender relations. Adonis and Pollard (1997) argue that the period since the mid-1960s has seen the rise of 'the Super Class' –

> a new elite of top professionals and managers, at once meritocratic yet exclusive, very highly paid yet powerfully convinced of the justice of its rewards, and increasingly divorced from the rest of society by wealth, education, values, residence and life style (67).

This is a critical development in class formation – as critical as the rise of organised labour in the past and the 'denigration of the manual working class' today. The professions now have much less status and are paid far less than the new elite, which is strongly located in the financial and multi-national business and administrative sectors. This affects the gender profiles of mobility in important ways. Women are increasingly entering professions that are de-skilled and devalued, while high-flying men are going elsewhere. Far from eroding this polarisation, Third Way politics deepens it, consistently supporting the very rich and disciplining the state professions.

At the same time, the reordering of working-class work in the new global economy has involved dispersion away from previously stable and organised male employment in the declining manufacturing sectors, and towards service industries based on individual contracts, piece work, home working and work in call centres, with a pressure to retrain and change jobs at frequent intervals. Labour is feminised at this level too. Women's employment is, therefore, divided between those who can acquire the education and skills to enter the professional and managerial sector and those who leave school with little or no qualifications and enter a job market defined mostly by poorly paid, often part-time work, little job security and periods of unemployment. A woman in such a job is frequently the sole breadwinner in the family.

This is the context in which girls and women must make themselves as modern neo-liberal subjects, and it is not surprising that women are still massively divided in class terms. In *Growing Up Girl*, the young middle-class women from professional and business families, aged 17 to 23, are succeeding spectacularly at school and are entering the labour market equipped with a degree from a well-established university (Walkerdine, Lucey and Melody, 2001). By contrast, no daughter of parents in working-class occupations in the study made it to a well-established university by a straightforward route. Indeed, the situation may be even worse than it was in the 1960s and 1970s, despite the expansion of higher education. A small minority of working-class women in the study got to university and in sight of a professional career, by a hard and painful route, but most did not succeed at school and entered a poorly paid labour market. Recent educational patterns, which have often been presented as girls in general outperforming boys, are actually changes in the gendered composition of middle-class educational outcomes, with middle-class boys not allowed to fail (Lucey and Walkerdine, 1999), while girls from lower income families are not doing well at all. This is more than the social exclusion of a minority; it is a re-assertion, after a few rather exceptional decades, of the systematic class divide in life opportunities. It is wishful or self-interested thinking to believe that class has disappeared as a major social dynamic – or as an indispensable tool of social analysis. Indeed Labour ministers, with footholds in Old Labour, are increasingly forced to recognise the class character of educational outcomes, especially in entry to Higher Education (e.g. Ashley and Hodge, 2002).

PRODUCING FEMININITIES

Much recent feminist work on class concentrates on the importance of identity and subjectivity (Walkerdine, 2003), whether as respectability (Skeggs, 1997), upward mobility and shame (Lawler, 1999), mothering (Reay, 1998), or consumption (Kenway, 1995). More is involved in successful aspiration to a better life than working hard and 'seizing opportunities'. Social aspirants have to be able to recognise themselves as the kind of person who is entitled to such a life. They have to want to be 'like that', and to be able to *envisage themselves* according to a particular social model. The kinds of discourses discussed so far explain, in a crude way, the psychological requirements for inhabiting the female future, or for failing, pathologically, to achieve it. 'Fran', in Demos' description, 'feels frustrated', 'feels cut off', 'lacks confidence', has 'poor self esteem'. She is 'angry', and a potential joiner of 'girl gangs'. She is evidently 'socially excluded' and a target for special measures, girl gangs being a recurrent nightmare in the struggle for 'decency'. Such discourses, therefore, provide sets of 'truths' through which both social welfare agencies and young women themselves are invited to recognise themselves and modify and manage their conduct, but only in self-demeaning ways, as 'losers'. Moreover, because of the pressures of regulation, a young woman may have to perform being a 'Fran' (if not a frustrated one) in order to qualify for the positive sides of 'inclusion'.

To become 'Mel', 'Barbara' or 'Naomi' is not the easy task which Demos' celebration suggests. It demands much emotional and practical work, which is often painful and difficult. This not only a striving for educational qualifications; it is a work of identity or self-production. It is very different work, depending on whether young women are brought up to expect success in middle-class homes, or are facing the apparently endless array of professional possibilities for the first time. In the new dynamics of class formation, where class itself is feminised, women become main carriers of what is both good and bad about the new economy. This is not a lessening of difference, inequality or exploitation, far from it. Inequality is differently lived today, however, because we are all constantly enjoined to improve and remake ourselves as free consumers and 'entrepreneurs of ourselves'.

'SUPER WOMEN'?: YOUNG WOMEN IN THE MIDDLE CLASS

In *Growing Up Girl*, we met many young women whose families had been characterised as professional middle-class in the 1970s, and who struggled to become the 'Super Women' they have been led to believe they can and must be. They are not immune from the pressures of class differentiation.

Their educational lives have been rigidly circumscribed by expectations of academic success, often to such an extent that quite outstanding performance is only ever viewed as average and ordinary. Some young women attended schools in which so much emphasis was placed on high performance that anything less than 10 grade 'A's at GCSE and three or more grade 'A's at A level was considered tantamount to failure.

> I actually complained to them [her parents] a few times about not feeling like I had any kind of recognition for my achievements, it was just like that it was expected that that's what was going to happen and I was going to do well and we didn't need to talk about it because it was just a foregone conclusion (Katherine, middle-class, aged 21).

Eleanor, a middle-class girl, achieved 9 A grades and 1 C grade at GCSE:

And I was really pleased. Yes, I hoped that I'd get a B in science, I knew I wouldn't get an A but I hoped to get a B but I was really pleased to get a C. And ... so I rang up my mum. And I said 'Oh, Mum I got a C.' And she said, 'Oh, well, congratulations on the A's anyway.' Fine. Bye.

Such high expectations of performance bring their own anxieties. Emma was studying medicine:

(...) it's difficult at Oxford because you've got the, kind of, top few people from every school in the country, and I mean, I was in the top five or ten at school, but it's so different. I mean, you're always kind of, in the middle. I just try and stay in the top middle ... [untranscribable]. I mean they're so quick on the uptake, it makes you feel, that's the one thing that's bad about it, it makes me feel a bit stupid sometimes. I mean some of these people are just so amazingly bright, you just think 'God, I shouldn't be here, I shouldn't be with people like that at all'.

In the complex relations between preparation for the labour market and the production of practices of subjection and subjectivity in schooling, a significant part of the work of achieving high performance has to be emotional. Despite the evidence of their success, feelings of not being good enough were endemic among the young middle-class women; they were anxious even when doing very well. Even if they do outstandingly, there is a feeling that no-one will praise them or even notice it. These anxieties are typically understood by all concerned as individual pathologies, only to be overcome by working harder and harder. Very few of the middle-class girls in the study made sustained connections between their sense of inadequacy and their social and economic position. We suggest that it was difficult for them to step outside an individualising discourse, because doing so would have undermined the sense of rightness and impenetrable normality necessary to sustain the very circumscribed educational trajectory leading to a professional career. Failure was simply not an option: whatever else happened, they were compelled to succeed educationally. This produced terrible psychic dilemmas: a struggle between feelings of not being good enough and feelings that one must not fail. Such a project involves a high degree of self-regulation, in effect part of their self-production as proto-professional subjects.

The process by which middle-class girls 'prove themselves' begins in the early years and is integral to the achievement of educational success (Allatt, 1993; Reay, 1998). It was common for teachers in the schools which the same middle-class girls were attending at age 10 freely to use terms such as 'natural ability' to describe top pupils. At the same time, these terms were rarely used to describe high-performing girls, even girls like Emma, who at ten were doing very well in test scores and teachers' ratings (cf. Walkerdine, 1998). It was noted, then, how 'flair' and 'ability' were opposed to 'hard work', an opposition which down-graded the 'quality' of girls' good performance because it was not *produced in the right way* (Walkerdine and Lucey, 1989; Walden and Walkerdine, 1985). Child-centred discourses and early mathematics education implicitly contrast the 'old' ways of hard work and rule-following with 'new' concepts of development, activity and discovery. The implications of this are serious – suggesting that children who make their work visible are rather lacking in those very qualities of 'flair', 'ability' and 'brilliance' which are most prized in the production of good performance. At ten, Emma's teacher said of her: 'If she comes across something new it needs to be explained to her whereas some of these will just be able to read what they're to do and do it'. Emma was certainly a 'good' girl and an 'ideal pupil'; her performance throughout her education has been outstanding. Isn't it all the more extraordinary that she should never have been attributed with 'flair', but seen as a good girl who only comes top through sheer hard work? Extraordinary yes, but by looking back to what was said about her as a child, we can begin to understand why girls like Emma deny them-selves the accolade 'clever'. At 21, Emma still believes the 'truths' told to her about her performance: that it can only be sustained by the kind of unremitting, exhausting and anxiety-provoking labour that she does indeed display. The opposition between flair and hard work she encountered at primary school continues to exert its influence into higher education. In the intensely competitive environment of medical school, being seen to be working hard signifies a lack of brilliance and so must be denied and hidden.

And then it's a kind of big competition and a game – you need to make out they've done the least work and get the best results. Which I find quite hard. I mean, I don't work that hard, but I do need to put quite a few hours into an essay.

'ALL RISE': TROUBLING ASPIRATIONS

If the work of becoming a successful professional woman involves sacrifices for middle-class girls, it is almost impossible for those facing the prospect of upward mobility through education. They too may have to face high social expectations. As Peter Mandelson puts it:

For me, the goal of social democracy is to create the sort of society in which the daughter of a Hartlepool shop assistant has as much chance of becoming a High Court judge as the daughter of a Harley Street doctor (2002).

On the face of it, Mandelson's expectations on behalf of working-class girls are implausible. As he admits, 'We have just tinkered'. In one of those eerie coincidences of evidence, however, *Growing Up Girl* includes one young women, the daughter of a security guard and a lavatory attendant, who expressed the desire to become a judge. Sharon's story shows how many things stand in the way of achieving such ambitions.

Her parents, despite their low pay, managed to buy their council flat through the Right to Buy scheme, sold up and moved away from the city. Buying a council flat, however, is a very different matter from affording the expensive private education offered to many middle-class girls, an 'investment' that also requires a close knowledge of the hierarchies of higher education. Young middle-class women are strongly pressured to take up positions in which the fertile body is relegated in favour of education, the academy and a profession. Young working-class women find it harder to escape becoming the embodiment of fertility, having children earlier, and foregoing an educational progression, at least for a time. Holding together the possibility of fertility with intelligence is no mean feat for women of whatever class position, but it is organised with stark differences for the two groups. It is much harder for some working-class women to escape the social exclusionary category of young motherhood.

Sharon's wants to 'be somebody', an ambition also encouraged by her family, who sees her as 'an Einstein next to her brother'. She says of her ambition:

> I don't know really, it's something different. Because my mates like, they want to be like hairdressers and nurses and things like that. It was something different. And ever since I was twelve I've always. My mum and dad think I can do it, but I don't think my Nan does, so I want to show the rest of the family that I'll be able to do it.

Sharon wants to be 'something different', to stand out from the hairdressers and nurses, by inventing herself as an extremely powerful professional – a judge. The fact that Sharon's choice is also a resonant example for Mandelson the publicist shows how potent a symbol of difference it is, of that new horizon for women. Sharon can imagine being a judge, but any career in the law is hard and painful to achieve. Neither she nor her family displays any knowledge of the long and complex path to realise her ambition. Before the interview quoted above, she had embarked on her second attempt at a BTec at a further education college and had found a supportive woman lecturer who nurtured her ambition. However, during one of the interviews for the research project, Sharon revealed that she was in a relationship with an older man and that they were not using contraception. She insisted to the interviewer that she was not trying to get pregnant, but 'if it happens it happens, cross that bridge when we come to it'. Her mother expressed a similar view in her own interview. It is known in the family that Sharon both wants to be a judge and is having sex without contraception; yet having a child and being on quite a low-status course are unlikely routes even to reading law at university.

We can perhaps understand Sharon's position by thinking about the deeply contradictory demands placed upon women today – that they should 'work' very hard and yet remain 'women' – fertile, feminine, and mothering. The fantasy here is that both are possible, even at the same time. Many middle-class respondents in the study resolved this dilemma, which was important for them too, by making sure that there was no possibility of ever getting pregnant, or if the impossible happened, by having an abortion and putting off mothering until a later date. For Sharon, the dilemma is being performed as though it were the result of chance. In this way, she does not have to decide to give up the fantasy of being a judge, nor does she have to admit that she does not want to become a mother just yet. Equally, becoming a young mother might make the possibility of failure and of not achieving her dream of 'being somebody' easier to bear in the short term.

While the middle-class parents in the study would not tolerate anything – and certainly not pregnancy – getting in the way of educational progress, working-class families may find some comfort in things staying the same; they may give less disapproving messages to their daughters about unplanned pregnancy. For the daughters, being successful would mean coping with enormous and far-reaching changes: leaving home and entering an entirely different world. While for many middle-class girls today a professional occupation is an expected destiny, the path of reinvention for working-class girls is still littered with obstacles. It is important that it is the fecund body that reasserts itself as the principle block in Sharon's pathway, the thing most opposed to the 'masculine', rational forms of ambition to which she also aspires. In effect Sharon, in the history of her short life, is trying to avoid being 'the Other' to successful middle-class girls, but continually risks falling back on it. Becoming a 'new woman' and becoming part of a socially-excluded group are shown, by these examples, to be based around different responses to the complexities of managing work and motherhood for young women today, differences explained not by pathology, personality or 'talent' but by the production of classed feminine subjectivities and the complex emotional investments involved.

CHANGING WAYS OF LIFE

These social patterns and psychic dynamics suggest longer-term developments in class and gender formations, in which not all costs are ascribable to New Labour politics. Rather, we are arguing that such socio-psychic dynamics are the context in which policies and rhetorics should be appraised. We are primarily interested here in the general social character of New Labour's politics and rhetorics, and in whether they are creating a political culture in which such issues can be addressed.

In what follows, we focus on three main questions. First, how is New Labour's regulation of subjectivity constructed in its general rhetoric? Second, what (dis)connections are suggested with the class-gender dynamics we have described? Third, how does all this help us to define the breaks and continuities of New Labour's politics and the past? Since Tony Blair's own speeches have been a major source, our analysis applies especially to the 'Blairite' elements in New Labour's repertoire.[2]

Initially, the Blair government seemed 'liberal' in the everyday sense of socially tolerant. Especially on matters of sexuality and ethnicity and race, its ethos chimed better with the diversity of ways of living in contemporary Britain than the cultural nationalism and moral traditionalism of the Major years. This was a government with a 'national quest for change', committed to 'change traditional thinking'. Its keywords included 'reform', 'radical reform', 'renewal, 'modernisation', 'social change', 'a new transformation and 'a second wave of reform' (e.g. in public services), a 'revolution' even – in education for example. Its rhetoric retained familiar socialist, feminist or anti-racist resonances: 'decent fair society', 'tackle social exclusion', 'extending opportunity' and 'combining economic dynamism with social justice' (Blair, 9 January 1998). Today it is easier to see that there was a war of persuasion going on in this re-use of older vocabularies. This was more than 'spin' or presentation. Major changes of political direction were being engineered, with language often leading. Key words were stolen from traditions of oppositional and alternative politics to re-assure key groups of activists and supporters. The words and concepts, however, were given different – sometimes directly opposed – meanings. This, in turn, opened the way for new policies.

Six clusters of key terms are especially revealing:

- Equality/equality of opportunity
- Decency or fairness (of society) or 'civic society'
- Social inclusion and exclusion
- Rights and responsibilities
- Culture
- Social justice

Equality/equality of opportunity

Historically, egalitarian principles and sentiments have been a way of subjecting asymmetries of power, resources and opportunity to ethical scrutiny, asking how far they breach human solidarity and a respect for persons. In one classic formulation, equality rests on 'common humanity' as a 'quality worth cultivating' (Tawney, 1964: 16). In Blairite discourses, equality is always qualified as 'equality *of opportunity*', though other terms, also transformed – 'community' and 'mutuality' for example – seem to carry some of equality's meanings. In the long history of Labour 'revisionism' this is new. Usually some degree of equality – or of equalisation of condition – is seen as necessary if equality of opportunity is to be achieved. Anthony Crosland, for instance, in prioritising equality of opportunity on 'the threshold of mass abundance', argued also for progressive taxation and comprehensive schooling to diminish 'the injustice of large inequalities' (1959: 231). In less optimistic times, even Anthony Giddens, a New Labour apologist, advocates minor measures of social equalisation (2002: 38-42).

By comparison, Blair extends the single logic of 'opportunity', by linking justice to merit.

> Social justice is about merit. It demands that life chances should depend on talent and effort, not the chance of birth; and that talent and effort should be handsomely rewarded (Blair, 18 March 1999).

The same speech cites the new Clause 4 of the Labour Party's constitution and other meanings of 'social justice':

> Social justice is about fairness. In a community founded on social justice, power, wealth and opportunity will be in the hands of the many not the few.

The contradictions between handsomely rewarding 'talent and effort' and redistributing wealth and power are obvious. Less obvious perhaps is Blair's redistribution of social responsibility. Where opportunity is stressed, it becomes possible to ascribe responsibility for inequality not to the rich, or to social arrangements, but to those who do not respond to 'opportunities'. The effects of this re -assignment are clearer in some of Blair's other redefinitions, but the strong aversion to taking anything from the very rich can be found in the formative texts of New Labour, including The Commission on Social Justice (Commission on Social Justice, 1994), and in the broad tendencies of policy while in power. New Labour conspicuously favours big business, individual tycoons and members of the Superclass in a range of policies and deals. Even after November 2000, when the government recommitted itself to 'social investment', it avoided progressive taxation at the top end. Rather, in its own way, New Labour attends to 'the socially excluded'. As Richard Sennett has argued, following Christopher Jencks, it is the 'unexceptional disadvantaged' whose position has declined most over the last forty years – in older language 'the working class' (Sennett, 2002).

Decency
'Decency', 'a decent society', a 'fair society' or a 'civic society' (not 'civil society') are also re-defined. 'Decency' does not on the whole refer to socially just institutions. It is closer to the cross-class but class-inflected idea of 'respectability'. It 'requires that any citizen of our society should be able to meet their needs for income, housing, health

and education' (Blair, 18 March 1999). In other words, citizens, without social distinctions, should, on the whole, meet their own needs. Decency isn't caring for others or attending to social differences, but is about looking after yourself properly, especially by earning a living and saving for a pension.

On the negative side, Blair is explicit about the connections between criminality and (in)decency. As he put it, off-island so to speak, to a Korean audience in 2000:

> We need to rebuild decent civic society. As we provide opportunity, we demand responsibility, order, law-abiding conduct. A tough crime agenda is not just good for the citizen; but for business. I am a tolerant person, Britain is a tolerant country. But I am intolerant of crime. That is also a choice (Blair, 19 October 2000).

This corresponds to a notably 'hard line' on crime, a mood extended to petty disorders – from litter and graffiti to 'vandals', begging and 'anti-social' or 'loutish' behaviour (e.g. Blair, 26 February 2001; 24 April 2001). Moreover, as Mac An Ghaill and Haywood argue in this volume, Blairite respectability is in part defined against a 'laddish' culture of consumption and enjoyment. Decency and 'civic society' are code for putting pressure on persons and behaviours who stand outside the respectable norms. Decency is not primarily about social solidarities or social care – values undervalued and under-rewarded by New Labour. Civic society is certainly not about citizen initiatives to make the world anew, more about picking up the litter and regulating the neighbours.

Inclusion / exclusion

In academic research and theory, 'social inclusion' and 'exclusion' are terms both widespread and deeply controversial (Levitas, 1998). We do not want to enter into debates about the social effects of inclusion policies – whether they reduce poverty for instance. Rather, we approach them as a politics of identity or of 'the subject'. From this perspective, calling a group 'socially excluded' is as significant as the treatment that follows – and this in two ways.

For Blair the socially excluded are 'a hardcore of society outside its mainstream' that 'needs a special focus' (Blair, 22 April 1999). Excluding a group in this way justifies intrusive policies and also helps to define what the 'mainstream' is. Policy can then insist on additional conditions for achieving normal citizenship. Thus single mothers must be serious about seeking work: their motherhood itself does not qualify them for social respect or support. So whatever their impact on poverty, these are policies of social regulation or control. As we have suggested, they help to redefine social injustice, not as the excesses of the rich but as the limitations of the poor or disorderly. In the first phase of its work the government's Social Exclusion Unit prioritised school truancy, drugs, street living and 'the worst estates', to which were added teenage parents, and 16-18 year olds (Annesley, 2001: 208). The key aim in most inclusion policies is to force people off benefits and into work, a policy which particularly affects women with children or other dependents. This is often presented as 'support' or 'compassion', so its coercive edge is softened and belied.

Rights and responsibilities

The re-writing of classical liberal ideas of rights – held by human beings or citizens – is achieved by pairing rights with 'responsibilities' and then often subordinating the latter. As Blair puts it:

> We must as a country decide what kind of society we want to be. For my part, I am in no doubt that it should be a society founded on rights *and* responsibilities, in which people accept more willingly their obligations to others not just the rights and benefits which they enjoy themselves (Blair, 30 December 2001, his emphasis).

Rights and responsibilities clearly *are* reciprocal, but in different ways. One person's rights are another person's responsibilities, and unlike Blair we have to recognise there are many situations in which rights are not in fact 'enjoyed'. Guaranteeing rights is commonly thought of as a responsibility of government or of the law. In Blairism, however, responsibilities and rights are attached to the same agent, so that we all have rights-and-responsibilities at the same time. This seems sensible enough, but the effect is that my responsibilities *qualify* my rights. I do not have rights as a citizen or as a person as such; I only have rights if I behave myself, according to someone's view of what is responsible. This must affect what rights I can hold and how they can be exercised. We can see this counter-definition operating in many domains today, notably in the mouths of Home Secretaries when introducing 'measures' on children and parents, asylum seekers and suspected terrorists, usually at the expense of their rights.

Culture

Culture is not a common term in the Blairite lexicon, but it nearly always carries negative connotations: 'the yob culture that intimidates so many people', 'changing institutional cultures' (e.g. in relation to racism), 'a culture of low aspirations and standards' (e.g. of schools). There are more positive tones in terms like multiculturalism and 'diversity', but also ambiguities here. In seeking to allay worries about Islamophobia after 11 September 2001, Blair repeatedly stressed his commitments to a multi-ethnic, multi-faith society (e.g. Blair, 27 September 2001). But he also foregrounded a conception of 'way of life' which must be defended at all cost from terrorist attacks, and it is this way of life which supplies the norms of inclusion or citizenship. In Blair's 'hot' version, in the aftermath of 11 September, this norm is implicitly middle-class in character:

> Today the threat is chaos, because for people with work to do, family life to balance, mortgages to pay, careers to further, pensions to provide, the yearning is for order and stability and if it doesn't exist elsewhere it is unlikely to exist here. I have long believed this interdependence defines the new world we live in (Blair, 2 October 2001).

It is particularly hard to imagine, within this framework, ways of living that are legitimate alternatives to one's own, and are not easy to assimilate – Islamic and peace-movement opinion with strong doubts about anti-terrorism and the wars on Afghanistan and Iraq for instance. More generally, ideas of culture are detached from a belief in positive popular agency outside of governmental regulation. This anti-popular emphasis distances Blairism from strands in New Left thinking that repose more hope in popular movements than in the politics of elites. As Ken Jones and Lisa Smyth argue in this volume, Labour's 'revolution' is 'passive' in that it robs the citizens or 'the people' of a positive independent role.

Social justice again

According to Blair, 'social justice' is 'our aim', 'our central belief', a declaration, which matches his endorsement of his predecessor's Commission for Social Justice. In his Beveridge Lecture of 1999, he redefined social justice in the ways we have suggested: equality of opportunity not equality, 'responsibilities' qualifying 'rights', 'decency' as respectability, social inclusion as an obligation to compete. Like 'rights', justice is a morally *qualified* category which depends on merit – ability plus hard work. Justice is primarily *the due rewarding of merit*; a just outcome, when someone 'gets their deserts' or when government gets 'something for something'. This amounts to a particularly uncritical embracing of meritocracy, with its notorious contradictions and dangers. (For a classic critique see Young, 1961.)

These redefinitions extract the critical potential from discourses of equality and of rights. Justice is still to be achieved by the mass of citizens, it is true, and not, as in neo-liberalism, by some hidden hand. Rather, citizens must respond to governmental tutelage that prompts, exhorts and monitors performance, rewards results and achievements, and applies 'special measures' (including shaming as 'failing') to those who err or are left behind.

BLAIRISM AND CLASS-GENDER DYNAMICS

There is little here to suggest an understanding of class/gender differentiation or its social costs. On the contrary, by attempting to install a *general* social ethos of merit and individual ambition, by denying, most of the time, that major class differences remain, and by administering, and not just in schools, multiple tests of success and failure, Blairism is likely to reinforce inequalities of all kinds. As social knowledge, the individual recipe of 'opportunity' excludes an understanding of the collective nature of social identities and the complexity of personal dispositions. Social exclusion policies target at best very specific social groups, leaving aside major structural differences. The dominant rhetorics construct, as their own working fantasy, a bland, unconflictual world where differences are only apparent, or are a product of ill will, or are relatively easily to reconcile. If some measure of social equalisation *is* indeed an aim of New Labour – and this has honestly to be doubted – the major social processes involved are not yet being addressed. As the biggest social experiment of them all – the United States of America – testifies, accumulating individual success stories does not touch the kind of structural inequalities which class, gender and racialised divisions of labour require.

A more critical reading is also possible, and perhaps more compelling. Consciously or not, Blairism takes sides socially; it constructs and services a particular social alliance. It takes as given – and as generally beneficial – the neo-liberal, market-led privatising drive of the transnational business and political elites. It seeks to conform institutions, ways of living and forms of subjectivity to the 'necessities' of work and consumption. In class terms, this means promoting the social rationalities and subjectivities of middle-class groups, and middle-class men in particular. There are striking correspondences between Blairite rhetorics of talent, hard work and merit, the contrived 'pressure' of its administration, and the cultural relationships of ambitious middle-class parents with their children. These mutually reinforcing demands press heavily on an over-examined, over-monitored, over-regulated generation of school pupils, reinforced for young women by a post-feminist belief that 'Superwoman' can 'have (or do) it all'. We fear that Blairite policies and discourses are sealing young people (no less than their parents) into over-work and pressured expectations that re-produce the personal problems, costs and casualties of both attempted 'excellence' and of 'failure'.

From this point of view, social inclusion policies are attempts to generalise a way of living to social groups that have, historically, given priority to local solidarities and other strategies of survival. At the same time, the stress on social accountability for all except the very rich and economically very powerful means that professionals are coming under similar disciplines to those that have subordinated working people – while plenty of room is left for blaming professionals for any unpopular outcomes.

We end, then, with three main conclusions. The first concerns the *novelty* of New Labour. One of its particular tasks is to recast the

keywords and social purposes of centre-left politics, including
Labour's own (ambiguous) tradition, but also radical liberalism and
'anti-oppressive' or 'emancipatory' social movements. The second
conclusion concerns its *continuities*. The continuities with the neo-
liberalism of Thatcherism are striking, especially the embrace of ways
of life and forms of subjectivity based upon a market-driven social
order. New Labour presents itself as different from Thatcherism,
through its *counterbalancing* stress on 'community' or 'the social'.
Our discussion suggests, however, that this too is a distortion. 'Social'
here (one linguistic root of 'social-ism') means the psychic and
cultural work of becoming a subject fit for a Britain which is dominated by global markets and transnational capital. It means reinforcing
existing middle-class practices and ambitious performances. It means
breaking down the alternatives which professional groups and working-class movements and communities have developed. It means
digesting and converting the challenges of feminism, sexual politics
and anti-racism.

    Our third conclusion concerns the government's difficulties in
seeing beyond its own redefinitions. Signs of growing inequality and of
the effects of 'pressure' and overwork continue to appear in statistical
and qualitative researches. Key instances for this chapter are the
continued, perhaps increasing predominance of middle-class students
in higher education despite overall expansion, and the continued
'choice' – conscious or not – of a minority of working-class girls for
youthful motherhood. The typical response has not been to attend to
'the evidence'. Rather, excuses are made, professional practitioners
blamed, and fresh targets set. What appears unthinkable – or politically
unsayable – is that current policies actually contribute to contemporary social divisions. The deepening of social inequalities cannot all be
ascribed, as in Labour's spin, to the Thatcherite past. Emergent differences in the experiences of young women are critical here, since a belief
in new femininities and women's achieved emancipations feature
strongly in modernising optimism. We are suggesting that this celebratory rhetoric of a new tomorrow depends on three crucial neglects: of
the work that women have to do to produce the new femininities; of
the burden they bear in servicing a neo-liberal agenda (in and out of
paid work); and of the deep divisions among women, on fundamentally
class lines.

NOTES

   1. See also Clarke and Newman, this volume, for discussion about the links
      between the reconstruction of gender and class politics in the wake of the
      new managerialism.
   2. For this chapter all of Blair's speeches on domestic issues available on the
      Downing Street website for the years 1998-2001 were read, plus some
      speeches on key themes from other years.

REFERENCES

Speeches of Tony Blair

(Source: unless otherwise stated: www.number-10.gov.uk)

9 January 1998 'New Britain in the Modern World' (Tokyo).

18 March 1999 Beveridge Lecture (Toynbee Hall, London).

22 April 1999 'Doctrine of the International Community' (Economic Club, Hilton Hotel, Chicago).

2 June 1999 To National Association of Head Teachers (Cardiff).

19 October 2000 To Asia-Europe Business Forum (Korea).

26 February 2001 To The Peel Institute (London).

24 April 2001 'Improving Your Local Environment' (London).

27 September 2001 'Meeting with Leaders of the Muslim Communities in Britain' (Downing Street).

2 October 2001 To Labour Party Conference (printed verbatim in *The Guardian* 3 October 2001).

30 December 2001 New Year Message (Downing Street).

Other References

Adonis, A. and Pollard, S. (1997) *A class act: the myth of Britain's classless society*, London: Penguin.

Allatt, P. (1993) 'Becoming privileged: the role of family processes', in Bates I and Riseborough, G. (eds) *Youth and inequality*, Milton Keynes: Open University Press.

Annesley, C. (2001) 'New Labour and Welfare' in S. Ludlam and M.J. Smith (eds), *New Labour in Government* Basingstoke: Macmillan.

Ashley, J. and Hodge, M. (2002) 'Blairite and Class Warrior: Jackie Ashley Meets Margaret Hodge, Interview with higher education minister', *The Guardian*, 24 June.

Commission on Social Justice (1994) *Social Justice: Strategies for National Renewal* London: Vintage.

Crosland, C.A.R. (1956) *The Future of Socialism* London: Jonathan Cape.

Foucault, M. (1979) *Discipline and Punish* Harmondsworth: Penguin.

Giddens, A. (1991) *Modernity and self identity: self and society in the late modern age*, Cambridge: Polity Press.

Giddens, A. (2002) *Where Now for New Labour?* Cambridge: Polity Press.

Kenway, J. (1995) 'Having a postmodern turn', in Smith, R. and Wexler, P. (eds) *After postmodernism: education, politics and identity*, London: Falmer.

Lawler, S. (1999) 'Getting out and getting away: women's narratives of class mobility', *Feminist Review*, 63, 3-24.

Levitas, R. (1998) *The Inclusive Society: Social Exclusion and New Labour* Basingstoke: Macmillan.

Lucey, H. and Walkerdine, V. (1999) 'Boys' underachievement: social class and changing masculinities', in T. Cox (ed) *Combating educational disadvantage*, London: Falmer

Mandelson P (2002) *The Blair Revolution Revisited*. London: Politico's Publishing.

Reay, D. (1998) 'Rethinking social class: qualitative perspectives on class and gender', *Sociology*, 32, 2, 259-275.

Rose, N. (1996) *Governing the Soul*, 2nd Edition, London: Free Association Books.

Rose, N. (1999) *The Powers of Freedom* London: Routledge.

Sennett, R. and Cobb, J. (1993) *The Hidden Injuries of Class*. Cambridge: Polity.

Sennett, R. (1998) *The corrosion of character: the personal consequences of work in the new capitalism*, New York, Norton.

Sennett, R. (2002) 'A Flawed Philosophy' *The Guardian* 17 June.

Skeggs, B. (1997) *Formations of class and gender*, London, Sage.

Tizard, B. and Hughes, M. (1984) *Young children learning*, London, Fontana.

Tawney, R.H. (1964) *Equality* (5th Edn., Intro. Richard Titmus) London: Allen and Unwin.

Walden, R. and Walkerdine, V. (1985) *Girls and mathematics: from primary to secondary schooling*, Bedford Way Papers, 24 London: Heinemann.

Walkerdine, V. (1998) *Counting girls out*, London: Falmer.

Walkerdine, V. (2003) 'Reclassifying social mobility: femininity and the Neo-liberal subject', *Gender and Education*, 15, 3 (September): 237-48.

Walkerdine, V. and Lucey, H. (1989) *Democracy in the kitchen; Regulating mothers and socialising daughters*, London: Virago.

Walkerdine, V, Lucey, H. and Melody, J. (2001) *Growing up girl: psychosocial explorations of gender and class*, London: Palgrave.

Wilkinson, H. *et al.* (1997) *Tomorrow's Women*, London: Demos.

Young, M. (1961) *The Rise of the Meritocracy* Harmondsworth: Penguin.

7. Blair's men: dissident masculinities in Labour's 'new' moral economy

Mairtin Mac an Ghaill and Chris Haywood

In this chapter we explore how New Labour politics, in the context of rapid social and economic change, is reconstituting contemporary gender relations. More specifically, we argue that state-led moral economies operate normatively to shape broader gender regimes or, as Connell (2000: 29) suggests, the *patterning* of gender relations. At the same time, these moral economies, understood as the '… norms which govern or should govern economic activity' (Sayer, 2000: 1), are systematically ordering masculinities. As a result, New Labour's attempts to establish their own moral economy is constituting a particular hegemonic gender regime. It is a regime where politically desirable masculinities become codified as appropriate (prescriptive) citizenship practices.

The first section of the chapter locates the gendered nature of moral economies within a historical context, and situates the current emergence of a politically ascendant masculinity – protective paternalism. The second section of the chapter focuses upon a number of dissident masculinities that are being shaped by New Labour's moral economy. 'Dissident' is used in this chapter to capture conceptually how certain practices antagonise social institutions and provoke the English/British cultural imagination. Thus, dissident masculinities occupy a strategic space in the cultural psyche, simultaneously contesting and supporting society's gendered/sexual hegemony. Spicer (2001: 202) argues that '… hegemonic types always provoke challenge by alternative and oppositional forms of masculinity, male types that embody the repressed desires and transgressive pleasures that official culture has denied'. In order to contain and manage this antagonistic dissidence, social institutions often discursively re-code masculinities by medicalising, psychologising, demonising or infantilising particular practices. Thus, state sanctioned masculinities are often rendered naturalised and normal by the political management of dissident masculinities.

In order to explore how state-led moral economies are shaping contemporary gender relations, we need to move away from an understanding of gender as anatomically determined. It is important to disconnect masculinities from embodied types – rejecting claims that 'male' bodies contain or carry inherent masculine attributes (see also Halberstam, 1998). This disconnection stresses the sociality of gender by suggesting that the bodily representations that constitute male and female are historically located. As Laquer (1990: 16) argues, 'the private, enclosed, stable body that seems to lie at the basis of modern notions of sexual difference is also the product of particular, historical, cultural moments'. In taking up a sex/gender approach that sees masculinities as inscriptions on political processes and practices, we explore historical traces of the current gender regimes articulated by New Labour politics.

SITUATING CONTEMPORARY POLITICISED MASCULINITIES

John Beynon (2002: 107) characterises the political and social upheavals of the 1980s and 1990s in terms of 'goodbye to the old industrial man'.[1] The idea of 'industrial man' as a key element of the post-second-world-war social democratic project helps to convey a state politics that was closely aligned to a nationalised economy, and dependant on traditional masculine occupational sectors such as ship building, agriculture and fishing, steel, mining and manufacturing. One aspect of the politically salient masculinities of the 1950s through to the 1970s was an English/British cultural connection of the body to the public sphere of work. During this period, occupational status emerged as a significant marker of English/British masculinity. The symbiotic relationship of men to their work gained sharper focus; men's work signified a broader epistemological way of being. Willis (2000: 91) suggests that the experience of being a man has been 'tied up historically with doing and being able to do physical work'. These working masculinities were often politically projected as emblems of 'Britishness', with productivity becoming nationalised; 'industrial man' was constituted by hard work, duty, determination, loyalty, responsibility and restraint – key attributes of post-second-world-war British identity.

At the same time, the Labour government of the 1960s blamed weak and insufficiently aggressive management practices for the rapid decline of Britain's identity as an economic world power.[2] An emphasis on Britain as a global economic competitor provided the context for the emergence of other politically salient class-based masculinities. For example, it has been suggested that men (and women) in management were developing masculinities that were shifting from emotional identifications with products to those inscribed by finance-based practices such as company acquisitions and mergers (Roper, 1994). Replacing military-led imperialism with state-sponsored economic and cultural colonialism, English/British working masculinities also contained important class and global inflections. Broadly speaking, the social democratic project of the post-second-world-war period fashioned a moral economy that placed 'industrious men' at the centre of the political agenda.[3]

The ascendancy or political viability of 'industrial man' was not to last. The long years of the New Right regime, from the late 1970s to the mid-1990s, were witness to profound social, economic and cultural change. The increasing numbers of women entering the labour market, alongside growing male unemployment, the increasing visibility of gay rights activism, and racial and ethnic awareness, began to trouble such connections. At the same time, a contained Conservative partisanship towards neo-liberal economic reform became a constitutive context for already fracturing gender order (McNeil, 1991). Severe disruptions, including the collapse of manufacturing industries, the explosion of young people's unemployment and the radical restructuring of welfare support, had direct impacts on the social ordering of multi-inflected masculinities and femininities (Hollands, 1990; Haywood and Mac an Ghaill, 1997). The contradictory position of New Right politics not only contributed to the fracturing of the traditional gender regimes, but was simultaneously involved in its re-establishment.

The rolling back of state regulation in favour of market forces cultivated a new sense of competitive individualism. The New Right fostered an enterprise culture and placed at its centre the entrepreneur, who took on a number of cultural representations (see Nixon, 1996; Edwards, 1997). One set of representations suggested an *embourgeoisement* of particular class sections. As McNeil (1991: 228) points out:

> The enticement of the aspiring working class into this form of consumerism may also involve changes in the modes of working-class masculinity. When buying one's own council house or purchasing education or healthcare are presented as essentials for working-class families … working-class men are adapting to more middle-class modes of masculinity.

Similarities have been drawn between the phenomenon of *the new money* in the early twentieth century and the *affluence* of the 1950s, both periods when concerns were voiced about the dislocation of people from their values, as people moved away from their class. One example of this was the emergence of the 'Yuppie'. Frank Mort's (1996) analysis of this city-based worker suggests that the Yuppie displayed all the traditional masculinised values of ambition, dynamism and ruthlessness. He points out:

> The Yuppie was a hybrid, the focal point for a wide variety of economic and cultural obsessions … the stress was on the yuppie as the representative of an aggressive personality, whose single minded dedication to work had displaced the older forms of gentlemanly amateurism' (171).

Connecting with a traditional English (puritan) work ethic, the commitment and dedication to work of the 'Yuppies' was offset by dislocated values towards wealth. They were vilified by the working classes for losing a sense of collective identity, and disparaged by the upper classes for crudely lacking 'high' culture. A neo-liberal conservative representation of the entrepreneur was also ethnicised, with the new Asian entrepreneur being paraded: traditional routes to success, with their loaded discriminatory practices, were being replaced by the logic of the market, which was not sensitive to gender or ethnic identities – *anyone could make it*.[4]

By the mid-1990s, with the New Right having imploded, a number of thematic priorities characterised New Labour's rise to power. Driver and Martell (1999) suggest a shift in Labour policy – drawing upon Charles Henry Tawney's 'remoralization of society' – that merged liberal individualism and ethical socialism. Labour's efforts to fill the gap opened up by morally vacuous, unrestrained market forces connected with their theme of a new land of economic, social, political and technological change (Andrews, 1996). This involved holding onto market forces and rejecting tax and spend policies, but was combined with a more responsible role for the state. As Gilbert (1998: 75) points out, this results in an emerging tension.

> The appeal to middle England, the rhetoric of caution, the implicit social authoritarianism, the attacks on single parents and the centralisation of power within the party itself can all be seen as attempts to articulate a basically conservative modernity. On the other hand, the commitment to constitutional change, to some re-instatement of workers' rights and to an ethical internationalism can all be seen as a democratising agenda.

New Labour is historically grounded in conflicting ideological positions, and such tensions have resulted in the ascendance of the 'Third Way', or communitarian politics: '... a political vocabulary which eschews market individuals, but not capitalism; and which embraces collective action but not class or the state' (Driver and Martell, 1999: 255). Internal tensions are also emerging from within New Labour's communitarian politics, via the relationship between social regulation and individual autonomy (Etzioni, 1996). This tension appears to be resolving itself in the form of an increasing social authoritarianism, suggesting positive policies that contain a strong social control agenda (James and James, 2001).

New Labour argues that community is an important dynamic in the generation of a shared collective conscience, existing as a key social partner in policing a morally responsible society. Aligned to this politics is a social control agenda that has a close affinity with a particular brand of Christian humanist ethics. This position stresses that people are likely to become good citizens if they are offered the opportunities to do so. The tension between individual autonomy and social regulation is producing the conditions for an increasingly visible political explanation of social deviance. As Pitts (2001: 198) suggests: 'Its rhetoric of social inclusion notwithstanding, New Labour appears to be locked into a politics of blame in which social problems, however complex, are ultimately explicable in terms of the indiscipline or moral failure of the people experiencing those problems.'

Within this context, a version of masculinity that constitutes and is constituted by the moral economy of New Labour's gender regime circulates through a protective paternalism (MacGregor, 1999). This protective paternalism – responsible, dutiful, 'fair but firm', steadfast and tolerant – replaces the moral vacuousness of Tory entrepreneurialism; or, as in a recent New Labour sound-bite, it is a combination of 'enterprise and fairness'. The gendered character of New Labour has been demonstrated in recent conference speeches that combine a 'duty to care' with metaphors of militarism, 'zero tolerance', 'a fight for freedom – economic and social freedom' and a 'battle of values'.[5] Themes such as nurturing and fighting have been juxtaposed in a political symmetry that combines a fight for social inclusion with a combat of social evils. This gender regime is politically expansive. Not only does a protective paternalism resonate with ways in which the government seeks to control the economy and develop social welfare policies; it also connects to broader themes of Britain's political and economic role at global levels.

STATE-LED DISSIDENT MASCULINITIES

New Labour's third way politics, which it is useful to conceptualise as operating through a protective paternalism, is concerned directly with the management of a moral conformity (see also Bell and Binnie, 2000). And its emphasis on social inclusion and exclusion can be seen as a direct response to unmanageable (immoral) gender/sexual practices (Scourfield and Drakeford, 2002). In light of this we are able to explore a number of unmanageable gender practices, and thus situate contemporary dissident masculinities. We will now turn to look at the significance of the 'absent father', the 'anti-social young man' and the 'dangerous man' to New Labour's moral economy.

The 'deadbeat dad': making good fathering

The late 1980s through to the 1990s brought lone (female) parents under increased state scrutiny, projected as they were by the Tory government as a major financial burden on public expenditure that needed reducing. The formation of the Child Support Agency was designed to respond not to father absenteeism *per se*, but rather to mothers' dependence upon benefits – the underlying political rational was to combat the 'nationalisation of fatherhood'. Historically, the state has played an important part in normalising certain familial masculinities (Collier,

1994). For the New Labour administration, fathering must now incorporate New Labour's communitarian morality. Building upon the politics of John Major, there has been a shift in which absent fathers have moved from being seen as an economic problem to become a mainstream political explanation of moral fragmentation; as disrupters of stable communities. In tackling social exclusion, father absence has been cited as an important aspect of children's poor mental health, increased criminal activity, greater involvement in violence, low educational attainment and experience of prolonged periods of unemployment (Morgan, 1995). The moral culpability of the absent father has been emphasised by New Labour's criminalisation of those fathers who fail to take responsibility for their children.

Set up in opposition to the 'absent father', New Labour's hegemonic vision of fatherhood is taking shape. Being located within the family, New Labour fathers not only carry the more traditional elements of responsibility and duty but also are distinguished by popular ethics of care and involvement. In terms of policies, there is evidence to suggest that New Labour has adopted a more positive approach to fathers, which has resulted in increased inclusion across a variety of government departments (see Scourfied and Drakeford, 2001). These commitments have been consolidated by New Labour's sympathy towards statutory paternity pay, and they resonate with a broader cultural significance for fathering, as illustrated by the increase in celebrities demonstrating their fathering integrity. At the same time, politicians' fathering practices have become a major part of a media-orientated spectacle. It is important to acknowledge here that New Labour has not articulated a new set of civic values. Rather, they have usurped the Conservative values of the patriarchal family and attempted to re-articulate them as national heritage, arguing: 'Don't let the Tories claim these as values as their own – they are our values' (Blair, 1996: 69).

In New Labour's moral economy, the family, alongside and as part of the community, operates as an important regulator of civil responsibility. Westwood (1996: 28) describes the state regulation of fatherhood as a classic example of the Foucauldian notion of power of surveillance in postmodern societies. She writes:

> It was constructed out of a series of discourses that generated a specific subject/object, one of which was the 'feckless father', who was to be the subject/object of surveillance, tracking and intervention at both the economic and moral moments. The feckless father had already forfeited his rights as a moral person to engage in self-regulation. Instead a refashioned state agency would regulate him and the woman and children to whom he was to be forcibly attached.

Stychin (2001: 11) suggests that, although New Labour does acknowledge the diversity of contemporary family forms, the monogamous heterosexual family remains for them the essential unit of community and economic stability. In turn, the absent father has enabled New Labour to mobilise a number of politically reparative discourses in its attempts to reinforce social stability. It is important to note that certain gender practices have always been represented as disobedient, out of control and uncontainable. The significance of New Labour's emphasis on fathering is that a respectable English masculinity is being generated, based upon paternal duties of responsibility and care.

Writing from a sociology of law perspective, Collier (1994: 203-4) makes a telling point in suggesting that the construction of the absent father as problematic in legal discourse involved establishing fatherhood as a desirable presence during marriage (the economic provider discourse). As he argues, the irony is that, given the logic of economic rationality in advanced capitalist societies, the breadwinner masculinity of the 'good father' entails many men being absent from their families. He suggests that evidence from divorce reveals that the presence of paternal masculinity was always open-ended. However, he makes clear what paternal masculinity, presumed by law to be desirable, actually entails. Hence, for Collier the absent father really signifies something else, namely the desirability of masculinity within the family embodying the three axes of authority, economic responsibility and heterosexuality, which constitute the idea of the 'good father' in law.

Civilising work: anti-social young men
A key theme of New Labour's rise to power in 1997 was the emphasis on youthfulness as a harbinger of social innovation. New Labour, emphasising a break with Old Labour, projected itself as a young political party, Britpop celebrated a young country and the government was aiming to increase the opportunities for the young. This emphasis on youthfulness contains a tension, since implicit within notions of youthfulness are discourses of risk, control and protection. Young people not only represent the 'promise' and imagined 'future' of the nation; they are also deemed central to its risk. In order to safeguard the future of the nation, particular lifestyles are targeted as threats. New Labour has continued to identify as a problem one particular lifestyle – 'the scourge of many communities ... young people with nothing to do who make life hell for other citizens' (Blair, in Fitzpatrick, 1999: 1). As a result, the Labour government has issued a range of contradictory legislation that insists on young people's independence, while simultaneously governing them with paternal protectionism.

In the mid-1990s New Labour politically vilified certain forms of masculinity which it saw as arising out of social exclusion. The discourse of yob culture, once again inherited from the Tories, became reconstructed within a frame of community responsibility and active citizenship. Thus men who have adopted particular lifestyles needed to be integrated and included (Scourfield and Drakeford, 2002). Laddism was one of the more antagonistic lifestyles that was identified. During the mid-1990s laddism became the focus of much cultural commentary. Magazines such as *Loaded* and *FHM* catered to, cultivated and established a legitimacy for the veneration of a hedonism associated with frequent sexual encounters, alcohol binges and football discussion. At the same time, they were part of a culture of consumption that focused on young men's bodies through retro-based practices linked to traditional forms of white working-class heterosexual culture. However this masculinity of laddism was deemed new, as it also contained a reflexive and self-mocking theme. This was particularly emphasised when it was taken up by middle-class men.

In many ways, the vocabularies of oppression that have mobilised identity politics around social groups such as women, ethnic minorities and gays/lesbians have a resonance with the middle-class Christian morality espoused by New Labour. Thus for New Labour, particular masculinities are construed as socially damaging as well as anti-authority. However, laddism also connects with a broader hedonism that rejects middle-class standards and the constant pursuit of consumer, political or spiritual enlightenment (for the middle class, non-commercial life can sometimes seem just one more learning experience). Laddism contests this cultural hegemony. What is also interesting is that laddism was not specifically about male bodies; it was about specific, socially-defined working-class masculine cultural forms: alcohol, aggressive sexualities, football. It operated as an alternative masculinised gender regime that could be taken up by males and females. Such sets of values have currently become part of New Labour explanations for school underachievement and social disorder. It is also charged that laddism is responsible for economic instability.

Other forms of hedonism were in place that might have challenged this cultural hegemony. For example, Gilbert (1998) suggests that the emerging dance culture of the first New Labour term allowed more hybrid identities to emerge, as club culture began dismantling the social categories of gender, ethnicity and sexuality. However, a queer politics of the dance floor did not appear.

Themes of laddism resonate and feed directly into New Labour's criminal justice and social welfare reform, as they target cultural concerns such as football hooliganism, young drunks, drug-pushers and anti-social families. In short, laddism is being fused with 'yob culture'. David Blunkett insists: 'We have to overcome what some call laddism – the belief that it is cool not to work'. The New Lads stand in tension with conventional lifestyles that have a work ethic as a central feature.

Sexual risk: beware the paedophile
The current concern with sexually dangerous men has contributed to New Labour's emphasis on citizenship, community duty and social

responsibility.[6] Given the current centrality of heterosexuality to protective paternalism, the presence of other sexualities challenges and reinforces the respectability of English masculinity. The high moral panic surrounding 'Stranger Danger' and the cultural demonisation of the paedophile have provided emphasis and momentum to New Labour's moral renewal of the nation. The social threat and risk carried by the paedophile has fuelled the political imagination and re-instated the centrality of the family to society, where 'strong families are the foundation of a strong community' (Mandelson and Liddle, 1996: 124).

At the same time, contained within New Labour's protective paternalism is the prescription for men to build caring and responsible relationships in the family and the community. For instance, the government has made a considerable economic commitment to funding nation-wide learning mentors. It has also placed onto the political agenda the importance of getting men into primary/nursery schools, alongside a consistently articulated view that men should be part of young people's lives in the form of good role models. Yet, at the same time, men's emerging protective paternal role in the family, community and nation has become a key source for current sexual anxiety. Public sector workers such as youth workers, social workers, school teachers, nursery nurses and social researchers are facing greater levels of surveillance and regulation (Owen, 2000). Although state sanctioned, there remains a cultural 'queerness' about men working with children.

There is also a specificity surrounding the English paedophile that troubles New Labour communitarian politics. The paedophile is anonymous. However, this anonymity of the paedophile – in terms of being an identifiable character – is the very dynamic that makes the phenomenon so culturally powerful. Ohi (2000: 204) points out:

> To sustain a stable picture of the paedophile, it is thus paradoxically necessary to assert that paedophilia cannot be detected, that a paedophile can not be pictured at all. The same gesture that renders him locatable and quarantined makes him unlocatable, omnipresent, and dangerously at large: just the way we like him.

Empirical evidence appears to show that child abusers are more than likely to be family members, especially fathers/step-fathers or brothers (Meloy, 2000). It is ironic that public surveillance techniques such as List 99, the sexual offenders register and criminal record checks continue to situate the sexual danger outside of the family and the community; sexual danger is projected onto the unlocatable, unknowable, anonymous bodies of non-citizens. Such practices are not simply prohibitive; they culturally produce the paedophile. For example, Foucault (1981) highlighted that in the Victorian period there was an intensified surveillance of the boy who masturbated. In the twenty-first century, the emphasis has changed, with the surveying gaze upon other people (adult men) masturbating the boy. Foucault suggested that the surveillance of the sexual child constituted the practices that were set up to eradicate it. It is argued here that a similar process is taking place in relation to the stranger, on whom a new 'truth of sex' is being written.

During recent debates on the age of consent, a familiar representation of masculinity was of the older male sexual predator (Waites, 1999). Whilst being a sexualised identity, the actions and descriptions of the sexual practices take on masculine forms; molesters, monsters and perverts operate through a masculinised but perverted biological drive discourse, and through a gendered crime dichotomy (Hollway, 1989; Collier 1998). Cultural representations of paedophiles tend to depict sad, lonely and socially disconnected individuals. Their dangerousness is illustrated by a suggested cleverness and cunning, as the paedophile remains part of the community without being identified. However, analytically, the cultural valorisation of a normative masculinity does not appear too abnormal. As Cossins (2000) suggests:

> ... it is necessary to consider the significance of a man's sexual behaviour with children in a social context that is pervaded by, and which valorises, images of hypermasculine toughness and performance (that is, a particular type of sexed male body, the Masculine Ideal), and in which power and sexuality are inextricably linked. In this way, far from being a deviation from such sexual norms, child sex offending could be said to be a celebration of them.

Currently, popular understandings of paedophiles as demonised others has legitimised the purging of safe spaces of danger. At the same time, New Labour policies that encourage the active participation of men in family life and the community are generating English cultural sexual anxieties.

CONCLUSION

We have argued that New Labour politics can be understood as contributing to a particular moral economy that is generating the conditions for a new ordering of masculinities. Part of that ordering has been the identification of antagonistic or what we call dissident masculinities. As social and cultural formations, the gender regimes that are contained within moral economies are subject to change. For New Labour and their communitarian moral economy, challenges are beginning to emerge. What has not been discussed here are the riots in northern towns by young Asian men. These may begin to highlight the limitations of a politics based upon communities. Furthermore, this social unrest makes visible the ambiguous nature of New Labour's 'community' (is it a location, a collectivity, a nation?), limiting our analytic purchase on central government's understanding of gender transformations. Another challenge to New Labour's moral economy is the increasing influence of European politics. In articulating a gender regime that is based upon the specificities of Englishness/Britishness, a shift to the gender regimes of Europe may create cultural fissures in what we understand as contemporary masculinities and femininities.

NOTES

1. Many thanks to Richard Johnson for pointing this out.
2. The Wilson government through the Industrial Reorganisation Corporation attempted to increase global productivity by encouraging company take-overs rewarded by financial incentives.
3. We use 'industrious' in a way that contains earlier associations with skilful and ingenuity with more modern meanings of labouring.
4. Indeed, it was the Asian entrepreneurs who could be seen to be taking the Tory minister, Norman Tebbit's advice 'to get on their bikes' as his father's generation had – an example of the socially marginal being culturally central – in this instance within conditions of late modernity.
5. Tony Blair's Labour Party conference speeches cited in the *Guardian* 27.09.00 and 03.10.01.
6. See also Weeks and Epstein, Johnson and Steinberg, this volume, for discussion about the reconstitution of discourses of male ('paedophilic') sexual danger as emblematised in the 'gay paedophile' (a key iconic folk devil of the Thatcher-Major years), in conjunction with new discourses legitimating (limited) claims for citizenship under the auspices of New Labour's investments in 'social inclusion'.

REFERENCES

Andrews, L. (1996) 'New Labour, New England', in M. Perryman (ed) *The Blair Agenda*. London: Lawrence and Wishart.

Beynon, J. (2002) *Masculinities and Culture*. Buckingham: Open University Press.

Bell, D. and Binnie, J. (2000) *The Sexual Citizen: Queer Politics and Beyond*. Cambridge: Polity Press.

Blair, T. (1996) *New Britain: My Vision of a Young Country*. London: Labour Party.

Cockburn, C. (1983) *Brothers: Male Dominance and Technological Change*. London: Pluto.

Collier, R. (1994) *Masculinity, Law and the Family*. New York: Routledge.

Collier, R. (1998) *Masculinities, Crime and Criminology. Men, Heterosexuality and the Criminal (ized) Other*. London: Sage.

Connell, R. W. (2000) *The Men and the Boys*. Cambridge: Polity Press.

Cossins, A. (2000) *Masculinities, Sexualities and Child Sexual Abuse*. Kluwer Law International: The Hague.

Driver, S. and Martell, L. (1999) 'New Labour: Culture and economy', in L. Ray and A. Sayer (eds.) *Culture and Economy After the Cultural Turn*. Sage: London.

Edwards, T. (1997) *Men in the Mirror: Men's Fashion, Masculinity and Consumer Society*. London: Cassell.

Etzioni, A. (1996) *The New Golden Rule: Community and Morality in a Democratic Society*. New York: Basic Books.

Fitzpatrick, M. (1999) 'Yob Culture Clash', *LM Archives*, No. 73.

Foucault, M. (1981) *The History of Sexuality, Vol. 1*. Harmondsworth: Penguin

Gilbert, J. (1998) 'Blurred vision: Pop, Populism and politics', in A. Coddington and M. Perryman (eds) *The Modernizer's Dilemma: Radical Politics in the Age of Blair*. London: Lawrence and Wishart.

Halberstam, J. (1998) *Female Masculinity*. Durham: Duke University Press.

Haywood, C. and Mac an Ghaill, M. (1997) 'A man in the making: sexual masculinities within changing training cultures', *The Sociological Review*, 45(4): 576-90.

Hollands, R. G. (1990) *The Long Transition: Class, Culture and Youth Training*. London: Macmillan Education.

Hollway, W. (1989) *Subjectivity and Method in Psychology: Gender, Meaning and Science*. London: Sage.

James, A. L. and James, A. (2001) 'Tightening the net: children, community and control', *British Journal of Sociology*, Vol. 52, no. 2, pp.211 –228.

MacGregor, S. (1999), 'Welfare, neo-liberalism and the new paternalism', *Capital and Class*, Vol. 67, pp. 91-118.

Mandelson, P. and Liddle, R. (1996) *The Blair Revolution: Can New Labour deliver?* London: Faber and Faber.

McNeil, M. (1991) 'Making and not making the difference: the gender politics of Thatcherism', in S. Franklin, C. Lury and J. Stacey (eds.) *Off-Centre: Feminism and Cultural Studies*. London: HarperCollins.

Meloy, M. (2000) '"Stranger Danger": Some problems with community notification', in K. Buckly and P. Head (eds.) *Myths, Risks and Sexuality: The Role of Sexuality in Working with Young People*. Russell House: Southampton.

Morgan, P. (1995) *Farewell to the Family?* London: Institute of Economic Affairs.

Mort, F. (1996) *Cultures of Consumption: Masculinities and Social Space in Late Twentieth-Century Britain*. London: Routledge.

Nixon, S. (1996) *Hard looks: Masculinities, Spectatorship and Contemporary Consumption*. London: UCL Press.

Ohi, K. (2000) 'Molestation 101: Child Abuse, Homophobia, and The Boys of St. Vincent', *GLQ: Journal of Lesbian and Gay Studies*, 6.2, 2000

Owen, C. (2000) 'Men as workers in services for young children: prolegomena', in C. Owen, C. Cameron and P. Moss (eds.) *Men as Workers in Services for Young Children: Issues of a Mixed Gender Workforce*. Institute of Education: London.

Pitts, J. (2001) *The New Politics of Youth Crime: Discipline or Solidarity*. Palgrave: Hampshire.

Roper, M. (1994) *Masculinity and the British Organization Man since 1945*. Oxford: Oxford University Press.

Sayer, A. (2000) *Morality and Economy*, Paper presented to the Equality Studies Centre 10th Anniversary Conference, University College Dublin, Dec. 15th.

Scourfield, J. and Drakeford, M. (2002) 'New Labour and the "problem of men"', *Critical Social Policy*, 22, 4.

Spicer, A. (2001) *Typical Men: The Representation of Masculinity in Popular British Cinema*. London: I.B. Tauris, 2001.

Stychin (2001) *Queering the Third Way: New Labour's Communitarianism, Social Inclusion, and the Politics of Sexual Dissent*, American Law and Society Conference, Budapest, Hungary, July 2001.

Waites (1999) 'The Age of Consent and Sexual Citizenship in the United Kingdom: a History', in J. Seymour and P. Bagguley (eds.) *Relating Intimacies: Power and Resistance*. London: Macmillan.

Westwood, S. (1996) ' "Feckless fathers": masculinities and the British state', in M. Mac an Ghaill (ed.) *Understanding Masculinities: Social Relations and Cultural Arenas*. Buckingham: Open University Press.

Willis, P. (2000) *The Ethnographic Imagination*. Polity and Blackwell: Oxford.

8. Virtual members? The internal party culture of New Labour

Estella Tincknell

This essay is dedicated to the memory of Terry Coello, a good comrade who would almost certainly not have agreed with some of its criticisms of 'old' Labour.

There are, of course, many histories of the transformation of the Labour Party into New Labour, but the way in which the party itself has been internally reconstructed has been relatively unconsidered. Yet New Labour's invention of itself in relation to an imagined 'other' – 'Old Labour' – onto which its fears, anxieties (and, perhaps, desires) were projected, has had major repercussions within the party's structures. Fundamental changes have been made in the name of 'modernisation', achieving legitimacy largely because the 'old' Labour Party was successfully cast – frequently by its own members – as an arcane and obsolete institution, tainted by a wholly self-interested 'activism'. Thus, for example, Peter Mandelson was arguing in 1996 that 'popular participation in the party started to decline and the party structure weakened, leaving by the 1970s an empty shell in many constituencies. Far too often this suited the small cliques of party loyalists who remained to run things as they wanted' (1996: 213).

The apparent break with party traditions that produced the invention of New Labour involved a process of cultural investment in a particular idea of the modern – one that seemed at odds with what I will call Labour's 'traditional modernity'. It also entailed a rhetorical emphasis on social and political inclusion, together with a distancing from class politics, as signified by the appropriation of the American political metaphor of 'the big tent' to describe Blairism's redefinition of the party's political culture. In place of the 'special relationship' between Labour and the old manufacturing-based trade unions, New Labour promised equal opportunities for capital and labour, and an extended definition of its own constituency. In order to do this effectively it therefore also had to redefine itself, its party base and its culture.

Yet New Labour's rhetoric of cultural modernity has neither endeared it to outsiders nor helped convince party members. Instead, it has produced a sense of the party as a hollowed-out entity without principles, purpose or even a 'real' membership. To draw on Jean Baudrillard's (1983: 2) flawed yet powerful argument about the collapse of the 'real' into the 'hyperreal', the relationship between policy and politics and their mediation seems increasingly blurred. The cultural investment in image and style, together with a professionalised (and obsessively reactive) approach to media management, means that the rhetoric of New Labour has begun to be perceived as standing in for real changes in policy, even where this is demonstrably not the case, and even among party members. The excessive rhetorical emphasis on the modern, the focus on the appearance of action and intervention (resignations, reports, speeches) and the intense relationship between political and media discourses, thus seem to me to be symptomatic of a bigger shift in New Labour political culture – towards a *postmodern* politics. It is this transformation, and the cultural significance of the modernisation project to the internal politics of Labour and to party members such as myself, that this chapter will explore.

1900 – COMPETING VERSIONS OF MODERNITY

The Labour Party has a contradictory and uneasy relationship with modernity and with modernist thought. In contrast to what appear to be sister parties in many other parts of Europe, which tend to style themselves as Socialist or Social Democrat and which are underpinned by the culturally modernist traditions of theoretical socialism, the British Labour Party's political allegiances were defined from the first as being to a class, 'labour', rather than to a specific ideological project. The Labour Representation Committee was formed in 1900, at the high point of British capitalism and imperialism and of mass forms of industrialisation, as a broad-based coalition to represent the specific interests of the organised (and largely industrial) working class in the Houses of Parliament. It was this grouping which formally became the Labour Party in 1906.

Though undoubtedly committed to the grand modern narratives of progress, morality and social order, Labour was never underpinned by a coherent and distinctively Socialist party ideology. As Eric Shaw points out (1996: 3), 'the original Labour Party exhibited a number of characteristics which have never been entirely lost. In contrast to continental social democratic parties, it was a party of *interest* rather than ideas'. These origins shaped the party's peculiar relationship to an 'epochal' modernity which tied it to processes and allegiances forged under industrialisation, urbanisation and the development of a mass society, while also cementing an intense hostility to overtly ideological forms of politics. It is this epochal modernity, including the links with the trade unions, which New Labour has struggled with in its attempt to redefine both itself and its membership.

Indeed, without a coherent and elaborated ideological model of society and of itself as a force within the social, the Labour Party responded in two ways. First, it developed a patchwork of beliefs and ethics drawn from Methodism, radicalism and trade unionism, all of which were underpinned by a single fundamental principle: the commitment to reform not revolution. Second, the party generated an attachment to its own history and to the actors in that history – Keir Hardie, Clement Attlee, Nye Bevan, Jennie Lee, Harold Wilson, Barbara Castle – as a way of making sense of itself. Instead of an ideology it had a story.

The patchwork of beliefs was effectively held together by a philosophical position whose links to common sense in the Gramscian sense effectively helped facilitate the New Labour project: pragmatism. It was pragmatism that made the party open to new ideas as long as they could be grafted onto its reformist version of modernity. It was pragmatism that enabled principles to be abandoned on the grounds that they no longer 'worked', and others to be adopted because they were voter-friendly. Indeed, it was pragmatism that was frequently defended as a British solution to a British problem – winning elections through the first-past-the-post system. And it has been pragmatism that has formed the basis of the New Labour approach to policy, an approach that may best be defined as instrumental rationalism.

The emphasis on history as a guiding narrative in Labour's self-definition has been complex and paradoxical. On the one hand, the party is opposed to 'tradition' when it comes in the form of 'Toryism' and pre-industrial models of power and privilege (although the monarchy has been perversely exempt); on the other, it is sentimentally attached to its own story as an explanatory framework and to the traditions of the labour movement. Even Tony Blair has argued that 'modernisation is not about diluting traditional values. It is about breathing new life into them' (1999: 157). Such 'traditional modernity' thus frames the party's complex relationship both to industrialisation and the development of liberal democracy, and to a more abstruse sense of national identity to which Britishness and 'tradition' are closely tied.

This history also worked to define the subject of its narrative, the hero of its action and the primary beneficiary of the changes it sought to bring about: the white working-class man. Indeed, the importance of 'labour' itself in the form of manual, usually industrial, work remains valorised in Labour Party discourse. This has meant that other kinds of work and other kinds of social identities have tended to be devalued or marginalised. Even as work was struggled over and redefined, 'feminised' and casualised during the 1970s and 1980s, masculinism remained central to the discursive structure of Labour politics.

However, Labour's relationship to the epochal modern is most explicitly if not very effectively expressed in its organisational structure, which is both rigorously 'democratic' and materially exclusionary. It may be useful to see this in terms of Raymond Williams's (1980) model of the presence of residual and emergent elements as well as dominant ones in any given cultural formation; and these elements can be clearly identified in the battles that marked the shift to New Labour. The culturally dominant version of the party, rigorously imposed by Blairism and widely mediated, is effectively of a 'post-modern' organisation, in its emphasis on multiculturalism and faith communities, sexual liberalism (within certain clear parameters) and 'meritocratic' individualism. This is the party of the posters and television advertisements, a party which offers space to the white nuclear family and to the stable gay couple, to the aspiring, 'post-feminist' young black woman and to the Muslim Asian man who came to Britain in the 1950s to make a better way of life: a party for whom the question of class and the economy has apparently been settled. Yet the residual culture of the Labour Party, the culture that is lived at the local level, remains dominated by the social relations of class power and male dominance, and by the 'modern' structures and conventions that were intended to transform them. So, at least *two* versions of modernity have been struggled over in the move from Labour to New Labour, and these can be identified in the gap between media representations of the party and the structures that continue to characterise its local base.

THE 1990S – 'MODERNISING' STRUCTURES/POSTMODERN PRINCIPLES

'The party' is still officially managed by a system of committees developed in the early twentieth century, all of which are empowered to debate issues and pass resolutions that are intended – in theory at least – to shape national policy. These range from the constituency-based General Committees, which are made up of delegates from local branches, through to the National Executive Committee, which is supposed to determine the overall direction of the party. These formal mechanisms are explicitly tied into both local and national government structures (local councils, parliamentary constituencies), so that elected representatives are, nominally at least, directly accountable to the party membership. At my local branch meetings in Birmingham, for example, the ward councillors, as well as the local Labour MP, attend meetings and can be variously questioned, reprimanded or congratulated on their actions. Moreover, any branch member can submit a written resolution on any topic, which will then be debated and voted upon. If the resolution is agreed it will be passed up the chain to the Constituency and Regional Parties and, in theory at least, to the National Party where it may become policy.

Branch and constituency meetings are further marked by their formality. Each has a Chair, Secretary and Treasurer with clearly defined roles; meetings are dominated by lengthy verbal or written reports by delegates about other parts of the meeting chain; there is a fixed agenda bound by the party's standing orders; and members are supposed to wait to be called by the Chair before they can speak. In principle, such a formalised way of operating ensures that important issues are addressed, that everyone has a chance to speak and to be heard, and that party officers are accountable for their actions. However, such a structure, with its hierarchies, bureaucracies and committee-room odour, has all the appurtenances of modernity to be found in a Victorian telegraph system or a tower block in Tashkent. Its continuation has led to the increasing visibility of contradictions around participation and activism in local Labour politics.

By continuing to operate through systems that are 'modern' but not especially contemporary, and through rules that are formally democratic but not especially inclusive, the localised base of the party has been weakened. The regularisation of meetings on weekday evenings means that those with family responsibilities may not be able to attend. The formality of discussion may mean that those who are unused to public forms of speech are silenced. Even the use of particular kinds of rhetoric – the register of Labourism – may confuse or alienate new members, and can look emptily gestural. At my local branch meetings, middle-aged white men far outnumber any other group attending and tend, still, to dominate discussions and decision-making. Most belong to the public sector middle class (or are retired from it), as teachers, lecturers, social workers, health professionals, council officers or trade union officials. Women have become increasingly absent from branch meetings over the last few years (although they were a significant presence during the 1980s and early 1990s), and those who do attend say less, despite the example of high profile female MPs. There are a number of black and Asian members, and in Birmingham at least a significant number of Asian city councillors and Asian-dominated branches, but in 'white' branches such as my own they rarely attend meetings. In this respect, the party's residual modernity seems to have been intensified: rather than extending inclusivity it appears to be withering away. More insidiously, while racism remains publicly (and very properly) identified as a significant political problem, it is increasingly difficult to put questions of gender and power on the agenda of local Labour Party activity, and casual sexism continues to underpin many aspects of social relations. The extent to which the national party was complicit in the trivialisation and then vilification of 'Blair's Babes' in the media is symptomatic of the way in which the party as a whole has failed to embed a genuine commitment to gender equality.

All this made the case for modernising the party in the early 1990s convincing. It enabled something called 'Old Labour' to be demonised and helped to secure consent to the first tranche of changes that signalled the party's transformation. First, the voting structures were completely overhauled, with OMOV (One Member, One Vote) replacing the complex system of union block votes at the party conference in 1993, and the procedures around NEC elections were made more transparent. Committee membership became – it seemed – genuinely more democratic and more open as a consequence. The removal of the block vote in particular seemed to signal the recognition that the 'organised' working class was increasingly a fraction of the real working class, and that the party was open to other, more diverse groups and interests.

The climax of the struggle between these two versions of the modern – between 'Old' and 'New' Labour – took place over the abolition of 'Clause Four' in 1994 and 1995. Clause Four of the original 1918 Party Constitution was drafted by the Fabians Sidney Webb and Arthur Henderson, and had been the key symbolic statement of Labour's commitment to the redistribution of wealth. It pledged the Labour Party, 'to secure for the workers by hand or by brain the full fruits of their industry and the most equitable distribution thereof that may be possible upon the basis of the common ownership of the means of production, distribution and exchange'.

Shaw (1996: 5-6) argues that Webb in particular did not actually believe in these principles (and suggests that the Clause itself was partly a pragmatic device, partly a product of its historical moment); and it is certainly true that even 'Old' Labour never attempted to carry out its promise when in government. Indeed, Clause Four was a symbolic text more than anything else – it represented the utopian dreams and desires of members rather than their expectations. Yet sentimental attachment to it was also symptomatic of the way in which Labour's traditional modernity could be cast as quaint and old-fashioned as well as tokenistic: what was the point of keeping a clause in the constitution that committed the party to a form of anti-capitalism that it didn't believe in and which was potentially alienating to the private sector, and to the conservative middle classes who had to be wooed? Its abolition was, then, also a symbolic act and was the most significant example of the playing out of the struggle around modernisation and modernity within the party.

The other significant change in the modernisation process has been much more difficult to trace or to challenge. It involved the stealthy introduction of a series of rival or parallel structures to the party's own system, in the form of focus groups, 'independent' advisers, media experts and press officers. These groups and individuals are frequently invisible within party structures, or operate outside them – and are wholly unaccountable because of this. They are either directly answerable to the Party's Head Office or to the prime minister's office at Downing Street, or contribute to the formulation of policy in ways that are unavailable to ordinary members. Indeed, the policy focus groups often appear to have been deliberately constructed without party members, presumably on the grounds that we were 'too political' to represent public opinion. Such groups represent the mythologised constituency of 'middle England' – a coded rubric describing the suburban, historically anti-Labour middle classes – that New Labour courted during the 1990s.

Yet, by the end of that decade party members were themselves being directly addressed in a glossy newsletter, *Inside Labour* (now replaced by *Labour News*), whose job was to 'spin' both the policies of the party and the main political figures. Although an apparently unimportant journal, *Inside Labour* was crucial to the redefinition of the party's image and identity: from the idea of Labour representing a relatively homogeneous, unified 'working class', to one of it as a coalition of diverse interests and identities, including women, ethnic minorities, gays and lesbians. *Inside Labour* thus helped to manage the party's shift to New Labour by representing it as a fait accompli.

These changes seem to me to be symptomatic also of the larger transformations taking place in British politics over the past decade, as well as of the ambivalences and contradictions around our understanding of what constitutes the 'modern' and how it relates to 'progress'. There is a great deal of talk about democracy, and a much more overtly articulated commitment to it in the form of what appear to be strenuously transparent codes and mechanisms for participation in politics and accountability to party members. Yet the emergence of a 'shadow' Labour Party, made up of anonymous advisers and focus groups whose precise relationship both to decision-making and to party democracy is unclear, shows not only that the presentation and management of public image is often regarded as more important than the social effects of politics in a 'real' world, but also that New Labour's commitment to internal democracy is questionable.

1997 – A POSTMODERN PARTY (1): CONSUMPTION

The final break between the old model of Labour Party membership as signifying (even in a limited fashion) active participation in public politics and the largely passive model that has become dominant under Blairism took place at some point during the mid-1990s. Up until 1995 the 'modernising' project had barely addressed the nature and status of party membership and the function of individuals within the party structure. The mass-based and largely urban model that had prevailed from the 1920s onwards had remained unquestioned. Within this model membership was a form of active volunteerism. Members were expected to contribute to meetings, take up posts such as those of Treasurer or General Committee delegate and, most importantly, declare their politics in public ways. This volunteerist paradigm structured the party's character: it helped to determine the issues that were at stake and the manner in which they were addressed.

The stated goal of the Blair leadership in the years immediately before and after the General Election of 1997 was to create New Labour as a 'mass membership' party by maximising the transformation of 'supporters' into 'members'. Paradoxically, this desire seemed to articulate the twin 'modernities' of both the 'old' and 'new' wings of the party; it drew on the language of 'Old Labour' with its attachment to the urban masses, and it spoke to the Blairite modernisers who were committed to drawing in as many potential supporters as possible by eschewing left/right political antinomies. What was not overtly acknowledged, however, was that this process would also produce a shift in power relations by turning the party's (troublesome) membership of 'activists' – already identified as a problem by Peter Mandelson – into a docile support base.

The new party model was partly achieved by the introduction of a national computerised membership system. This had several consequences, both for the 'modernisation' of the party and for the shift in power between the local and national strands. The most significant was the way in which it effectively redirected the dynamics of party organisation from the 'roots' of the constituencies and local branches back to the centre. From being a party whose membership was largely organised around localised recruitment and activism, especially at the level of local elections, Labour became a centralised, overtly hierarchical organisation, whose membership was directly controlled at a national level. The 'mass' party that subsequently developed had little in common with the socialist – and properly 'modernist' – model of a mass movement, and much more in common with the post-modern phenomenon of the fragmented, individualised internet customer, 'massified' in terms of numbers rather than consciousness.

The 'post-modern' New Labour party is a much more contingent, fluid and 'floating' entity than the old Labour Party – involving coalitions of interests that are not defined primarily by class, caste or ideological commitment. While the process of extending and redefining both the nature of membership and the politics of a 'Labour identity' is clearly crucial, it seems to me that the specific version of the postmodern that has been taken up is one that is reductively commodificatory. Culturally, the party now resembles a cross between a business and a club (despite the 'mass membership'), with an annual return to make to its stake-holders, and a centralised and autonomous organisational structure. This also means that membership itself has been destabilised. Are party members activists or share-holders? Are they entitled to expect a 'profit' from their investment or are they to be seen as akin to charitable givers – donating without expectation of a specific return other than the warm glow of knowing that they have done some good in the world? In addition, because the party *member* has been stealthily recast as a *supporter* (despite the declaration of a desire to do precisely the opposite) – that is, as someone who has little power to change or intervene in policy – joining New Labour closely resembles joining the RAC or supporting a charity: membership is increasingly represented in terms of specific, individualised and consumerist benefits.

The post-modern party supporter appears in party literature defined largely in terms of individualised lifestyle and consumption practices that are wholly uncoupled from a wider social context (a perennial 'floating voter' perhaps). For example, I have a nicely glossy brochure entitled 'Benefits of Labour Party Membership'. It offers me discounts on insurance services, a Co-operative Bank Visa card and personal loan service, and access to a telephone-based travel club (which promises to be open 364 days a year – I wonder if they are unionised?). In case I become nostalgic for the picturesque, I can purchase a series of Labour Party poster reproductions so that, in a piece of exquisitely post-modern irony, I might have Keir Hardie's 1900 address to the impoverished voters of Merthyr Tydfil to hang on the walls of my post-industrial loft apartment if I am so inclined. Supporters, it seems, must be repeatedly wooed, their commitment secured and reclaimed on a regular basis and their membership guaranteed by the promise of material benefits to themselves if they are to be retained.

Inside Labour especially exhibited profoundly symptomatic anxieties about the party and the nature of political commitment. And because New Labour promised to achieve its goals painlessly and consensually, making things better for everyone, including those who already enjoy a comfortable life, the tension between the expression of that position and older, socialist values was especially visible in such texts. In the October 2000 edition, for instance, an editorial letter from then General Secretary Margaret McDonagh, began with an emphatic assertion of the 'funda-mental differences' between Labour and the Conservatives, and went on to remind readers of the effectiveness of the government's policies on the economy, presumably on the basis that party supporters, unlike party members, may take their custom elsewhere.

Equally problematic was the magazine's emphasis on members as 'willing hands' rather than thinking individuals. For example, a 2001 pre-election edition of *Inside Labour* featured a series of snapshots of party supporters, showed them stuffing envelopes, campaigning with national politicians and recruiting new members. Later editions featured strenuous attempts to demonstrate party openness through columns in which 'ordinary' members quizzed ministers about govern-ment policy. All offered in the name of openness and communication; and, in the sense that we are now receiving regular letters, missives and documents from party headquarters, this is the case. In contrast to the dog days of the early 1980s, when Labour Party members were fortu-nate to be sent a parcel of stickers in time for an election, we are now bombarded with literature: personalised letters from Tony Blair and John Prescott, leaflets to hand out, pocket policy guides, all clearly setting out what we are supposed to say – and think. Yet the political thinness of so many of these texts, together with their high glossiness, makes them powerful reminders of New Labour's investment in style and simplified 'messages'.

One key moment in the run up to the general election in 2001 marked this process for me most clearly. It was a Saturday morning in early February and, with a general election originally expected in May, plans for the forthcoming campaign were under way both locally and nationally. I answered the telephone to a caller who identified himself as speaking from Labour Party Head Office in London, and who launched into a scripted plea for a donation. 'We would like to thank you for your support', I was told. 'The Labour Party is very appreciative of the money you donate'. Although this method of soliciting funds has become familiar to most party members over the last few years, this particular moment assumed the status of an epiphany for me. I responded angrily and somewhat futilely with the retort, 'actually, *I* am the Labour Party, not somebody sitting in an office in London. Political parties are made up of people like us who do the work locally – they are not something that exists beyond their members'. Even as I spoke I wasn't sure whether what I was saying was 'true', or could even be said to have been true once. Nonetheless, I was convinced that the moment was symptomatic of the way in which party members like me were being systematically marginalised from the decision-making process and transformed into the 'docile bodies' (in Foucault's phrase) required to leaflet and canvass but not to think or debate. The caller's (also prescribed) response was illuminating – it was to repeat his thanks 'on behalf of the Labour Party' for my good work, which wasn't really the point.

The main issue that arose out of this brief encounter was the way in which it crystallised for me the shift that had taken place around the status of party members in the current structures of the organisation. It offered a brief shaft of light onto the way in which my – and others' – membership of the party had been redefined without my consent or knowledge and probably outside the existing, if somewhat creaky, internal political structures – structures that were supposed to deliver a democratic decision-making process. Someone somewhere had decided not only that the Labour Party should establish a national call-centre system that would effectively by-pass local recruitment and fund-raising mechanisms (with all the implications for local party funds that this suggests), but also that the discursive address through which members would be solicited should emphasise the need for financial support rather than political activity. Nobody has ever telephoned me from London to remind me to go out canvassing. They may prefer me not to.

1997 – A POSTMODERN PARTY (2): PASTICHE

Importantly, this recasting of the role of the party member has been accompanied by a powerful rhetorical emphasis on our importance, but only in this limited, redefined capacity. If anything, as the sense of belonging to a political movement has declined, the rhetorical emphasis on party membership has become more insistent. There is plenty for us to *do* but this doesn't include thinking about the politics in which we are supposed to be involved. This specific moment emphasised for me a larger, ongoing process: that of the party's effective split between a powerful, centralised, and undoubtedly metropolitan (and masculine) executive 'Labour Party', and a disempowered, symptomatically provincial and individualised membership.

In his attempt to identify and define the characteristics of postmodern culture, Fredric Jameson (1984) has explored the extent to which post-modern texts are themselves both 'knowing' and nostalgic about the modern, while eschewing an overt commitment to its precepts or ideals. One could argue, of course, that Tony Blair's insistent restatement of certain ideals that may be said to be 'modern', such as fairness, moral probity and a just world, is clear evidence of New Labour's genuine modernity in ideological terms. But one could also see them as a postmodern evocation of nostalgia of the kind that Jameson discusses. Blair's grandiose claims to speak for the oppressed or to be able to bring world peace appear excessive and therefore hollow: they have the style and rhetorical appearance of the modern, but the strong performative aspects involved – especially Blair's own self-consciousness about his performance of matey masculinity – make them unconvincing. This may be because post-modern culture itself can make little space for grand claims or big ideas, so that the sense that such speeches are a pastiche of a political mode now largely residualised becomes inevitable. Similarly, the nostalgic references to Labour's own traditions seem to situate them in quotation marks.

Jameson (1984: 53-92) goes on to argue that these nostalgic texts render a historical period, or more generally a concept of 'pastness', through a process of stylistic connotation, in which meanings are invoked through cultural references, but the specificities of historical change, especially struggles over power, are removed. In postmodern culture the 1960s are recast as 'the sixties' – a condensed, barely periodised moment in which mods and rockers, Carnaby Street posers, hippy counter-culturalists and mini-skirted dollybirds are part of the general maelstrom, and the Vietnam War becomes a groovy epiphany. For Jameson (1985: 120), such texts are 'schizophrenic', occupying the present and the past simultaneously and with a heightened intensity. They offer a condensed and largely empty history, dominated by popular and pop culture, in which the ambience of 'pastness' is produced by a flattening out of temporality and a knowing stylisation of its artefacts and commodities, as though history were simply a story of 'things'. The television series *I Love the Seventies* (BBC TV) is an interesting instance of this trend, exemplifying a genre that is both excessively knowing and hardly knowledgeable enough.

This tendency to flatten out the past or to see it in terms of changes in consumption practices is most visible in media culture. But the extent to which the New Labour project depended upon style, spectacle and a gestural attachment to Labour's own history came through to me most forcibly at a particular moment during the General Election campaign in the summer of 2001. Activist members of my local branch and constituency, already somewhat depleted in enthusiasm by the loss of faith engendered by the Blair administration's conservatism, reluctantly but with a sense of fateful obligation duly began to organise the nightly canvassing and the weekly street stalls that mark an election. As part of the election materials from national office, our local constituency received something extra to be used on the street stalls and on polling day: a set of ready-made card placards mounted on short poles, uncannily resembling those traditionally carried on marches or at demonstrations, yet this time emanating from party headquarters and bearing a Labour-endorsing slogan: 'Be Part of It: Vote Labour, June 7'. The placards were somewhat self-consciously waved at a couple of street stalls organised by my own branch and constituency, and I have a set of photographs of friends and members holding them aloft, but the experience of receiving and using them seemed to be a further symptom of New Labour's effective emptying out of the politics from the political. In a bizarre simulacrum of a tradition of protest, the boards successfully managed to be both a pastiche of 'Old Labour' and an effective incorporation of its traditions. By carrying Millbank-approved placards which bore messages only the most die-hard anti-democrat might object to, the weary foot soldiers of New Labour could, with a brave heart and a clear conscience, occupy both 'old' and 'new' ground simultaneously. They invoked a kind of 'Labour pastness' that was mysteriously redolent of public protest, of organised labour, and even of 'the masses' themselves in their Jarrow Marchers romanticised form. Yet they did this without once offering a proposition that could be interpreted as genuinely radical or resistant – unless we assume that voting is now sufficiently unusual for it to constitute a challenge to the status quo. As Jameson observes, the sensation was one of occupying the present and the past simultaneously – a whole tradition condensed into a single object – yet the politics of protest and of Labour's own militant history was erased in that very moment.

PERFORMING THE POLITICAL

During the 1990s the annual Labour Party conference was slowly transformed from a forum of political exchange and decision-making into something else: an increasingly spectacular 'performance of the political', in which the appearance of measured debate replaced the admittedly dismal spectacle of the union block vote and the heated exchanges between the floor and the platform that had marked the

1970s and 1980s. This remodelling of the Labour Party conference seemed at first to mark a genuine commitment to democratisation, as I have already noted. Its status as an annual spectacle of power rather than a forum for policy-making was, however, confirmed by the 2001 conference. Coming so rapidly after the securing of the mythologised 'second term' in June of that year, the conference might have been expected to at least gesture towards the implementation of the radicalism and innovation that had been repeatedly promised and rarely delivered by the Blair government's first period in office. However, notwithstanding the high drama of Tony Blair's 'post-11 September' address, much of the conference was marked by an emphasis on stage-managed speeches, underlined by a highly mediated style of presentation, including digital video screenings, 'mood music' as conference delegates filed into the main hall, and intermittent 'feelgood moments' during which party workers were rewarded for their faith with suitable baubles. All of this seemed in important ways to be part of an appropriation of the *style* of the party without the political substance. It looked like the Labour Party, and there were plenty of symbols of the Labour Party, but the substance of politics – ideas, debates, plans – was largely absent except at the level of rhetoric.

For example, on the morning of 10 October I watched a television transmission of a public discussion carefully staged in the style of the BBC topical debate programme, *Question Time*. It was chaired by Tom Sawyer, the ex-General Secretary of the party, and featured three impeccably Blairite government ministers, Stephen Byers, Alan Milburn and Estelle Morris, who were shown responding to a series of questions from the conference floor. The four main participants were seated on stage in leather bucket chairs rather than behind a table, and the style of the proceedings was relaxed and informal, signified by the flourishing of shirtsleeves and the unbuttoning of jackets. This, the semiotics of style suggested, was to be a friendly, civilised discussion between fellow party members. The exchange between the floor and the ministers that followed was illuminating, but not because it was marked by radical policy declarations or by lively and engaged debate. Indeed, the register of the 'discussion' – the rehearsal of well-worn phrases, the avoidance of explicit policy promises and the reduction of political argument to 'on message' platitudes – made it clear that it was primarily addressed to another audience, one located outside the conference hall: the imagined television audience of uncommitted voters whose support evidently had to be secured. It was the emphasis on the *appearance* of debate, rather than on debate itself, that was important.

Two further things were striking about this elaborate charade. The first was its clear articulation of contemporary forms of hierarchy: the government ministers were informal in manner yet seated 'above' the conference floor, comfortable with and sure of their authority. The second was the way in which it staged more effectively than anything before or since the transformation of 'the conference' – that is, the delegates – from equal participants in a political decision-making process into an audience for a political spectacle. The performative aspects of the conference signified its shift from a genuine forum of debate to a spectacle of political exchange. Once again, I was struck by the extent to which New Labour has become a 'virtual' party, full of members whose status is closer to that of a ready-made audience or a customer-base for specific products than to a truly 'modern' mass movement with the political power to change anything. I remain wondering whether New Labour's official discourse of 'modernity' is little more than a postmodern simulacrum.

CONCLUSION

By winning two successive general elections, by effectively marginalising the Conservative opposition, and by developing a political discourse that remains powerfully hegemonic, New Labour has successfully established itself as the major political force in the Britain of the twenty-first century. As I have argued, it was Labour's specific characteristics – its traditionalism and commitment to pragmatism, and its refusal of ideology – that facilitated this triumph, through the deployment of instrumental rationalism in policy and the remaking of the party in a hollowed-out form. However, this process also needs to be situated within wider changes in political culture, both in Britain and globally. There has been a real shift in the *idea* of the political party, not, despite the rhetoric of modernisation, towards a 'modern' model, but rather to a postmodern one, in which membership is about consumerism, power structures are diffused, and political commitment is contingent. Indeed, the rhetorical excess of the modernising project, its 'noisiness' about modernity, is precisely what points to a postmodern reading – it is concerned largely with the modern as style and as image. And while there is something profoundly disturbing about the way in which Labour's tradition of principled (if frequently puritanical) dislike of consumer culture seems to have been replaced by an uncritical embrace of markets, it is difficult to see how else the party could have remade itself within the context of postmodern flux.

All this suggests more than a crisis for the Labour Party, however; it suggests a significant transformation in the practice of politics that New Labour's current hegemony disguises. The general election victory of 2001, for example, was secured with the smallest voter turnout – 59 per cent – since 1918. New Labour is a symptom of the ways in which political interests and concerns have re-focused, both at local and global levels, so that conventional 'left' and 'right' political parties are no longer always identified as the primary means to effect social change, and are uncertainly (frequently antagonistically) related to emergent social groupings, such as the anti-capitalism movement that appeared in the late 1990s. The large-scale international economic and social shifts that produced such resistant groups also suggest that the confinement of electoral politics within a strictly national context is increasingly difficult. New Labour began as a Labour Representation Committee in 1900, an organisation that articulated the interests and ambitions of a very specific historical social formation – the British working class. There is no reason to believe that it is the only appropriate vehicle for other kinds of formations – with other interests and ambitions.

However, despite this, and notwithstanding my concerns and reservations about my own membership of the Labour Party, about the centralisation of power and the disappearance of accountability, and about the persistence of masculinism as a dominant feature of New Labour, I am left with a dilemma. I remain committed to a reformed version of left politics and to those of the electoral variety, until something that can deliver democratic accountability genuinely appears to replace it. I also want to be able to engage practically in political activity, not to confine myself to academic commentary or express my politics wholly within intellectualised terms. While I remain within the party I can at least feel that I am doing something – however alleviatory, however small-scale – to make a material difference. Perhaps that is an appropriately diminished ambition in these postmodern times.

BIBLIOGRAPHY

Robin Blackburn (1997), 'Reflections on Blair's Velvet Revolution', *New Left Review*, 223, May/June: 3-16.

Jean Baudrillard (1983), *Simulations*, New York: Semiotext(e).

Michel Foucault (1977), *Discipline and Punish: the Birth of the Prison*, London: Penguin.

Jane Franklin (2000), 'What's Wrong With New Labour Politics?', *Feminist Review*, 66, Autumn 2000:138-142.

Antonio Gramsci (1971), *Selections From Prison Notebooks* (edited by Quintin Hoare and Geoffrey Nowell-Smith), London: Lawrence and Wishart.

Andrew Gray and Bill Jenkins (1999), 'British Government and Administration 1997-98: Modernisation and Democratisation?', in *Parliamentary Affairs*, 52 (2): 136-166.

W.H. Greenleaf (1983), *The British Political Tradition. Vol. Two, The Ideological Inheritance*, London: Routledge.

Fredric Jameson (1984), 'Postmodernism, or the cultural logic of late capitalism', *New Left Review*, 146, July/August.

Fredric Jameson (1985), 'Postmodernism and Consumer Society', in Hal Foster (ed) *Postmodern Culture*, London: Pluto: 112-120.

Andrew Rawnsley, (2001), *Servants of the People: The Inside Story of New Labour*, London: Penguin.

Eric Shaw (1996), *The Labour Party since 1945*, Oxford and Malden, Massachusetts: Blackwell.

9. Summer of discontent: New Labour and the fuel crisis

Lisa Smyth

INTRODUCTION

In September 2000 daily life in Britain was severely disrupted when oil refineries across the country were blockaded by road hauliers and farmers protesting at the increasing price of fuel. This apparently spontaneous and uncoordinated action, taken in the name of 'the People's Fuel Lobby', was directed at the Blair administration's high rate of tax on petrol, approximately 72 per cent of the purchase price (*Guardian Unlimited*, 14.11.00). The 'people's party' appeared to be under attack from 'the people' themselves.

This chapter is concerned with New Labour's response to the fuel crisis in particular, as an illustration of the dependency of Blairism on what can be described as a politics of 'passive revolution' (Gramsci 1971:106-114). The party's time in power has been marked by crisis management, from the death of Princess Diana during its first months in office, to the rail disasters, widespread flooding, the spread of foot and mouth disease, anti-globalisation protests, and, most recently, the 'war on terrorism'. The action of the 'People's Fuel Lobby' represented the first major 'popular' criticism of New Labour's political legitimacy since it took power in 1997, and the party's successful management of this crisis depended on making explicit the main currents of its cultural politics. New Labour's response to the People's Fuel Lobby, who appeared to have successfully appropriated the distinctively Blairite category of 'the people',[1] illustrates the ways in which the party's hegemony depends on 'the people's' political passivity. In order to maintain its hegemonic position as the political expression of 'the people's' will, New Labour was dependent on preventing the development of alternative 'popular' forms of politics.

Specifically of interest in what follows is the way in which the initial clash between New Labour's 'spin' on the crisis and the popular news media account of what was going on was resolved. How did the party respond to the apparent revolt from the very people it claimed to represent? How did the national news media construct the crisis, and the relationship between the party and 'the people'?

THE CRISIS

The actions of the People's Fuel Lobby, blockading oil refineries across Britain in order to prevent the distribution of petrol supplies, took the Blair government by surprise. Although France had experienced popular protests against the escalating cost of fuel in the summer of 2000, similar action seemed unlikely in Britain. Indeed, an attempt to urge motorists to 'dump the pumps' during August 2000 in protest at the rapidly increasing price of petrol failed to stimulate public action (Glover 2000). However, as the price of crude oil reached US$35 per barrel in September 2000, pushing petrol prices in the UK up to new levels, a group of hauliers and farmers blockaded an oil refinery in Stanlow, Cheshire, on 7 September. Within three days the protest blockades had spread across Britain, and motorists began stockpiling petrol supplies. Tanker drivers refused to leave refineries, claiming that they had been intimidated by protesters. Long queues appeared at petrol stations as supplies began to run out.

The protests lasted for one week, and were called off on condition that the government act to reduce fuel duty within 60 days. However, by the time this deadline had expired, the protests had lost the public support they appeared to have enjoyed in September, for a number of practical reasons. Public attention had shifted towards coping with the chaos caused by severe flooding and with serious long-term disruption on the railways following a fatal train crash at Hatfield (Clark et al 2000). In addition, Chancellor Gordon Brown announced his plan to cut tax on low-sulphur fuel, and introduce a 'Brit-Disc' system aimed at charging truckers from abroad for using British roads. He also declared an increase to the basic state pension, something which, he claimed, could not be funded if fuel tax were to be cut. Thus, he placed the interests of the fuel lobby in conflict with the interests of impoverished pensioners, as a zero-sum option. Finally, the fuel protesters' plans to organise a slow-moving convoy of vehicles to drive from Jarrow to London in November, in an effort to draw comparisons with the Jarrow hunger march of 1936, was reported in unsympathetic terms. The convoy was strictly controlled by the police, and remained insignificant in size and public impact.

THE 'PEOPLE'S REVOLT'?

As Hall (1980) has argued, the media encode 'news' events with 'preferred readings' through which meaningful discourses are constructed and reproduced. The news media's survival depends on its ability to articulate a national 'we' with whom a national audience can identify (Anderson 1983: 40; Billig 1995: 115). News media are key sites where political consensus and discourses of nationhood combine, not least in times of crisis, when the relationship between a national 'we', a political perspective, and a national 'news' audience becomes destabilised (Hartley 1982; Mattelart 1986).

This media preference for national consensus in times of political crisis was evident in coverage of the fuel protests. The crisis was constructed initially as a popular revolt against the government, which suggested that 'New' Labour's newness was questionable. Was this simply a re-run of the 'Winter of Discontent' of 1978/79 which ended Labour's last term in power, when widespread strike action caused massive disruption to daily life in Britain? Was the 'New' Labour party now capable of managing the economy successfully, engaging with 'the people', and maintaining law and order?

The headline on the front page of the *Sun* newspaper at the height of the fuel protests read 'Great Petrol Revolt 2000' (12.9.00). In the background were scenes of motorists queuing for petrol across Britain as supplies ran out. As the paper explained, 'Although all of Britain could be out of fuel TONIGHT [sic], most drivers at the pumps were backing the protest.' It seemed that 'all of Britain' was united in its revolt against the 'people's party'. The fuel revolts were constructed, particularly by those popular news media that supported the actions, as a popular protest against a government that was acting against the people's economic interests.[2] Even the Labour-identified daily newspaper the *Mirror* urged the government to drop the price of fuel in the face of the apparently widespread public anger, despite its opposition to the blockades (Editorial, 'Time to give motorists a break, Tony' 12.9.00).

NEW LABOUR AND THE PEOPLE'S ECONOMY

> 'Well, at the moment I'm running ten trucks and we're gradually losing work, month by month, to continental hauliers that can just come over to our country with tanks full, disappear back to Germany, Belgium and Holland. They've worn our roads out and not contributed a penny to this country's tax, and we're trying to compete with that' (Fuel Tax Protester, interviewed on *Channel Four News*, 12.8.00).

The capacity of New Labour to manage the British economy in the interests of 'the people' was specifically in question through the actions of the fuel protesters, as the above statement indicates. Reports relied explicitly on a nationalist construction of protesters and their supporters as a British 'we', who were not going to let 'them', i.e. the French and other Europeans, get away with paying lower prices for fuel. This national 'we' evoked memories of the Blitz spirit of co-operation, and was a way of minimising public discontent at the disruption the blockades were causing. Indeed, one petrol station owner, who doubled the price he charged for petrol, was attacked in the press and on television news, presumably for his attempts to make a personal profit out of a national crisis, although this was not made explicit.[3]

The attack launched by the People's Fuel Lobby on New Labour's ability to run the economy in the interests of 'the people' was significant. Labour had lost the 1992 election precisely because of a popular perception, particularly evident in the tabloid press of the time, that the party would be incapable of running a successful economy. Labour was, in the well-known conservative phrase, the 'tax and spend' party, and could not be trusted to keep 'UK plc' afloat (Philo 1994: 62-5). 'New' Labour's claim to be the party of 'the people', a national-popular, non-ideological party which would support both industry and labour, the City and the public sector (Gartside 1998: 61), was explicitly under attack in this 'people's revolt'. According to news reports, 'New' Labour appeared, like 'old' Labour, to be incapable of managing the economy in the interests of 'all' the people.

NEW LABOUR AND THE POLITICS OF INCLUSION

The Labour Party under Blair has articulated a distinctly populist politics, which Ryan (1999) describes as reliant on the management of a public sense of loss, achieved through a concern to re-engage the public voice in the wake of Conservative elitism. However, this Blairite discourse of popular inclusion came directly under attack through the fuel crisis. Newspapers and news broadcasts sent messages from 'the ordinary people' of Britain to the Prime Minister, who was accused of not listening, and of being out of touch with 'the people'.[4] The prime minister's apparent easy access to petrol placed him in an entirely different category from others who were reliant on their cars, something which the *Sun* newspaper reinforced in its ongoing depiction of transport minister and deputy prime minister John Prescott as 'Two Jags Prescott' throughout the crisis (e.g. '2 Jags, One Hell of a Shambles on TV', *Sun,* 14.9.00). Again, the Labour-identified *Mirror* condemned Blair's attempts to 'snub' the fuel campaign, pointing out that the blockades didn't affect his access to his Jaguar ('I'm All Right Jag' 12.9.00).

Thus, Blair and New Labour were constructed in the popular news media as presiding over a people they not only refused to listen to, but also actively appeared to be profiting from. As the *Mail on Sunday* insisted, 'the fundamental point of the protest is a rejection of this Government's policy of creaming off ever greater tax revenue while blaming the world markets' (Leader, 10.9.00). Was this the sort of action to be expected from an 'inclusive' 'New' party, particularly a party that constructs its 'inclusive' project in explicitly economic terms (Levitas 1998)?

NEW LABOUR AND PUBLIC ORDER

Lengthy queues are forming on the forecourts in scenes which we have not seen in this country in the 20 years since the overweening power of the trade unions was broken. Britain has changed beyond recognition in that time. We no longer tolerate in this country unions that hold us to ransom. Unlike France, where the government has caved in over the same issue of fuel prices, we in this country no longer elect governments that appease blackmailers. This was a battle hard won and there is no appetite, even among activists, for a return to industrial anarchy (Leader, *Mail on Sunday*, 10.9.00).

As Fowler (1991) argues, editorials play a particularly significant role in constructing or evoking a national consensus, particularly in the face of confusion or crisis. This is achieved not least by relying on categories of 'us' (namely the newspaper and its audience) and 'them', against whom 'we' define ourselves (1991: 210).

The explicitly national point of view articulated by the *Mail on Sunday* editorial, quoted above, positioned 'us' both against France, and against the 'old' Labour politics of the pre-Thatcher era. The editorial concluded by warning that unless he cut fuel taxes, Gordon Brown would face his own 'Winter of Discontent'. While insisting all but a few of the protesters were not militants or extremists, the newspaper constructed an anti-strike, anti-protest national consensus which high fuel tax was placing under severe pressure. These protests were constructed as being unlike those presided over by 'old' Labour during the Winter of Discontent, since these were spontaneous protests by non-militant, 'ordinary', farmers, hauliers, and motorists. High fuel tax provoked the ordinary British voter to adopt a form of action normally associated with militant anarchists, and New Labour had consequently placed public order at risk. This law-and-order failure on the part of New Labour was not superficial, but raised questions concerning where the party stood in relation to 'us'. Was Blairism simply 'old' Labour in disguise, creating a culture of 'lightning pickets', blackmail and industrial anarchy, because of its distance from 'the people'?

The news media suggested that 'the people' were staging their own revolution, bringing the country to a halt in order to demand that New Labour live up to its claim to be the 'people's party'. How did New Labour contain this apparent threat of rebellion?

DISARMING 'THE PEOPLE'
The threat posed to New Labour's populist hegemony during 'the people's revolt' was successfully reversed, not only as a result of the impact of unforeseen events such as the widespread damage caused by flooding and travel chaos, but through a strategy of passive revolution, aimed at reasserting the party's position as the only legitimate expression of 'the people's' political will. This was achieved by officially constructing fuel protesters themselves not as representatives of 'the people', but instead as a threat to the nation's economy, to its democratic institutions, and to public order. The ultimate success of this

strategy was such that, by November 2000, when the protester's 60-day deadline had expired, the media had adopted New Labour's construction of what was at stake. Blair insisted in his daily press conferences that New Labour was indeed 'new', and would manage the protests in a way which would protect 'the people's' economic, political and community interests.

THE PEOPLE'S ECONOMY

there is one very simple difference with the greatest of respect between now and the 1970s: we have one of the strongest economies, perhaps the strongest economy at the moment in Europe. We've unemployment at historic lows, we've our long-term interest rates, for the first time [...] in my adult life, below that of Germany, we've an immensely strong economic position. There are problems with particular groups, but this is a protest that is being caused by a small number of people at oil refineries. It's not an industrial dispute, it's nothing to do with industrial relations who want to force a change of policy on the government (Prime Minister's Press Conference on Fuel, 13.9.00).

During his daily press conferences, Blair attempted to reassert the identification between New Labour and 'the people' by insisting on the difference between the events of September 2000 and those faced by the previous Labour government in the late 1970s. As the above quote demonstrates, Blair was at pains to point out that 'New' Labour was presiding over a strong and successful economy, whereas 'old' Labour's regime was associated with economic crisis and mismanagement. He insisted that a successful economy depended on strict regulation. Thus, he argued that to devise economic policy in a context of crisis, particularly where pressure groups appeared to be attempting to extract concessions which were not necessarily in the interests of 'the nation', would be a mark of bad government.

Blair reasserted the central position of economic management to his government, insisting that the 'national' economic interest took priority over any particular interest or lobby. As he argued:

To put all that [economic success] at risk by emergency budgets in response either to blockades or temporary fluctuations in the world oil price would be a gross betrayal of this country's true national interest and I will not do it. I do not in any way minimise the plight of some of the hauliers and farmers who are genuinely suffering, but the way to help them is not to harm the rest of the country (Prime Minister's Press Conference on Fuel, 12.9.00).

The government's *refusal* to respond to the demands of the protesters was precisely what, in these terms, made it the government and the party of 'the people'. Blair could therefore characterise the possibility of making tax concessions to the fuel protesters as an act of gross national betrayal.

'GOVERNING IN THE ROUND': NEW LABOUR'S POLITICS OF INCLUSION

> We are still listening. But there is a process to decide a Budget [sic]. We receive representations. There is a pre-Budget report in November and then there is the actual Budget in March. That is the proper way to listen and if necessary to respond to what we know are genuine problems (Prime Minister's Press Conference on Fuel, 13.10.00).

Blair denied the popular news media's construction of the protests as indicative of New Labour's refusal to listen to 'the people'. Clearly, the investment of Blairism in a discourse of inclusivity, which marked itself out as a 'third way', distinct from previous Conservative government elitism and 'old' Labour socialism, was at stake. Blair's response was simply to announce that he and his party were indeed listening to 'the people', but that they had to, as he described it, 'govern in the round'. In other words, a truly inclusive government should not act in response to particular pressures, but should consider the broad effects of political actions, while observing established democratic procedures for decision-making, in this instance the annual budget process.

It is at this point that New Labour's populism is most fragile, since clearly 'the people' are divided, and make conflicting demands on government, something that Blair himself recognised:

> Some of those people, out as farmers, asking for a cut in duty are the same types of people I saw a short time ago asking for an increase in government subsidy to the farming industry. Some of those hauliers who want us to cut duty also want us to increase spending on public transport. Now, in the end, you've got to balance these things as a government, and recognize you have to govern in the round, and that means occasionally saying things to people that they don't want to hear as well as things that they do (Prime Minister's Press Conference on Fuel, 14.9.00).

The idea of 'governing in the round' suggests that New Labour could simply take account of local conflicts between 'the people' in ways, which would ultimately reunite them. Thus, the party would not only represent 'the people' in all their different locations, but could actually reconstruct 'the people' as a coherent nation in situations of conflict, through the decisions that it made.[5] Again, this insistence that New Labour were listening to 'the people' relied on constructing protesters as a threat to national unity, a threat which 'the people' could depend on Blair's government to assuage. It seems that there is little room for democratic deliberation or persuasion in New Labour's populism. The need to insist that the party is in tune with 'the people' depends instead on a politics of 'decisionism' that obscures substantial disagreements in the interest of popular unity (Habermas 1996: 295-6).

RESISTING INTIMIDATION AND TERROR: NEW LABOUR AND PUBLIC ORDER

> Whatever the strength of feeling, there can be no excuse whatever for this type of action which is hurting our people, businesses and emergency services severely. Legitimate protest is one thing. Trying to bring the country to a halt is quite another, and there can be absolutely no justification for it (Prime Minister's Press Conference on Fuel, 12.9.00).

Blair located the activities of the fuel protesters on the terrain not of politics but of law and order. As the above widely reported quote demonstrates, he both isolated the protesters from 'our people', and constructed them explicitly as a threat to social order.[6]

This law-and-order response was characteristic of New Labour's discourse of community, security and consensus, through which, as Levitas notes, Blairism defines the arena of political inclusion (1998: 125). Blair constructed the protests not only as illegal, but also as a threat to democracy. What he termed the 'violence and intimidation' practised by the protesters was contrasted with a distinctly British form of democratic culture. As he argued, 'no-one can seriously think that it would be right for a British Government to allow policy to be decided by direct action of this kind' (Prime Minister's Press Conference on Fuel, 13.9.00).

Again, this uncompromising construction of the protesters marked what was 'new' about New Labour, a party that would not preside, as the last Labour government had done, over another Winter of Discontent. Britain was not, Blair indicated, entering a period of extended national crisis, when public health itself would suffer as a result of the government's inability to manage, or prioritise, competing interests successfully. The health service had indeed been placed on 'red alert' in response to the fuel crisis, and Blair insisted that blockades were placing lives at risk. He signalled his government's intention to use the police and the army, as well as the oil companies themselves, to ensure that fuel supply would return to normal. While this again raised the spectre of the Winter of Discontent, when the police and striking workers were involved in clashes, Blair's law-and-order discourse, combined with his discourse of democratic inclusivity, constructed the possibility of clashes between the state and the protesters as a necessary risk, in 'the people's' interests.

A key aspect to this 'law and order' response relied, ironically, on a contrast between illegal 'direct action' and legal industrial action. Unlike 1978/79, when the Labour Party's link with the unions was seen as the source of the government's inability to run the country, in September 2000 New Labour relied on the fact that the blockades were not legally organised through established industrial action procedures to label them as an illegitimate attempt to influence policy. Indeed, the government suggested that the success of the blockades relied largely on the protesters' ability to intimidate unionised drivers. New Labour's discourse of democratic 'inclusivity' could accommodate trade union representation, albeit within a framework of community and consensus. It would not, as Levitas points out, engage in overtly adversarial debate, an 'old' style of politics which 'New' Labour had cast aside.[7]

CONCLUSION

What is remarkable about this episode in New Labour's story is the extent to which the issue of fuel tax disappeared from the political agenda. By the time the sixty days had expired in November, the news media constructed the protesters not as representatives of 'the people', but as a self-interested lobby group. New Labour had apparently succeeded in pacifying 'the people's revolt', and re-establishing its own hegemony as the representatives of 'the people'. As journalist Bill Neely commented, in his report on the protesters' slow convoy which set out for London on 10 November 2000: 'They passed through Tony Blair's constituency. The numbers dwindled. It's now clear to him, and to them, this is no mass protest' (*ITV Evening News* 10.11.00).

New Labour populism, reliant as it is on a political strategy of passive revolution, produced two outcomes. Firstly, because its hegemony depends on refusing to recognise the legitimacy of any form of 'popular' political agency, it responds to direct action in terms of law and order, rather than politics. In the case of the fuel crisis, the party failed to engage seriously in any political debate over high fuel taxes, for example by defending the high rate of fuel tax for environmental reasons. Instead, during the height of the crisis, Blair insisted that protest politics was anti-democratic, and consequently should not be engaged with seriously by the government.

The second, related, effect of New Labour's 'passive revolutionary' politics is that, because 'popular' political mobilisation must necessarily be directed by 'the people's party', Blairism is unable to build alliances with potentially popular social movements, for example, in this instance with environmentalism.

The fuel crisis illustrates the ways in which the New Labour project relies on and re-produces a consensual and passive form of British political culture, also noted by Kelleher in this volume. The party is consequently unable to respond to publicly expressed dissent on a range of issues in democratic political terms. For example, the May Day Demonstration in London in 2001 was very heavily policed, despite the fact that there was no illegal activity and no evident threat of violence. Indeed, more than 1,000 protesters were imprisoned within police cordons for six hours.[8] Furthermore, Blair's uncompromising response to the street protests against the visit of US president George W. Bush to Gothenburg in June 2001, when he characterised protesters as an 'anarchist travelling circus' whose leaders should be prevented from travelling for political reasons, illustrates his efforts to define all public protest, whether of left or right, as at the least illegal, and, at the extreme, a form of terrorism (*Guardian* 18.6.01). Similarly, he refused to criticise the policing of the anti-globalisation protests in Genoa in July 2001, when one protester was killed and a number of British citizens, among others, were seized and assaulted by the Italian police.[9] The fuel crisis indicates the ways in which New Labour's claim to be a distinctly new, revolutionary, party of 'the people' depends on a form of populism which refuses to recognise the political force behind competing expressions of 'the people's' will. Such expressions are treated as problems of law and order, as well as opportunities for New Labour to demonstrate its 'new' inclusive cultural and political programme.

I am grateful to Deborah Lynn Steinberg and Richard Johnson for their help in writing this chapter. I would also like to thank to Cillian McBride and Louise Ryan for helpful comments and discussion, and to the staff at the British Film Institute, for their assistance.

NOTES

1. This is illustrated for instance in Blair's designation of Diana as 'the people's Princess' following her death in 1997 (Kear and Steinberg 1999).
2. *Five News*, for example, characterised the mid-week situation as one where the government was refusing to back down, and the people in no mood to surrender (12.9.00). This construction was not, however, universal in the media coverage. See, for instance, *Channel Four News*'s coverage of the events on the same day as the above, where the presenter, Jon Snow, asked 'Is this the 21st century people's revolt? We discuss whether this is the new direct action or just plain old self-interest' (12.9.00). The evidence subsequently presented by the programme, including interviews with motorists queuing for petrol they did not particularly need, suggested the latter explanation.
3. For instance, he was labelled 'the meanest man in Britain' by *Five News* (12.9.00).
4. See, for instance, the editorial published by the *Sun* newspaper on 13 September: 'The Prime Minister is in a mess for one reason: He has not been listening. He and Gordon Brown were WARNED [sic] time after time about the people's anger about fuel prices'. Only *Channel Four News* (12.9.00) explicitly challenged this construction, by pointing out that

motorists had ignored the call to 'Dump the Pumps' during the summer of 2000. This news programme also characterised motorists who supported the fuel protests as typical Conservative voters, by interviewing, 'Basildon man and woman', and subsequently running an interview with Conservative leader William Hague, thereby underlining the convergence of views between all three interviewees.

5. Ruth Levitas (1998) demonstrates the centrality of this Durkheimian emphasis on social cohesion and integration to New Labour's politics.

6. As he argued: 'whatever the protesters feelings, and I repeat I understand the real difficulties people have over the high price of petrol, it cannot be right to try to force a change in policy by these means. No Government, indeed no country, could retain credibility in its democratic process or its economic policy-making, were it to give in to such a campaign.' (Prime Minister's Press Conference on Fuel, 13.9.00)/

7. This point is well illustrated by Blair's speech to the 1996 Labour Party Conference: 'Forget the past. No more bosses versus workers. You are on the same side. The same team. Britain united' (quoted in Levitas 1998: 114).

8. Vikram Dodd 'Blair praises Met for control of protesters' *Guardian Unlimited* 3 May 2001.

9. As he was reported as saying: 'to criticise the Italian police and the Italian authorities for working to make sure the security of the summit is right is, to me, to turn the world upside down' (*Observer* 22.7.01).

REFERENCES

Anderson, Benedict (1983), *Imagined Communities: Reflections on the Origin and Spread of Nationalism*, London: Verso.

Billig, Michael (1995), *Banal Nationalism*, London: Sage.

Clark, Andrew, Keith Perry and Sarah Hall (2000), 'A broken rail – new safety alert at 100 sites on the network', *Guardian*, 19 October.

Dougan, David (1968), *The History of North East Shipbuilding*, London: George Allen and Unwin Ltd.

Fowler, Roger (1991), *Language in the News: Discourse and Ideology in the Press*, London: Routledge.

Gartside, P. (1998), 'Bypassing politics? A critical look at DIY culture', in Rutherford, Jonathan (ed.) *Young Britain: Politics, pleasures and predicaments* London: Lawrence & Wishart: 58-73.

Gramsci, Antonio (1971), *Selections from the Prison Notebooks of Antonio Gramsci*. Edited and translated by Quintin Hoare and Geoffrey Nowell Smith, London: Lawrence and Wishart.

Habermas, Jürgen (1996), *Between facts and Norms: Contributions to a discourse theory of law and democracy*, translated by William Rehg, Cambridge, Mass: MIT Press.

Hall, Stuart (1980), 'Encoding/decoding' in Hall, Stuart, Hobson, Dorothy, Lowe Andrew and Willis, Paul (eds) *Culture, Media, Language: Working Papers in Cultural Studies, 1972-1979* London: Unwin Hyman: 128-138.

Hyman Hartley, John (1982), *Understanding News*, London: Routledge.

Kear, Adrian and Steinberg, Deborah Lynn (eds.) (1999), *Mourning Diana: Nation, Culture and the Performance of Grief*, London: Routledge.

Levitas, Ruth (1998), *The Inclusive Society? Social Exclusion and New Labour*, London: Macmillan.

Mattelart, Michele (1986), *Women, Media and Crisis: Femininity and Disorder*, London: Comedia Publishing Group.

Philo, Greg (1994), 'Politics, Media and Public Belief', in Perryman, Mark (ed.) *Altered States: Postmodernism, Politics, Culture*, London: Lawrence & Wishart, 46-72.

Ryan, Mick (1999), 'Penal Policy Making Towards the Millennium: Elites and Populists; New Labour and the New Criminology', *International Journal of the Sociology of Law* 27:1-22.

10. 'Our radius of trust': community, war and the scene of rhetoric

Joe Kelleher

John Humphrys You've been in power for six months and a bit now, and you've had a quite extraordinary period in office, I mean, you have been the most popular Prime Minister since *ever*. Now people are saying the issue surrounding you is one of trust. Do you believe that as a result of what has happened in this past week or so that you have lost the trust of the British people?

Tony Blair No I don't believe that ... er ... and I hope that ... people ... know me well enough, and realise that I've, person I am, to realise that, that I would never do anything either to harm the country or anything improper, I never have. I think most people who have *de*alt with me think I'm a pretty straight sort of guy and I *am*. And I think that ... what I would say to you about that, and I, I do find that, erm, these, these things difficult, and er upsetting ... is ... I think there's been a desire ... *[pause]* ... to say right from the word go. This can't be as good as it looks. You know. They're all the same. The Tories were sleazy, Labour's no different. I don't believe we're like that, at all.

The exchange is from the opening of Tony Blair's television appearance in late 1997, at the climax of a week of mounting criticism of the government over what was known at the time as the 'Bernie Ecclestone affair.'[1] In these opening moments, Blair performs the 'straight sort of gu' he claims to be: blushing (or at least rouged up), stuttering towards sincerity, his focus internalised as he struggles with self-examination, but becoming open-eyed to meet the gaze of his interrogator as the words themselves open out into hard-won assurance. The prime minister owns up to a badly handled business, 'And I apologise for that.'[2] Meanwhile the performance makes its claim upon us, weaving our uncertainty into the very texture of its rhetoric. It says, trust me; and, in trusting me, trust my party. But most importantly, trust me when the chips are down not to try and persuade you with the convincingness of a mere *performance*. Because the ethos of the party, nay the ethos of the government – and, indeed, this is an issue of ethics, of right and wrong, or at least proper and 'improper' behaviour – is wrapped up in the 'straightness' of the 'guy' you see right here. That is the gambit: to douse the sting of political contestation in the supposedly consensual balm of ethical common sense – because we all know deep down what doing bad and doing good is, don't we, and how much the difference really matters? ... or how much it might appear to matter, ground up in the rhetorical machinery and spat out into the theatre of public life.

Because we also all know that 'theatre' is not real life. Nobody is being taken in here. Although, of course, as auditors of the performance maybe we do buy it – just a bit. Just enough. Maybe we do feel *persuaded*. Although again, if we are 'taken in' we might ask ourselves: taken in where precisely? And taken in as what?

This chapter seeks to examine the complex of theatricalisms embedded in New Labour's political rhetoric. I am interested in how this government's bid for trust so often takes the form of a moralistic discourse projected as an imaginary dramaturgy. My conviction is that political rhetoric is neither trivial nor superficial, but functions as a key means of including and excluding people from the arena of what is offered as 'politics'. What this rhetoric stages, particularly in speeches given by Tony Blair, is a dramaturgy that summons 'us' into its scene, to inhabit roles already hollowed out for us; to work through conflicts already marked up as a moral agon, in terms of friends and enemies, good and evil and so on; and to reap the rewards of a destiny that already has 'our' name on it. This chapter will follow this dramaturgy by focusing on some of the key terms deployed in this rhetorical summoning. Those terms are 'trust', 'people', 'globalisation', 'contract', and 'community'. I shall argue, though, that this summoning, even as it gathers us, in its aspiration to an 'ethical' politics predicated on 'shared values', also threatens to undermine the trust it seeks to produce. It may be – as I shall argue – that some of the figures gathering at the edge of the stage, while they remain crucial to the plot, are not those to whom the spectacle is addressed. This is particularly the case when the arena of action extends beyond the immediate, as in the theatre of war.

THE BID FOR TRUST

If New Labour is 'about' anything, surely it has to be about trust. At least that has been so at the level of the party rhetoric – wherein 'trust' is the refracting medium through which rhetorical pledges would appear transformed, in time, into policy and real-world changes. From the distribution of watch-this-space pre-term Pledge Cards, to devolutionary policies, and the various promotions of the party leader – as informal normal-bloke glottal-stopper on the one hand, and clued up *über*manager on the other – trust has been the currency of exchange between New Labour and those under the sway of its governance.

But trust is a currency of uncertain value. It is a commonplace of the criticism directed against the current Labour Party that the bid for trust is all there is, that what is offered up is all appearance without intrinsic value, 'all spin and no substance', as the tired saying goes. At the level of this everyday anti-rhetorical prejudice, trust is opened to doubt through denunciations of a pernicious political culture of press secretaries and focus groups, of mediatised soundbites and photo-ops. (Of course, some of those who denounce rhetoric tend not to acknowledge their own part in the production of the rhetorical machinery – as if there were such a thing as journalistic objectivity devoid of interests and 'values', or as if the popular 'common sense' to which political opponents claim to have a direct line were not the very fuel with which that machinery (in its most banal and brutal manifestations) fills its tanks. All the same these denunciations, when presented to the Court of Public Opinion, seem to offer up a more or less constant set of charges.)

What makes itself felt across this spectrum of scepticism is the problematising of trust in the face of a politics that comes across as altogether 'staged'. It is not that staging itself is at issue (what else can a poor Prime Minister do ...); it is more a question of the politics 'of' that staging – its poetics let us say. In pursuit of the most literal of instances, we might take the example of the rather clumsy launch of the 2001 general election at St Olave's School, and recall Blair in pious preacher mode hijacking the children's school assembly – spinning his image through and beyond the assembled schoolgirls, directly through the assembled news media onto the screen in the corner of our living-rooms, for our approval and, as it turned out, amusement. What is indexed in such performances, projections, and relays is the promise of a politics to come, a politics already underway in the engagements and practices that we – us others – are summoned to by this or that staging (to the extent, that is, to which political rhetoric does indeed summon our critical engagement, rather than merely representing its desire for our applause).

POWER TO THE PEOPLE

If this talk of rhetorical summoning sounds like some sort of political necromancy, then let us say right off that New Labour does not believe in ghosts. In fact, it so doesn't believe in them, it is unafraid to chant the magic words. To quote from Tony Blair's 1999 address to the Labour Party conference: 'And all around us the challenge of change. / A spectre haunts the world: technological revolution. /... / People are born with talent and everywhere it is in chains' (Blair 1999a). However, there is a declared purpose sustained throughout the New Labour rhetorical corpus, which, if not exactly concerned with summoning the dead to divine the future, does seem to have something to do with coaxing breath out of collapsed clay. Blair's own rhetoric peoples its projected vision of a future scene with ... well... 'people'. And although we might ask what, precisely, *are* 'people', that, it seems, is not the question Blair is asking. He knows what people are, even if his version does tend to focus upon a rather enigmatic interiority. To quote again from the 1999 speech:

> The challenge is how?
> The answer is people.
> The future is people.
> The liberation of human potential not just as workers but as citizens.
> Not power to the people but power to each person to make the most of what is within them.

In spite of those famous verbless phrases that imply, on the one hand, future aspiration, and on the other a vision of rather mysterious processes already in train (never mind the transitive intervention of motivated human agents), on the face of it this seems the sort of call that offers a direct, political address: a challenge, an invitation, an opening. That would be a contractual opening that weaves a promise with an injunction – the promise to break our chains and restore our 'right' to exercise our talents; and the injunction upon us to take 'responsibility' for investing those talents constructively by establishing a stake in the greater social body. And there is at least consistency here. This contract has long been a key New Labour topic, from the 'stakeholder' speech delivered ostensibly to an audience of Singapore business leaders in 1996, to the more coy rendition of that same trope in the 2001 general election manifesto, where the prime ministerial preface revisited the theme of 'rights and responsibilities' and concluded: 'New Labour is proving that it is only by using the talents of all that we get a healthy economy, and that it is only by giving a stake to all that we are a healthy society' (Labour Party 2001: 5). It is indeed people, *the* people (and that is us, presumably), who matter. And what could be the matter with that?

Well, throughout these several manifestations there remains something phantasmatic about the 'people' that are evoked (called forth) onto the stage of the Blairite rhetoric – something spectral indeed, as if they were all mask, sculpted in abstract form and hollowed out, awaiting the ignition or inspiration of some spark or breath, call it 'talent', 'potential', 'opportunity', before they might figure forth as regular embodiment. In short, the drama is being scripted, but something else is called for – something of 'us' – before it kicks into life and pursues its proper destiny. The effect is given in part, I think, by the tendency of the Blair speeches to do scene-setting, to exhibit what Norman Fairclough has diagnosed as 'a logic of appearances that manifests itself grammatically in a propensity towards lists', a pageant, let us say, of would-be-affective signifiers (Fairclough 2000: 28, 53).

This pageant is usually displayed in the context of discussions of the irreversibility of global 'change'. 'Globalisation' figures throughout Blair's speeches as the ever-intensifying occasion upon which 'people' and social relations shimmer with the threat of some sort of imminent dissolution, losing shape, losing momentum – all that is solid melting into disorientation. For example, Blair brings before our gaze, in a 2000 speech given to the Global Ethics Foundation in Tübingen, first of all a masque of 'fear':

> Globalisation has brought us economic progress and material well-being. But it also brings fear in its wake. Children offered drugs in the school playground; who grow up sexually at a speed I for one find frightening; parents who struggle in the daily grind of earning a living, raising a family, often with both parents working, looking after elderly relatives; a world where one in three marriages ends in divorce; where jobs can come and go because of a decision in a boardroom thousands of miles away; where ties of family, locality and country seem under constant pressure and threat (Blair 2000).

What follows is a logic of governance that applies itself to the scene as nothing so much as a mode of *stage*-management:

> So the change is fast and fierce, replete with opportunities and dangers. The issue is: do we shape it or does it shape us? Do we master it, or do we let it overwhelm us? That's the sole key to politics in the modern world, how to manage change.

At stake is a labour over signs and their meaning. As semiotic labour this involves the 'shaping', enabling and relocation of whatever (humanoid) signifiers are thrown up by the storm in such a way as to make those signifiers re-appear both fixed and purposive. To put the 'people' on stage as proper players. And there is no other way to achieve that than to insist we all (is that really 'all' of us?) sign up to a contract of agreed conventions, agreed ways of acknowledging and recognising whatever phantom comes into view. We need, in short, to agree that this or that figure 'stands' for something – something 'we' can agree to understand – and trust that it will continue to do so.

THE SPECTRE OF COMMUNITY
Blair tends to speak about this mutual understanding as a matter of 'shared values' (from the Tübingen speech again: 'it is only by clear commitment to shared values that we survive and prosper in a world of change…'). That word 'values' seems to incorporate an understanding of contract. ('But you can't build a community on opportunity or rights alone. They need to be matched by responsibility and duty. That is the bargain or covenant at the heart of modern civil society'.) Then again, this is a particular sort of contract, because what binds it (what

binds us *to* it) is trust: 'habits of co-operation, the networks of support, our radius of trust', which we learn in 'families, schools, congregations and communities'.

That last word turns us to what has been the dominant theme throughout the speech – 'community'. This is also perhaps the most spectral, the most hollowed out and looming of all the figures evoked by the Blair rhetoric to date. In the Tübingen speech this figure of 'community' seems to summon up some greater social body that retains in the hollow of its belly a special space just for me. It is the figure that summons me, but summons me with spooky presentiment to a consensus already inscribed – like the junk-mail credit card contract already filled in with my name and address.

In September 2001, in his annual speech to the Labour Party conference, shortly after the attacks on New York and Washington of 11 September, Blair gave his most elaborate meditation on the term 'community' to date. 'Amidst all the talk of war and action, there is another dimension appearing. There is a coming together. The power of community is asserting itself' (Blair 2001). Again, community functions not as a set of practices or shared knowledges, not even really as an idea; it functions rather as a quasi-theatrical 'appearing', something that looms behind the dialogue, a rather mysterious 'power' that is already amongst us and summoning us – or at least, amongst *those representations of ourselves* that people the stage of the Blair rhetoric. Again, this emergence of community appears as an effect of ongoing processes of dissolution and disorientation linked to 'globalisation' ('We are realising how fragile are our frontiers in the face of the world's new challenges …'). Indeed, it might not be unfair to suggest that the notion of 'community' being put over in this speech is, basically, a diagnosis of globalisation (as a set of irreversible social and economic processes, functioning like nothing so much as natural forces), but re-inflected as a sort of ethical aspiration, with a view to managing some of globalisation's more pernicious effects – or appearances:

> The state of Africa is a scar on the conscience of the world. But if the world as a community focused on it […] The issue is not how to stop globalisation.
> The issue is how we use the power of community to combine it with justice.

There are good intentions throughout the speech; that is, Blair's heart appears to be in many of the 'right' places (social justice, the relief of poverty, wealth distribution, environmental protection, improvement of public services, and so on). At the same time there is no disguising, even in Blair's own discourse, 'community's' rather spectral appearance as an ethical aspiration hitching a ride, and an ambitious world tour at that, on the back of the pursuit of globalising self-interest. When we consider what the most powerful vehicles may be in the world right now for the pursuit of interest, and how far these may be trusted to turn their focus towards that 'sense of justice [through which] community is born and nurtured', we may remain unpersuaded by the rhetoric, whatever its own ethical claims.

PRONOUNS AT WAR

To return to earlier evocations of the community spectre at times of international political crisis, we might suggest that 'community' has long functioned as a sort of rhetorical ectoplasm, as the doctrinal jelly that might hold together the several and not necessarily compatible interests that compete in any given political situation. One set of examples are the various and not necessarily differentiated first person pronouns evoked by Blair during the time of the NATO military action over Kosovo. Pronominal slippages over specific, immediate and, perhaps, unspeakable 'interests', rhetorically repackaged as 'shared values', have been convincingly analysed by Norman Fairclough (2000). In his discussion of New Labour language around the Kosovo war, Fairclough analyses Blair's keynote speech 'Doctrine of the International Community', delivered in Chicago (again to business leaders) in April 1999. Fairclough gives credit to Blair's attempt to represent the NATO action in relation to a complex construction ('globalisation') constituted by the domains of economy, security, and politics. He picks up, however, on a vagueness as to how these domains actually operate – a vagueness exacerbated by Blair's ambiguous use of the word 'we':

> The title of the speech ... refers to 'the international community' as if it were something well-defined (it presupposes that there is an international community), yet what we get in the speech is a series of disjunctions between different 'communities' referred to as 'we' (Fairclough 2000: 152).

In order to make sense of what Blair says, *we* have to be assuming something along his lines, and *we* go along with that assumption until we realise (if we do, or if we choose to do) that what is being assumed is not something that could have been explicitly said. Not in public, as it were. Not in 'our' hearing.

A 'rhetoric-reality' dichotomy opens then, according to Fairclough, between the speech and the 'real' economic and 'strategic interests' of the western powers and their corporate allies, which are not being fully acknowledged. At this level we may doubt the human face that is turned to us in the representation of US foreign policy as down-home good neighbourliness. We might also pick up on questions about who is and is not included in this or that 'we'? Who benefits, how and where, and from the spread of whose 'values'? We may even come round to questioning the oracular given-ness of the plot itself, with its sometimes simplistic division of the world into good guys ('us' – and again, who is that?) and bad guys (and these could sometimes include democratically elected bad guys, or onetime business partners of 'us').[3]

It is not the case, though, that the other stories we might tell are any the less 'rhetorical' than the ones Blair tells. No public intervention could ever be less than rhetorical. That does not mean, though, that we cannot identify rhetoric's material supplement – its flesh and blood leftovers. That is to say, there are actual bodies involved: all of the phantasmatic bodies put up for view in the rhetorical theatre are stitched together, propped up, and paid for, by people who are real enough, and real enough to be with-held (we might say detained) at this side or that of the rhetorical prophylactic. Political rhetorics, after all, are not just about inclusion but also exclusion. And the prophylactic, when it takes the form of a closed border, or elsewhere a sweatshop factory line, or an order of command, a line of soldiers or police, a computer screen, a line of tracer fire, the wire of a camp compound, a hidden grave, can also be 'real' enough.

Slavoj Zizek asks us to hold together in the same thought:

> ... war as a purely technological event, taking place behind radar *and* computer screens, with no casualties, and the extreme physical cruelty too unbearable for the gaze of the media – not the crippled children and raped women, victims of caricaturized local ethnic 'fundamentalist warlords,' but thousands of nameless soldiers, victims of anonymous and efficient technological warfare (Zizek 1999: 78-9).

This is, however, incompatible with the sort of rhetoric that would seek to function as a technology of *trust* – which is to say a discourse that asks 'us' to take it on trust that an ethically-minded representation is but a rhetorical shadow for a no less ethical *action*, in the real world as it were. Anything *but* 'purely technological', anything *but* 'anonymous', this rhetoric of ethical action turns out to be a *discourse* of pronouns and negotiable distances. An 'I' speaks to a 'you' about a 'them' over there, a there too close for comfort, where – as in the classic humanist dramas – destiny sets challenges for those who would make decisions.

Let me try to be clearer. Whether soliloquising in the theatre of war or stage-managing social exclusion in the domestic arena, the Blairite rhetoric – rather than drawing a scrim of vagueness across the scene – itself deploys a clear and principled dramaturgy. This dramaturgy depicts a peopled space. Again from 1999, on a stage within the stage, arranged in tableau, pitched to catch the conscience of us all, are the abject bodies that signify the victims of events:

> As far as the eye could see, a queue of humanity stretched through no man's land to Kosovo. Dignified in their pain and terror. Eyes glazed,

mothers trying to soothe children under a blistering sun. Old men staring vacantly into a new country, and a future they could not predict. Slowly, they were processed from one queue to the next (Blair 1999b).

The spectacle is gathered then into the conscience of Blair's first person pronoun, an ethical subject who is neither glazed, vacant, nor uncertain, who speaks on behalf of those who can not speak for themselves. This subject ('I') speaks 'their' unspoken message and answers it on behalf of an undivided 'we' that is itself, already (never mind the United Nations as an alternative option, never mind China's objections, or the possibility of Russia promoting a negotiated settlement), entrusted with the agency of righting wrong, of taking care of that unpredictable future, which is to say delivering revenge and reparation:

> Their message was simple, and it was dignified. We are leaving for now, but please, please help us to go back.
>   I felt an anger so strong, a loathing of what Milosevic's policy stands for, so powerful, that I pledged to them, as I pledge to you now; that Milosevic and his hideous racial genocide will be defeated. NATO will prevail. And the refugees will be allowed to return in safety to their homes.

This particular pledge is itself, though, performed for the benefit of another constituency, a 'you' (in this instance the Romanian parliament) who will themselves be beneficiaries of an analogous pledge: a pledge of communal belonging. This is the reward measured, after all these years ('for 2000 years [...] Romania has survived'), by the radius of trust. Indeed, more than a pledge, provisionality is elided here in the scenic evocation of nothing less than a communal 'destiny'. Can there, even amongst such a plethora of pronominal interests, be any argument?

> You can and will be part of the new Europe we are creating. At long last you will take your rightful place, confident and secure, on equal terms with the other European nations of the world. You will walk tall. And I extend the hand of friendship of my country, also a proud nation with a great history, and say we will walk with you into that brighter future. It is our common destiny.

This is a rousing cadence, and it returns its listeners to the tonic of communal harmony, projecting behind the masque of fear the humane features of international community, features that seem to promise untold returns to those who turn to embrace this shimmering brotherliness, no matter how shimmering, no matter how virtual the projection.

THE REMAINING WITNESS

What, though, of those who still labour on the other side of the rhetoric, the anonymous ones on whom the images, so to speak, depend? What do they do – do they put down their props and unmask? Blair himself would seem to suggest not, arguing in a speech to the Newspaper Society at the height of the Belgrade bombing that 'the conflict does not begin or end on a TV screen'. There is a danger, he tells journalists, that media 'refugee fatigue' only serves the interests of the other side in the propaganda conflict. And Blair draws attention to an actual backdrop now, a map behind his own podium, which he insists – and he may be right – serves no less as a cartography of the 'real' than the reality-effect of the news photograph:

> You may be wondering why I have a map of Kosovo behind me, and what it shows ... it is a story that has to be told, day after day, pictures or no pictures ... These are real places, real people. Real stories of burnt villages, devastated families, lootings, robberies, beatings, mass executions. These people are the reason we are engaged and the fact that we cannot see them makes us more determined to get in there and give them the help they need. This is more than a map. It is a montage of murder (Blair 1999c).

This is creditable. It is as if, in the theatre, one were to be reminded at the close of *Oedipus Rex* of the plague-ridden bodies on whose behalf the dramatic action was pursued in the first place. Or, at the end of *Hamlet*, as if the unquiet ghost might still recount his wounds. But then again, in the image of Oedipus's self-blinding, or in the overt accumulation of corpses in the revenge tragedy, that is precisely what the theatre does do. Furthermore, the theatre also credits these abject others – 'real people', 'real stories', – not as faraway victims of an ultimately unimaginable, because altogether exterior, power of evil. In the theatre *those* victims are only ever intimate with *this* scene. In the mediatised, technologised long-distance theatre of modern warfare it has seemed at times as if war does not occur 'in our time and place', but always in someone else's. The theatre *per se*, though, tells a different story. In the theatre of real illusions and made-up stories *that* scene (the scene of mythology, for instance) is always intimate with *this* stage, *these* combustible and corruptible presences, here. So for example, Oedipus can only prosecute a promised action on behalf of the plague victims by coming to recognise his own complicity in what ails these people – a 'criminal' complicity, even, that was established even before he arrived here, when another was in power.

Indeed, the suffering of 'people' may be the price being paid, beneath the makeup as it were, for the reification of community effected in the present spectacle.[4] Something of this sort of recognition is demanded by Slovoj Zizek in the essay already quoted above, wherein, recalling how the western powers supported Milosevic earlier on, he wonders whether phenomena like the Milosevic régime 'are not the opposite to the New World Order, but rather its *symptom*, the place at which the hidden *truth* of the New World Order emerges?' (Zizek 1999: 79). Within the radius of this thought, those 'real people' Blair insists we do not forget are set strangely, enigmatically, upon the scene: gathering at its edge with 'messages' but without passports; citizens of the spectacle but, within the remit of trust, aliens, asylum-seekers.

There is a peculiar economy of rhetorical reproduction at work, whereby 'real' bodies are constantly emerging, only to be incorporated – virtualised – as subjects of the party political plot. At the same time, however, the rhetoric can only incorporate so much; it has to exclude as well, and the figures it is least able to deal with are those who are least able to speak, *even as* these are identified as the ones most suitable to be deployed in a dramaturgy that would claim to speak on their behalf. In the wake of this dramaturgy, I want to suggest, may appear a certain sort of belligerent witness – a witness who remains, after the speeches have been made. This is a witness who appears and remains as much in the domestic arena as in the theatre of war, as we may see if we return to that 1999 conference speech. 'There is no more powerful symbol of our politics', Blair tells us – and one must assume it is New Labour's 'politics' he is symbolising – 'than the experience of being on a maternity ward'. From the subjectless opening – 'Seeing two babies side by side. Delivered by the same doctors ...' – careful not to obscure our unmediated spectation, the Prime Minister takes us through the scenario of a rich kid/poor kid cautionary tale. He incorporates the newborn as figures in a rhetoric that enables him to locate himself as their articulate representative, and from that position open up a contractual pledge that offers up a promise in exchange for trust. The 'pledge' here is 'to end child poverty in 20 years', a pledge that we should trust (those of us in the conference hall, and those others indirectly addressed through broadcast) precisely because it is backed up – 'not just as a politician, but as a father' – by the rhetor's claim to ethos.[5]

Blair describes the scene of a particular life. What the scene hinges upon, however, is the enigmatic and solipsistic behaviour of the child dispossessed of the radius of trust. This alienation serves the Prime Minister's rhetorical purposes, while at the same time depositing a remnant that may cause the whole machinery to shudder. The child whose life-story Blair outlines is fashioned into a familiar enough phantom upon the scene of domestic political rhetoric in Britain – the so-called 'single mother', culpable, irresponsible, incapable, dependent. It is her very predicament as a mute witness that suits her to her rhetorical role. Not even a proper player in her own drama, she is figured by Blair as witness to the scene of her dispossession. 'A child is a vulnerable witness on life. / A child sees her father hit her mother. / A child

runs away from home. A child takes drugs. A child gives birth at 12.'
This scenario, though, gives way to the overcoming and expanding
rhetoric (family, community, nation) of belonging. 'That every child
can grow up with high hopes, certainty, love, security and the attention
of their parents. / Strong families cherished by a strong community. /
That is our national moral purpose.' And that, presumably, is the
payoff for the trust we are asked to invest in the New Labour rhetoric.
However, even as the phrases swell we cannot help but recall that the
shared values, the communal 'moral purpose', evoked in the rhetoric
are predicated upon a montage of alienation. There on the scene the
radius of trust snaps, and the protagonist of the scenario – like that
queue of humanity at the Kosovo border – is witness to the snap, and
struck dumb. In any of these instances the ostensible human objects of
political concern are displaced, dazed, incapable, and silent. Nothing to
say, that is, apart from what the politician pledges to say – and, it is
implied, do – on their behalf.

Acting on another's behalf seems imaginable enough. There are
always, surely, things that can be *done*. An ethical foreign or domestic
policy is indeed, at the very least, *imaginable*. And that doing, the
imagining of that doing, might yet be contested in a politics (a 'struggle
amongst groups of people over substantive aspects of social life'). But
can the imagination engage to the same extent with the ethical pretensions of a *rhetoric*, and a rhetoric that asks us not to contest but to
consent and trust? A rhetoric predicated more on the semiosis of
governance ('the management of relations between groups') than the
agon of politics need not acknowledge trust as a 'two-way dialogue'
(Fairclough 2000: 11, 160).[6] This is a rhetoric that already knows best.
It is, let us say, a straight guy rhetoric, more and more assured of the
weight of its own ethos, and assured too of its capacity to speak on
another's behalf. But how does one speak on behalf of a witness, particularly if the witness's 'own' testimony is, for one reason or another,
inadmissible, unavailable, inaudible? Is not the witness's predicament,
as a living 'supplement' to rhetorical exclusions and inclusions, and as
a vantage on whatever it is that rhetoric indexes but can not incorporate, such that it precludes ventriloquism? What do we know, after all,
of what the witness witnesses, unless he or she may speak on his/her
own behalf? Although again, how would or could 'we' trust them even
if 'they' did?

NOTES

1. A one million pound donation to the Labour party from the motor racing
   promoter Bernie Ecclestone came to public attention, just at the time the
   government appeared ready to go back on its decision to ban tobacco
   advertising at sporting events, after lobbying from Ecclestone. The television programme was BBC1's *On the Record*, 16.11.97. The transcription is
   my own.

2. Blair: 'I didn't get it all wrong in relation to the original decision as I'd be very happy to explain. But it hasn't been handled well and for that I take full responsibility. And I apologise for that. I suppose what I would say to you is that perhaps I didn't focus on this and the seriousness of it in the way that I should, as I was focusing on other issues', *Guardian*, 17.11.97.

3. For more on the complicity of the NATO powers in the Milosevic regime, see for instance the essays Fairclough recommends in *New Left Review* 234, 1999.

4. See Ulmer 2001.

5. See Aristotle book 1 ch. 2 § 3-6; and book 2 ch.1.

6. For an extended analysis along these lines of New Labour 'good governance' see Mair 2000, who in turn develops arguments out of Marquand 1999.

REFERENCES

Aristotle (1991) *Aristotle*, On Rhetoric: *A Theory of Civic Discourse*, tr. and ed. G. Kennedy, New York and Oxford: Oxford University Press.

Blair, T. (1999a) 'Tony Blair's Full Speech,' (Labour party conference address), September 28. last accessed July 20, 2001.

Blair, T. (1999b) 'Speech to the Romanian Parliament,' May 4. last accessed July 20, 2001.

Blair, T. (1999c) 'Speech to Newspaper Society,' May 10. last accessed July 20, 2001.

Blair T. (2000) 'Values and the power of community' (Prime Minister's speech to the Global Ethics Foundation, Tübingen University, Germany), June 30. last accessed July 20, 2001.

Blair, T. (2001) 'Blair's Speech,' (Labour party conference address), September 2. *Guardian*, September 3.

Fairclough, N. (2000) *New Labour, New Language?* London and New York: Routledge.

Labour Party (2001) *Ambitions for Britain. Labour's Manifesto 2001*.

Mair, P. (2000) 'Partyless Democracy: Solving the Paradox of New Labour?' *New Left Review* 2, March/April, 21-35.

Marquand, D. (1999) *The Progressive Dilemma: From Lloyd George to Blair*, 2nd edn. London: Phoenix Press.

Ulmer, G. (2001) 'The Upsilon Project: a post-tragic testimonial', in P. Campbell and A. Kear, eds., *Psychoanalysis and Performance*, London and New York: Routledge.

Vidal, J. (2001) 'Blair attacks "spurious" May Day protests,' *The Guardian*, May 1.

Zizek, S. (1999) 'Against the Double Blackmail', *New Left Review* 234, March/April, 76-82.

11. A sympathy for art: the sentimental economies of New Labour Arts Policy

Michael McKinnie

When Labour was elected in 1997, arts workers and observers hoped that the change in government would herald a different approach to the arts. Conservative governments had displayed a deep suspicion of the arts during the Thatcher years and a slightly patronising tolerance under the Major administration. The main thrust of arts policy under successive Conservative governments had been consistent with the rest of their legislative agenda during their eighteen years in power: the arts, comprising activities heavily dependent on public subsidy, needed to be submitted to the 'discipline' of the free market through greater reliance on private sponsorship; and arts organisations needed to recuperate a greater proportion of their costs through the box office than through public grants. Though the practical achievement of these neo-liberal policy goals was often imperfect (and in this respect the arts were no different than many other areas targeted by the Conservatives for marketisation), the Conservatives' approach effectively ended fifty years of political consensus that the arts were a public good that required state patronage in order to provide access to all. This consensus may have been somewhat idealist in conception and paternalist in practice, but its attempt to define a democratic role for the arts in the political life of Britain was incompatible with Conservative policy-making, which viewed the arts as yet another space, albeit a particularly recalcitrant one, in which to entrench free-market economics.

Labour has, at least superficially, appeared more sympathetic to the arts than were the Conservatives. The party's 1997 election manifesto proclaimed Labour's support for the arts, stating that the Tories 'consistently undervalue[d] the role of the arts and culture in helping to create a civic society'; and though it offered no commitments regarding public expenditure on the arts, Labour's rhetoric seemed to offer the possibility of a warmer relationship between artists and the government than had been the case under the Conservatives (Dale 372). And to some degree this possibility has been realised, insofar as the Labour government has devoted considerably more attention and energy to the arts than their predecessors. The Department of Culture, Media and Sport (DCMS), the successor to the Major government's Department of National Heritage (DNH), has produced a flurry of studies, ranging from big-picture 'mapping' plans to tightly-focused analyses of the nether-regions of its purview. The DCMS has also secured the thing that tends to matter most to artists and arts organisations: more money from the Treasury. After a lean first few years, when Labour controversially adhered to the previous government's expenditure forecasts, the DCMS managed to win over the Treasury to such high-profile moves as the abolition of museum charges and the first substantial, above-inflation, increase in arts funding for more than two decades. These rather 'old' Labour achievements may have been accompanied by a very 'new' Labour regime of technocratic bureaucracy, but, at least in the blunt fiscal terms in which artists and arts organisations tend to measure their relationship with government, Labour has been more than a passing acquaintance, if not yet a close friend.

The purpose of this essay is to theorise the ideological anxieties of arts policy under New Labour, rather than gauging the achievement or failure of specific policy objectives. Though Labour returned to government in 1997, it is difficult as yet to measure the results (as opposed to the motivations and discursive content) of Labour arts policy, since much of it is long-term in focus but relatively recent in formulation. This should not, however, preclude an analysis of how New Labour is attempting, awkwardly, to shift the terrain on which the arts, the state, and private capital meet, especially since this attempt circumscribes to some degree the role that the arts might play in the British public and industrial spheres. New Labour sees itself and the arts – or the creative industries, to use the term it prefers – as sharing a broad ideological affinity, and believes that the arts can help in 'recreating a sense of community, identity and civic pride that should define our country' (Dale: 372). This is not a novel idea, but, in formulating its methods of achievement, it is important to recognise that New Labour has neither wholly resuscitated older Reithian models of cultural patronage nor simply extended a Conservative market-led model of arts sponsorship. Arts policy under New Labour does not abandon the marketisation promoted by the Tories, but instead recasts how the arts relate to society, private capital, and the state in more harmonious ways, and introduces a barrage of tests to measure the success of this new relationship. New Labour's arts policy tries to reconcile a number of conceptions of the arts that no British government has previously attempted: a particularly affirmative reading of the social function of the arts themselves – the arts as a medium through which social inclusion occurs, the arts as a virtuous form of economic production ('creative industries'), and the arts as an object of technocratic 'modernisation'. This arts discourse contains a tension between a desired social harmony and the market-inflected quantitative testing of its achievement – something that New Labour hopes is a harmonious process, but one which, as its policies reveal, is fraught with anxieties about the possible social efficacy of art and the ability of the state to regulate the terms of that efficacy.

ARTS POLICY AS A SENTIMENTAL ECONOMY

New Labour's arts policy attempts to define a culturally affirmative and sympathetic sentimental economy: it is seeking to imagine a policy structure through which the arts can create relations of social accord – in the economic, civic and institutional spheres. It assumes that the paramount function of the arts is to confirm and reproduce dominant social ideals, and, in the process, encourage a sense of mutual well-being. New Labour's understanding of the arts, therefore, is wholly affirmative. Its policy does not acknowledge that art might be critical, subversive, or socially dissonant, conceptions of art which Labour Party policy once thought possible, and, to a limited degree, tried to encourage.[1]

In order to understand this affirmative logic of New Labour's arts policy, it is useful to look at the work of two theorists, one a twentieth-century Marxist (Herbert Marcuse) and one an eighteenth-century liberal (Adam Smith). In characterising arts policy as culturally affirmative, I have drawn on a conceptual framework outlined by Herbert Marcuse, whose contribution to materialist critical theory is widely acknowledged (albeit usually in the past tense), but whose work is rarely invoked in performance studies or analyses of the arts today. This is regrettable, as Marcuse offers a productive way to conceive how the arts are simultaneously aesthetic and institutional practices. He argues that art, whether 'high' or 'low', is characterised by a tension between social negation and social affirmation. Thus art can, depending on historical circumstances, either sustain dominant social ideology by reproducing the mystifications on which that ideology rests, or it can undermine that ideology by making its premises – and the hierarchies those premises serve – visible in a way that they had not been previously.[2]

Marcuse argues that art's dual potential lies in the ambiguous nature of representation (through which all art functions), and in art's demand that its audience negotiate imaginary and social worlds simultaneously. He argues that 'negating' art provokes a schism between these worlds in the consciousness of the audience member by dialectically opposing them in the moment of representation and reception. This rupture undermines the accepted, and often unquestioned, way that the spectator-subject has come to view its world, or its 'given reality'. 'The world formed by art is recognised as a reality which is suppressed and distorted in the given reality', Marcuse argues. 'This experience culminates in extreme situations ... which explode the given reality in the name of a truth normally denied or unheard' (6-7). Art's representation of an alternative reality opens up the possibility of creating a 'rebellious subjectivity' and calls into question the 'rationality and sensibility incorporated in the dominant social institutions' (7).

Affirmative art does exactly the opposite, using its representational power (its 'overwhelming presence') to reinforce the given reality, thereby 'reconciling' the subject to dominant social ideals and institutions (6-7). An example from the theatre – in terms of the changing perceptions of naturalism – is one way of illustrating the tension between, and historical contingency of, negating and affirming art. Theatrical naturalism sees the ideal representational relationship between the stage and its social formation as one of verisimilitude, where the appearance of subjects and objects onstage mimics, as closely as possible, their surface appearance in the 'real world'. This has been the dominant form in Western theatre since the early twentieth century, and many critics now argue that naturalist plays have become culturally affirmative because naturalism privileges the imaginary representation of the social world as it is, rather than as it might be. But this view does not deny the fact that naturalism was, in its inception, a new and radical form, whose use in a play like Henrik Ibsen's *Ghosts* changed the ways that audiences saw the relationship between their imaginary and social worlds.

Though Marcuse is extending a line of Marxist aesthetics inaugurated by the Frankfurt School, his identification of the arts as a 'reconciling' activity has a much earlier precedent, one which also helps theorise New Labour's arts discourse. In *The Theory of Moral Sentiments* [1984], Adam Smith identifies 'sympathy' as the intersubjective bond that creates social accord. Like Marcuse, Smith is concerned with social negation or affirmation (to use Marcuse's terms) or sympathetic or unsympathetic social sentiments (to use his own terms); but he locates the production of these sentiments in a different, though complementary, place. Whereas Marcuse discusses the production of affirmative or negative sentiments largely in terms of the way in which a subject engages with the representations of a pre-existing artistic product, Smith discusses social sympathy in terms of the ways that subjects represent themselves to each other in a pre-defined social process that functions according to an artistic logic. Marcuse, then, provides a way to think about a subject's engagement with an artistic product; Smith provides a way to think about a subject's participation in a social process whose logic is essentially artistic. For Smith, social accord is achieved through an imaginative subjective transposition: a subject imagines itself in another's place, and, as a result, achieves a 'concord with the emotions' of the other ([1984]: 22). This process of imagining, measuring, and moderating behaviour creates an impartial subject and achieves the 'harmony of society' he strongly desires

([1984]: 22). Smith's social model, as David Marshall points out, is fundamentally based on an artistic paradigm – and specifically a theatrical one. Smith describes social subjects as spectators of each other, and Marshall describes Smith's version of a harmonious society as 'a theatre of sympathy' (173). This theatre is not only a forum where sympathetic social relations are achieved, it is also a forum where sympathetic social ideals are established: 'The spectator enters by sympathy into the sentiments of the master, and necessarily views the object under the same agreeable aspect' (179). The artistic/social scene, then, is at once harmonious and hierarchical. Smith imagines the socially affirmative tautology that is at the heart of New Labour's emphasis on 'participation' in its arts policy: social sympathy is art and art is social sympathy.

It is also true, however, that Smith is worried that social subjects will be unsympathetic. Since an unsympathetic subject is a failed spectator in Smith's social imaginary, he betrays an anxiety about social discord that is rooted in an anxiety about the operations of art itself. Having based his social model on a wholly affirmative conception of art, this affirmation cannot help but reveal the potentially negating force of that art, and the instability of the model of social relations upon which it is based. New Labour suffers from much the same unease. Its desire to use an affirmative art to create civic, economic, and institutional sympathy reveals profound and unacknowledged anxieties about the historically ambiguous position of the arts within the British political system and, ultimately, about the potential for art to provoke a rebellious subjectivity that is unwelcome in New Labour's Britain.

CIVIC SYMPATHY

Labour's 1997 election manifesto makes clear that the party is attracted to the civic role that the arts might play in British society. Such an interest is not without precedent; the arts have at least a two thousand year-old history as a civic enterprise in Western culture, and have generally contributed to the civic as a social ideal, both at the local level and at the national level.[3] A long list of civically-inflected activity could be compiled from theatre history alone, and it would certainly include: the City Dionysia, a civic and religious theatre festival that began in Athens in the sixth century BCE; the mystery plays sponsored by town guilds throughout England during the Middle Ages; the local pageants of the Renaissance in Britain and France; and the civic theatre movement throughout North America in the twentieth century. Each of these artistic events was part of the training of what it meant to participate in the public (though not necessarily democratic) life of the societies in which they were produced.

Rightly or wrongly, New Labour viewed the British public sphere as diminished after eighteen years of Conservative government, and saw the arts as a particularly effective forum through which to rebut

Margaret Thatcher's infamous claim that society did not exist. Soon after the 1997 election, Chris Smith, the first Secretary of State for Culture, Media and Sport, claimed that the arts and New Labour shared the same core belief, one which was sanctioned by the electorate: that 'after eighteen years of a contrary doctrine, there *is* such a thing as society' (Smith, 1998: 15). 'Without culture, there can ultimately be no society and no sense of shared identity or worth', Smith argued. 'For a government elected primarily to try and re-establish that sense of society that we had so painfully lost, this is a very important realisation' (16). Though the importance of society may have needed stressing in the immediate aftermath of a long period of Tory rule, Smith's representation of the arts as civically recuperative is nothing new; if the immediately celebratory function of the arts has an extensive lineage, then the notion of the arts as a transhistorical marker of community dates back at least two centuries in British history as well.

It is significant, however, that Labour's 1997 manifesto explicitly positioned 'culture' – by which it meant the traditional forms of high art and other representational media such as film and television – as a central means by which 'civic society' is created. The use of the phrase 'civic society' in the 1997 manifesto, as opposed to the Habermasian 'civil society', reveals a subtle semantic distinction in New Labour's arts discourse: the arts are not a forum in which public debate occurs, but rather the means by which training in pre-determined civic values takes place. This function recalls Adam Smith's theatrical scene, in which the spectator gains sympathy by learning the 'sentiments of the master' and then viewing the world 'under the same agreeable aspect'. But this hierarchical sense of civic training through the arts is also intended, somewhat ambiguously, to promote 'social inclusion'. A key policy document released by the DCMS in 1999 focused on how the arts 'provide powerful positive role models' (DCMS, 1999: 29) for those who reside in neighbourhoods that fail on 'key indicators' of community 'performance' (the artistic metaphor is appropriate) (DCMS, 1999: 22). In this way of thinking, the arts embody a range of civic ideals that, if instilled in 'those living in deprived neighbourhoods', could lead to the rehabilitation of communities in crisis (29). Moreover, the results of this process can be measured by the state through technocratic (though vaguely defined) instruments.

New Labour's conception of the arts as a tool for civic training in disadvantaged areas uneasily echoes the dominant state interest in the arts during the nineteenth century in Britain, when the arts were 'valued chiefly as means of inculcating middle-class attitudes in the working-class mind' (Minihan: 229). It also recalls the Reithian ideal of cultural training through entertainment, education, and information. But to infer that New Labour's arts discourse simply resuscitates older models of cultural education would be to misrepresent the distinct understanding of artistic efficacy and artistic labour processes on which this discourse hinges. Whether old Labour or Conservative, welfarist or monetarist, the consistent preoccupation of post-war arts policy was the nation. In contrast, local communities (the smaller the better, it would seem) are the subject and object of New Labour's civically-minded arts discourse. The social subject's location within these civically sympathetic arts has also shifted, from the consumption of a civilised artistic product to participation in a civilising artistic labour process. According to New Labour policy, the arts 'lend themselves naturally to voluntary collaborative arrangements which help to develop a sense of community'; they 'help communities to express their identity and develop their own, self-reliant organisations'; and they 'relate directly to individual and community identity: the very things which need to be restored if neighbourhoods are to be renewed' (DCMS, 1999: 30). Furthermore, the arts 'are things in which people participate willingly'; they 'give individuals greater self-respect; self-confidence and a sense of achievement'; and they 'can contribute to greater self esteem and improved mental well being' (31).

These are highly affirmative glosses on art's social efficacy and its labour processes, resting on a series of assumptions that are empirically dubious, and logically difficult to sustain. The communitarian function of the arts is more presumed than proven under New Labour. That the arts *can* help communities define and articulate themselves is not in question; that the arts *will* perform this function in an ideal way is another matter. Contrary to the claim that artistic activity is 'voluntary' and undertaken 'willingly', participation in the arts is not necessarily any less coercive than any other community activity, and the arts are not an inherently 'healthier' form of community participation than any other. If the arts are supposed to recuperate a supposedly absent 'community identity' through providing a sense of self-esteem, self-reliance, and general well-being, the concrete mechanisms by which these results are achieved are effaced; though 'participation' is ostensibly the means of achieving them, the definition of participation is so broad as to be virtually meaningless: 'creative expression, co-operative teamwork or physical exertion' (DCMS, 1999: 21). Since there is little human activity that does not involve some measure of these things, artistic participation becomes a black box where civic aspiration can masquerade as civic outcome.

Furthermore, the assumption that the arts are inherently collaborative is rarely borne out in practice. While many artistic practices do involve groups of people working together in order to create an art object or event, others, such as writing, may involve a single producer for much of the duration of the labour process. Additional participants may become involved along the way, but this is little different than when groups of people work together during any labour process, making the supposed distinctiveness and normative superiority of the artistic labour process difficult to discern. Moreover, the peripatetic way that artistic collaboration is usually funded in Britain – which means that it is frequently short-term, badly paid, and punctuated by extensive periods of unemployment and uncertainty – actually mitigates against building the types of sustained creative relationships that might prove useful models for disadvantaged neighbourhoods. And though artistic labour processes may sometimes be collaborative (and one should not assume that a group of people working together is necessarily collaborative in the normative sense implied by New Labour), they are also often rigidly prescriptive and hierarchical. It is rather ironic that the arts should be vaunted for their flexibility when most theatre rehearsal processes in Britain rely on a strict definition of occupation and task that has remained largely unchanged for more than a century: whether one is a director, an actor, or a technician, one usually has a very clear sense of the boundaries of one's job and its position within a sharply defined pecking order. Though New Labour uses the arts as models of civic collaboration and training, they are just as readily models of self-interest, anxiety, and hierarchy.

ECONOMIC SYMPATHY

It would not be an exaggeration to describe New Labour's relationship with the market economy as the friendliest yet seen in a Labour government. This is not to say that previous Labour governments did not arrive at a kind of détente with the market, but New Labour has vigorously extended, rather than checked, the process of marketisation undertaken by the Conservatives. It has done so, however, in a particular way: whereas the Conservatives viewed marketisation as a form of combat, with the forces of the free market triumphing over the state, New Labour seeks to extend the market through more sympathetic means. The counterpart to participation under New Labour, therefore, is 'partnership', where the arts, the state, and private industry not only collaborate in investment, but where the ideal relationship is one in which the historic economic ambivalence between the arts and private industry begins to dissolve. By refashioning the arts as part of the 'creative industries', New Labour attempts to place them in a more harmonious relationship. The creative industries are the industrial prerequisite for the arts and private capital imagining themselves in each other's places, and joining together within New Labour's industrial strategy.

While the Conservatives attempted to force arts bodies into articulating their social value in monetary terms, and were successful in achieving this to some degree, they could never completely reconcile the different conceptions of the arts that they advanced. Even after two decades of arts marketisation, the Conservatives remained suspicious that the arts, in economic terms, were a throwback to a time before the frontiers of socialism had been rolled back. At the same time, however, the Conservatives' arts discourse was relentlessly backward-looking, seeing the function of the arts as preserving Britain's 'national heritage' (the phrase that the Major government chose for its culture ministry), and thereby invoking a whole range of social ideologies – such as patriotism, historical nostalgia, and familial allegiance – that may reside outside the interests of an increasingly transnational market economy.

New Labour, in contrast, has 'modernised' the economic relationship between the arts and private capital by refashioning the arts as the creative industries. According to New Labour, the creative industries are 'those industries which have their origin in individual creativity, skill and talent and which have a potential for wealth and job creation through the generation and exploitation of intellectual property' (DCMS, 2001: 5). Arts like theatre and sculpture are now allied with computer software and advertising, seamlessly linking the old with the new through 'individual creativity', 'wealth and job creation', and 'intellectual property'.[4] Though the term 'cultural industries' had been in use by both right-wing and left-wing observers since the 1980s, New Labour has taken pains to disavow it and promote the creative industries in its place. 'Some say [the creative industries] is just the cultural industries under a new label, but that's not true', Arts Minister Alan Howarth claimed in 2000. 'We take creative industries to include sectors such as advertising, architecture, design, designer fashion, software and music in addition to what we would recognise as the more traditional cultural industries' (DCMS, 2000: 1). Competing connotations of 'cultural' and 'creative' underpin Howarth's distinction, and New Labour clearly wishes to be associated with the sentiments implied by the latter term: creativity connotes dynamism, individuality, modernity, and inventiveness, while culture implies heritage, stasis, the 'forces of conservatism', and collectivity. Significantly for a government that wants to encourage artistic and commercial sympathy, creativity is a word that is used by their respective advocates to describe both artists and markets.

The incorporation of the arts into a sympathetic industrial strategy salves an anxiety about the limits of the economic value of the arts, limits that the Conservatives encountered in the early 1990s. Prior to the 1980s, the arts in Britain were valued mostly for their contribution to 'the public good', which meant the way that 'the arts are pleasurable *and* contribute to our spiritual, emotional and moral health' (Shaw 1987: 24). Though the arts may also have been an economic good, this benefit was seen as secondary, and the relationship between artistic and economic production was ambivalent at best. Roy Shaw, who was Secretary-General of the Arts Council of Great Britain (ACGB) between 1975 and 1983, acknowledges that the economic function of the arts is 'vital', but it 'is more important to demonstrate that the arts … remind us that man does not live by bread alone' (27). Shaw suggests that the arts possess a moral calculus that the market does not, and, while the arts and the market are not necessarily antipathetic toward each other, the former possesses a system of value that is not reducible to the monetary calculus of the latter.

This economic scepticism is reflected in the fact that, until relatively recently, data on the arts as industrial activities were not systematically gathered. As Baz Kershaw comments: 'Statistical analysis of the arts in Britain was not considered a priority until the mid-1980s, when the pressures of neo-Conservative monetarism forced onto the funding agencies the issue of their contribution to the nation's economy' (Kershaw, 1992: 46). Data collection began principally as a way to place the arts and the market in a more sympathetic relationship; it was impossible for the market and the arts to comprehend each other if they did not employ the same financial measurements of value. For Kershaw, this statistical emphasis was part of a general move away from the *status* of the arts (with which Shaw and much of Britain's post-war arts discourse was preoccupied) to the *scale* of the arts. John Myerscough's 1986 landmark study, *The Economic Importance of the Arts*, marked the first comprehensive attempt to quantify the monetary value of the arts as an industry, refashioning artists as producers supplying commodities to be purchased not by audiences but by consumers. 'Expressed in these terms', Robert Hewison argues, 'the arts become purely instrumental, a matter of "value for money", and the opposition between culture and industrial society has disappeared' (1994: 30).[5]

The results of this shift, however, were not completely sympathetic in the ways hoped for by the Conservatives or by the advocates of marketisation at the funding councils. If anything, the attempt to submit the arts wholesale to the logic of the free market threw the tension between the arts and private capital into sharper relief. Arts marketisation may have opened up a new avenue for artistic advocacy by using a monetary logic familiar to the governing Conservatives and private capital, but the quantitative results of statistical analysis tended to show that the arts, at least as traditionally defined, were a relatively small proportion of the national economy. 'The argument that the arts return more to governments in taxes than they cost governments in subsidy should not be taken seriously', Hewison comments. 'Certainly the British Treasury does not appear to do so' (31). Attempts by the state to attract more private investment for the arts were also largely unsuccessful, as corporations saw little benefit for their bottom line in financing art. Despite successive Conservative governments trumpeting the role for private capital in the arts sector, the Department of National Heritage reported in 1993 that the Business Sponsorship Incentive Scheme, introduced in 1984, 'with the aim of raising the overall level of business sponsorship' of the arts, had managed to attract only £32 million during the previous nine years (Central 16). To put this in perspective, the Arts Council allocation for 1992-93 alone was £221 million, and this figure excludes the £192 million spent on 11 national galleries and museums in England and other substantial grants to organisations like the British Library, the British Film Institute, and the Crafts Council (Central 16). Despite the rhetoric of 'industrial and commercial concerns offer[ing] vital sponsorship', the arts were largely ignored as an economic good by private capital (Central: 16).

Boundaries between different expressive and aesthetic media needed to be dissolved for the arts to enter into commercial partnership in both quantitative and qualitative terms. The shift from the arts to the creative industries places the arts within a wider range of activities and implies that they are more conceptually and economically homologous than previously imagined. As a corollary, it creates an industrial sector whose quantitative economic output is much greater than previously accounted for. Whereas the arts, traditionally conceived, were estimated to account for £6 billion of economic activity in 1990 (Central Office of Information, 1993: 1), the combined creative industries were estimated in 2001 to account for £112.5 billion (DCMS, 2001: 10), a level of growth that could only be achieved by expanding the definition of the industrial sector being measured. As the creative industries, then, the arts became part of much larger industrial strategy, and New Labour has situated the arts squarely within its promotion of the 'new economy' and export-led economic development.[6] The qualitative benefits of this shift are equally important: the ostensibly collaborative nature of the arts supplies the ideal labour process that New Labour desires for the broader economy, and the arts also embody a pre-industrial ideology of artisanship that is sympathetic to the new economy's post-industrial privileging of individual entrepreneurs.

This approach helps to explain New Labour's attempt to redefine the boundaries of cultural production – direct private investment in arts projects matters less when the industrial sector as a whole is seen to combine not-for-profit and commercial enterprise – but it does not completely efface the contradictions within that redefinition. While New Labour is somewhat concerned about the arts in terms of their quantitative economic output, the commercial, profit-making side of the creative industries is responsible for the vast majority of the revenues generated by the sector; the economic value of the traditional arts remains small relative to the rest of the creative sector and to the larger economy. It is also clear that the fit between the traditional arts and the other creative industries in DCMS strategy is uneasy, resulting in either the complete elision of the 'older' arts or the awkward insistence that a commercial funding rationale remains applicable in spite of its acknowledged failure. When the DCMS promotes 'connecting creativity with capital', the creativity with which it is concerned is almost exclusively that located in high-technology, commercial, and mass production industries like computer software development (DCMS, *Creative Industries Finance*). The section of the 2001 *Creative*

Industries Mapping Document on music is devoted to the commercial pop record industry, with no mention of opera companies, orchestras, experimental, or traditional music (15). The section on the performing arts is rather paradoxical, and illustrates New Labour's inability to find a coherent economic logic for the 'old' arts: the *Mapping Document* admits that 'attendances overall are static [and] the sector does not demonstrate strong growth', and partly attributes this to 'a higher level of dependence on market support than in other European countries, resulting in a fear of creative risk-taking' (DCMS, 2001: 15). The solution to the problem of overdependence on the market, however, is not greater public funding (as in many 'other European countries'), but rather 'more private support' (15). The new system of economic value in which New Labour has placed the arts features as many compromises, albeit of a different sort, than the supposedly unsympathetic value system it replaces.

INSTITUTIONAL SYMPATHY

The groundwork for an institutionally sympathetic arts model, which attempts to bring together the arts and the state harmoniously, was actually laid by the Major government. After the 1992 election, Major created the Department of National Heritage, which assembled 'the whole range of governmental activity that constitutes the state's cultural policy within Britain' (Gray: 59).[7] The DNH assumed responsibility not only for the arts councils but also for such things as media regulation, sport and tourism promotion, administration of the national lottery, heritage buildings, libraries, and the national galleries, museums, and theatres. Though the DNH was not intended to be a grand Ministry of Culture on the French model, it was intended to provide a broader policy-making framework than had previously been possible. Equally importantly, the Secretary of State for National Heritage was made a Cabinet-level position, implying that the state would take a higher-level interest in artistic production.

The Conservatives may have created a basic institutional structure, but New Labour set out to exploit it for their own ends. In doing so, they were attempting to break with the awkward and distinctive institutional arrangements within which the arts in Britain had existed since the Second World War – the time when systematic state patronage of the arts in Britain began. While individual and business patronage of the arts had existed in Britain for centuries, the modern structure of substantive public subsidy for the arts dates from the establishment of the ACGB in 1946. As Clive Gray observes:

> Prior to 1940 about the only direct state involvement with the arts in Britain was to be found in local and national museums, financial support for broadcast opera on the BBC and in the post of Poet Laureate. Apart from these small areas of activity the British state displayed a marked

reluctance to become involved in a field that was seen to carry as many political problems as it did opportunities (Gray: 35).

The 1946 foundation of the ACGB codified a tension that was to dominate arts policy for much of the next four decades: that between a democratic rationale for artistic subsidy – the ACGB was mandated to provide 'access for all' – and a patrician one based on the dissemination of pre-determined ideals of beauty and civilisation.[8] New Labour's cultural policies can thus be understood as efforts to resolve some of this a tension and muddle.

Although Jennie Lee was made Britain's first Minister for the Arts in 1965, the post-war consensus around the institutional structures of arts policy-making was more motivated by convenience and obfuscation than by thoughtful design. Because public subsidy for most arts organisations was directed through arm's-length bodies rather than through an arts ministry with Cabinet-level representation, the state could provide resources for the arts without the government having to answer directly in Parliament for their final allocation (Gray: 44; Hutchison: 16-19). The system permitted general state influence over the direction of arts councils through the government appointment of their members, but reassured arts organisations and artists that specific decisions over the funding of companies and individual works would be insulated from direct governmental fiat (though in practice artists discovered that ministers did not have to issue specific orders for progressive arts organisations like theatre company 7:84 to be targeted for funding cuts during the 1980s). This arrangement was also reassuring in a populist sense, in that its development seemed to mimic the conventional understanding of constitutional evolution in the United Kingdom, and therefore appeared to be an innately 'British compromise' rooted in political incrementalism (Hutchison 16). Janet Minihan may not theorise this compromise in a way sympathetic to the approach of this essay, but she usefully describes its logic, which was promoted by both the state and arts advocates:

> The nation's lawmakers were not asked to approve a dangerous, unprecedented step into uncharted cultural realms, but merely to transform a temporary arrangement, and one of proven worth and popularity, into a permanent body dignified by Royal Charter. Over the centuries, the organs of British Government had developed in just such a way, through precedent becoming custom and ultimately being embodied in legal form (228).

Until the 1980s (and arguably the 1990s), state influence on the arts was present but diffused, and – albeit for different reasons – this arrangement broadly suited all the participants in the system.

The consequences of this structure, however, were two-fold. In the first place, it largely devolved arts policy-making to a relatively small number of quango staff outside government and the state bureaucracy, making an already minor government interest in the arts even smaller (Gray 44-47). Gray argues that arts policy formation, though rhetorically committed to access for all, was determined by a tight group of officials cut off from the major state policy apparatus that was actually making accessibility a broad reality through the formulation of more wide-ranging public projects and services. It could also be argued that the ad hoc devolution of arts policy-making to intermediary organisations like the ACGB stifled within government any political imperative to fund the arts at levels similar to those in other parts of Europe (something that was more likely to make universal access a possibility), and deflected artistic disaffection away from the government and towards bodies like the ACGB. Even with the appointment of a Minister for the Arts, the fact that this person was effectively a junior minister within the Department of Education (and therefore outside Cabinet), and that responsibility for the arts, broadly defined, was scattered amongst various departments, made intra-institutional pressure on the government difficult to assert successfully (Abercrombie 23-25).[9] In addition, this structure implied that the arts owed allegiance as much, if not more, to the nation (or the union) as to the state. The Major government allied the arts more explicitly with the state by creating a single Department specifically responsible for them, but the name of this Department – National Heritage – served to extend a preoccupation with the arts' national, rather than state, relationship.

If the 'creation' of the creative industries sought to create an economic homology between various forms of aesthetic and expressive activities, New Labour's 'performance agreements' (again, note the artistic metaphor) attempt to create a bureaucratic homology between the creative industries and all other areas of state involvement. While the arts have historically been a distinct forum of policy-making (for better and worse), they are now subject to the same objective standards of measurement as other activities that come into contact with the state. Many of these standards are deeply technocratic and entrench a market-inflected system of value: the arts are measured according to their 'performance' in 'key indicators', their 'expenditure and outputs' are analysed, they are subject to 'best value' audits, and they must develop 'modernised management arrangements' and 'improve value for money' (DCMS *Policy*: 11-12). Above all else, they must 'join up' with other policies being formulated across other government departments (DCMS, *Culture*: 5).

The arm's-length relationship between arts funding, the DCMS, and the Treasury has also been weakened, as the arts have become an increasingly indistinguishable part of public policy-making. The Arts Council of England (ACE), for example, may be an independent royally-chartered body, but it is now governed by a 'performance agreement' with the DCMS that is similar to those agreed with (or imposed on) other quangos. This agreement outlines the ACE's commitment to achieving a variety of government objectives on such things as social inclusion, partnership, participation, and efficiency. The ACE agreement is, in turn, mirrored by a performance agreement between the DCMS and the Treasury that contains much the same set of objectives – and many of these goals would not look out of place in the agreements between most other government departments and the Treasury. This arrangement, while perhaps a logical next step for most areas within government, binds the arts to the central policy-making apparatus of government in a way that is unprecedented.

New Labour's more sympathetic structure further entrenches a strict bureaucratic hierarchy, with the Treasury firmly positioned at the top. The inclusive language of creativity, participation, and partnership trumpeted in numerous DCMS documents arises from the Treasury's continued scepticism about public funding for the arts and its desire for the arts to articulate their value in the preferred discourse of New Labour. Buried deep in Policy Action Team 10's report on the arts and social exclusion is the admission that partnership 'has arisen out of a political imperative to reduce the public sector funding requirement' (DCMS, *Policy* 92). The civic and economic ideals espoused by New Labour's arts policy, then, compensate for a blunt fiscal imperative.

While the value of the arts should be expressed and measured as transparently as possible, New Labour's sympathetic arts policy privileges a technocratic calculation of value whose ultimate arbiters are government ministers, and, in the final instance, the Treasury. Other value systems that could be used to articulate the significance of the arts have difficulty in being accommodated. For example, it is difficult to imagine the case for the arts laid out by the Labour Party during the Callaghan government being understood by New Labour. That case focused on the institutional governance of the arts, and conceived of participation very differently: as the direct, elected involvement of arts workers and audiences in the administration of arts bodies. Moreover, the ultimate measure of artistic efficacy was whether or not the arts challenged, rather than confirmed, dominant morality and accepted beliefs (Labour 7). Even the more patrician and institutionally-friendly case outlined by Shaw in the mid-1980s, in which the role of the arts is to transmit national and international 'cultural tradition', would have difficulty being understood within the technocratic context of New Labour (37). Whether radical or patrician, these discourses imply institutional roles for the arts that are incompatible with the institutionally sympathetic position in which they have been placed by New Labour.

CONCLUSION
Writing after the first decade of arts marketisation in 1990, Justin Lewis commented, 'We live in an age of priorities, not ideals' (1). New Labour

places an interesting twist on Lewis's observation: it promotes its priorities as ideals. New Labour imagines that the arts perform wholly affirmative civic, economic, and institutional functions, and assumes that each role brings them into more sympathetic relationships than had been previously imagined: first with the social formation, then with private capital, and, finally, with the state itself. But after a long period during which the arts were hectored by successive Conservative governments, it should not be assumed that New Labour's more sympathetic approach is any less disciplinary or, equally importantly, any less anxious. Instead, New Labour's arts discourse must be seen as an attempt to subtly define the terms on which the arts enter the British public and industrial spheres.

However, the possibility that the arts might still be negating or unsympathetic is not completely extinguished in New Labour's approach to the arts. Indeed, the ministerial shuffle after the 2001 election confirm this possibility: the entire ministerial team at the DCMS was dismissed and replaced by one led by Tessa Jowell, a Blairite and, most importantly, former minister at the Department of Trade and Industry. It is hard to avoid the implication that, with Jowell's appointment, the new government wanted to encourage even tighter ties between the state, industry, and the arts. New Labour appears to be amplifying its sympathetic overtures in its second term, but strictly on the affirmative grounds laid out in its first. That it believes this amplification necessary betrays the fear in New Labour's political unconscious that a rebellious art might yet surface.

I would like to thank David Grant for sharing his insights into, and professional experience with, arts policy-making in the United Kingdom.

NOTES

1. This does not mean that the last Labour government was wholly committed to a radical arts policy during its period in office; however, the Labour Party continued to debate what an explicitly socialist arts policy might be during the Callaghan administration and formulated proposals on that basis. See Labour Party, *The Arts and the People*.

2. Marcuse's debt to the early Frankfurt School theorists is clear here. His discussion of cultural affirmation and negation echoes Theodor Adorno and Max Horkheimer's earlier attempt to theorise 'autonomous' art, which they viewed as art that exposed the premises of social relations through novel representational strategies.

3. I have discussed this elsewhere in the context of theatre practice, but the same statement hold true, in various ways, for the arts in general. See McKinnie 257-258. It should be noted, however, that this general tendency does not diminish the culturally and historically-specific nature of these practices.

4. The complete list of creative industries used by the DCMS is: advertising, architecture, the art and antiques market, crafts, design, designer fashion,

film and video, interactive leisure software, music, the performing arts, publishing, software and computer services, television and radio.

5. For an excellent discussion of how this 'monetarist' discourse for arts advocacy began to supersede all other discourses in the mid-1980s (to the extent that public funding bodies began using it in embarrassingly hyperbolic ways), see Kershaw, 'Discouraging' 274-275.

6. See, for example, DCMS, *Creative Industries Exports*.

7. It should be noted that the creation of the DNH may have resulted as much from the tradition of personal interest rather than thoughtful design as earlier institutional arrangements. The Secretary of State for National Heritage, David Mellor, had been a strong and early supporter of John Major's leadership of the Conservative Party and it is an open question whether the Secretary of State for National Heritage would otherwise have been a Cabinet-level position.

8. The Arts Council was the successor to the Council for the Encouragement of Music and the Arts (CEMA), which had been founded in 1940 as the artistic wing of the war effort. CEMA's role was to promote British art as part of the wider campaign against fascism, and, though initially created by a private charity, the Pilgrim Trust, the government had assumed the full operating costs of CEMA in 1941 through the Board of Education. The wartime government saw CEMA as a useful tool for promoting national morale and for propaganda purposes, and, as Gray observes, it inaugurated an institutional cosiness that has dominated the relationship between the state and arts bodies ever since (though this cosiness should not be reduced to a crude form of political control).

9. While the ACGB reported to the Minister for the Arts, its remit was limited to a fairly restrictive group of 'fine' arts like theatre, visual art, and classical music. Responsibility for related arts industries lay with other departments; for example, the film industry was overseen by the Department of Trade and Industry, radio and television communication were supervised by the Home Office, and the Treasury and the Environment Department were responsible for arts activities, such as the national galleries, that were relevant to their remits.

REFERENCES

Abercrombie, Nigel (1982) *Cultural Policy in the United Kingdom*, Paris: UNESCO.

Central Office of Information (1993) *The Arts*, London: HMSO.

Dale, Iain (Ed.) (2000) *Labour Party General Election Manifestos 1900-1997*. London: Routledge.

Department of Culture, Media and Sport (1999) *Creative Industries Exports: Our Hidden Potential*, London: DCMS.

—— (2001) *Creative Industries Mapping Document 2001*, London: DCMS.

—— (2001) *Culture and Creativity: The Next Ten Years*. London: DCMS.

—— (1999) *Report of Policy Action Team 10*. London: DCMS.

—— (2000) *Report on the Creative Industries Finance Conference: Connecting Creativity with Capital*. London: DCMS.

—— (2000) 'Speech by Arts Minister, Alan Howarth, to UNESCO Round Table of

Ministers of Culture'. 13 December 2000. London: DCMS.

Egan, Michael (Ed) (1972) *Ibsen: The Critical Heritage*. London: Routledge and Kegan Paul.

Gray, Clive (2000) *The Politics of the Arts in Britain*. London: Macmillan.

Hewison, Robert (1984) 'Public Policy: Corporate Culture: Public Culture'. *The Arts in the World Economy: Public Policy and Private Philanthropy for a Global Cultural Community*. Ed. Robert Freeman et al. Hanover: UP of New England.

Hutchison, Robert (1982) *The Politics of the Arts Council*. London: Sinclair Browne.

Kershaw, Baz (1999) 'Discouraging Democracy: British Theatres and Economics, 1979-1999'. *Theatre Journal* 51.3: 267-284.

—— (1992) *The Politics of Performance: Radical Theatre as Cultural Intervention*. London: Routledge.

Labour Party (1977) *The Arts and the People: Labour's Policy Towards the Arts*. London: Labour Party.

Lewis, Justin (1990) *Art, Culture and Enterprise: The Politics of Art and the Cultural Industries*. London: Routledge.

Marcuse, Herbert (1978) *The Aesthetic Dimension: Toward a Critique of Marxist Aesthetics*. Trans. and Rev. Herbert Marcuse and Erica Sherover. Boston: Beacon.

Marshall, David (1986) *The Figure of Theater: Shaftesbury, Defoe, Adam Smith, and George Eliot*. New York: Columbia UP.

McKinnie, Michael (2001) 'Urban National, Suburban Transnational: Civic Theatres and the Urban Development of Toronto's Downtowns'. *Theatre Journal* 53.2: 253-276.

Minihan, Janet (2001) *The Nationalisation of Culture*. London: Hamish Hamilton.

Rawnsley, Andrew (2001) *Servants of the People: The Inside Story of New Labour*. London: Penguin.

Shaw, Roy (1987) *The Arts and the People*. London: Jonathan Cape.

Smith, Adam (1984) *The Theory of Moral Sentiments*. Indianapolis: Liberty Fund.

Smith, Chris (1998) *Creative Britain*. London: Faber and Faber.

Willett, John Ed. and Trans (1964) *Brecht on Theatre*. London: Methuen.

Worthen, W.B. (1992) *Modern Drama and the Rhetoric of Theater*. Berkeley: U of California P.

12. Balancing acts: empire, race and Blairite discourses of development

Pat Noxolo

INTRODUCTION

During its first year in power, in November 1997, the new Labour government presented a white paper on international development to the British parliament: *Eliminating World Poverty: A Challenge for the 21st Century* (EWP). By presenting this white paper, the first since 1980, so early in its term, the government signalled the importance of development issues in its own self-definition. Its declarations in favour of poverty alleviation and global equality served as guarantees, addressed both to interest groups within Britain and to other governments, of the Blair government's moral character. It is one of the arguments of this chapter that development policies have been one important instrument for shaping the economic and political relationships between new Labour and other governments (both those in the so-called third world, and those in the first).[1]

In this chapter I explore New Labour's development policies by taking the EWP as the point of departure. My method is to read the report critically, and to place it within a larger historical context, particularly the history of imperial and post-imperial discourses. I suggest that many of the themes that emerge – especially the stress on Britain's fulcrum role, the representation of power as 'partnership', and the peculiar, one-sided constructions of 'agency' in the world – testify to the persistence (though not necessarily conscious) of imperial and racist frameworks. This only partly conscious colonial legacy is a pervasive feature of New Labour's production of Britain's relationships in the world more generally, especially in relation to questions of global poverty and the third world.

BALANCING MANY RELATIONSHIPS

The document is at pains to mark out a network of international relationships that gives to the British government its external shape. It outlines the concept of 'partnerships' to describe the relationships the British government proposes to have with selected third-world governments. It places the British government's development targets firmly in the context of international development targets agreed at United Nations (UN) conferences. At the same time it proposes for the British government a peculiar position, unlike that of any other 'on the fulcrum of global influence' (EWP: 20). This fulcrum or pivotal role is based on simultaneous membership of the Group of Seven industrialised countries (G7), the European Union (EU), the UN Security Council and the Commonwealth, to which is often added the 'special relationship' with the United States. The Blair government's distinctive identity is seen as directly derived from its relationships with other governments.

Managing so complex a network, with such diverse responsibilities and roles, is a difficult balancing act. Maintaining a visible role in international development is one way of keeping these relationships going. This integral relationship between development and self-definition can be seen, in a contrasting mode, in the Fundamental Expenditure Review (FER) which was the previous Conservative government's Overseas Development Administration's (ODA) final major document on international development, published in 1996. FER overtly debated the value of overseas aid for the British government at a time when international development seemed a low priority for a number of reasons. It noted how international development was now subsumed under the Foreign Office, was tied increasingly to spending on British goods, and had dropped from 0.50 per cent of Gross National Product (GNP) in 1979 to 0.31 per cent in 1994, a reduction continued through to1997/8 when aid was a mere 0.26 per cent of GNP (FER: 22). FER pointed out that, apart from any moral arguments, countries that receive aid from Britain were much more likely to buy British goods (with or without tying). Aid could also be used to exert influence on third-world governments to maintain stable political environments, and to create economic environments that promote trade with first-world countries; in addition, membership of the G7, the UN Security Council and the EU carried with it an obligation to contribute to the collective aid-giving of these organisations, alongside security and other costs (FER: 18-22). All this provided the context for the Conservatives' Aid and Trade Provision (ATP) – which enabled aid to be tied to trade – and for the resulting Pergau Dam scandal of 1994.[2]

In the face of such Conservative scepticism and instrumentalism towards aid, the Labour government early signalled its strong commitments to aid, and constructed its patterns of international relationships somewhat differently. It created a new government department, the Department for International Development (DFID). It abolished the Aid and Trade Provision, and advocated the untying of aid (EWP: 43), although bilateral aid is not yet completely untied.[3] It committed itself to reversing the decline in government aid spending, pushing the percentage up from 0.27 per cent in 1998 to a projected 0.33 per cent in 2004.

However, international development policy not only helps to ensure continuation of important relationships; it also helps to maintain their quality, and specifically their power differentials. My argument is that these power differentials are underpinned not only financially – by the ability to give aid and the need to receive it – but also discursively – by post-imperialist and neo-imperialist structures of power that draw their moral force (their impression of rightness, of inevitability) from racialised assumptions.

POST-IMPERIAL DISCOURSE? BALANCING PAST AND PRESENT

EWP begins with a context-giving narrative. It is a story exclusively of 'the last fifty years' (EWP: 8), this being the third in a series of white papers on international development published by Labour governments within a year of taking office (the first two were in 1965 and 1975). This fifty-year time frame defines New Labour as part of a *post*-imperial British tradition in its relationships with a formally independent third world. The first white paper (1965) is said to have been a response to the challenge of 'manag[ing] the transition from colonial empires to a world characterised by independent states' (EWP: 8). EWP also places current British interventions *within* a development era, the parameters of which are officially defined by the UN and the Bretton Woods institutions (EWP: 8). This was an era, ostensibly, of international co-operation to eradicate poverty – but *it precedes* the late 1970s, since when, according to the document, international development has been dominated by the Cold War and the neo-imperial preoccupations of the US and USSR (EWP: 9, see also Esteem 1997, and Escobar 1995). The 1997 white paper itself arrives *after* the Cold War, at the beginning of a 'new era' (EWP: 9), which is characterised by the end of neo-imperialism and the start of a 'global society' (EWP: 10). So the new government deliberately excludes itself from the traditions both of imperialism and neo-imperialism, but includes itself in its own Labour tradition. The opening narrative describes a 'quest for international development' (EWP: 8), during which Labour governments have done battle repeatedly on behalf of a third world defined by poverty, but also by incompetence and division. All this has taken place in an 'international climate' (EWP: 9) that is as impassive and as destructive as the weather, and quite unconnected, of course, with what is benignly described as the 'international community'.

In this opening narrative, therefore, the new government gives itself a decisive international shape by shearing off the imperialist and neo-imperialist past and aligning itself with an international harmony of purpose. Whatever Labour is, whether Old or New, it is not imperial, whether old or 'neo'-.

However, the internationalism that remains is not, for all this, imperialism-free. A brief look at the narrative's thumbnail sketch of the new

era of globalisation illustrates the ways in which imperialism continues
to breathe in Blairist international development discourse:

> Decisions taken in London, New York or Tokyo can have a profound
> effect on the lives of millions far away. We travel to distant places and
> trade with people of whom our grandparents knew little. We are mutu-
> ally dependent. If our grandchildren are to have a safe future, we must
> improve opportunities for all the children of the world (EWP: 10).

The three major global cities, situated at the heart of former imperial
and neo-imperial centres, still stand in neo-imperial relationships of
power and influence over former colonial outposts. As Michael Manley
put it: 'If America sneezes, we all catch a cold' (Manley, 1987: 8). The
'we' and 'our' in the passage from the EWP are (deliberately?) ambiguous, yet the context establishes clear 'us' and 'them' boundaries in the
very same geographical and political places as before. The slippage of
time and space through which both 'our grandparents' and 'we' are
coeval with the same timeless 'people' – and equally 'distant' from
them (despite numerous migrations) – taps into racialised assumptions
of timeless civilisations, kick-started into meaningful history only by
the catalyst of a dynamic western civilisation, and always remaining
distinct. The threat to the safety of 'our grandchildren' posed by 'the
children of the world' taps into imperial and aristocratic fears of
'revolting peasants/natives' that are centuries old. Moreover, these
latent imperial geographies cast shadows over the character of the
'mutual dependency' that 'we' share – after all, imperial centres have
always relied on their colonies to bring them wealth, whereas for
colonies and 'post-colonies', 'dependency' has not always been either
desirable or lucrative for any except a small minority.[4]

I am not of course suggesting that instead of trying to disengage
itself from the old imperialisms, New Labour ought to embrace them.
This opening paragraph of the Blairite document can be read, as can its
policies, as a direct (and welcome) reaction to the attitudes of the previous administration towards international development. The previous
Conservative administration proclaimed all too proudly that Britain's
formal development efforts began with the Colonial Development Act
of 1929, when 'the British Government's responsibility for the development of her colonies on a continuing basis was first recognised'
(FER: 27). Here the possessive pronoun 'her' activates the dual force of
'natural' maternal belonging and an 'imposed' military subjection
related to the colonial iconography of the great Britannia. And the
document which followed this Conservative administration's preamble
uncritically characterised Britain's post-war development role as an
extension of this same relationship.

What I want to suggest in this chapter, however, is that a decision to
disengage from imperialism will require much more radical change

than anything we have seen so far from the Blair government. Imperialist assumptions continue to infuse Blairite development discourse, despite attempts to claim otherwise. They are expressed in the ways in which power relationships – and, as we shall see, agency – are rendered into spatial and temporal relationships. Race is purposely not voiced within twenty-first century international discourses: after anti-imperialist movements, the rise and containment of European fascism through two world wars, US civil rights struggles, and arguments over South Africa in the Commonwealth (see Chan, 1988), overt racism has become unutterable in international arenas. Yet the postcolonial underpinnings of British governmental relationships mean that race continues to form the base for its discourse of development.[5] In the rest of this chapter I am going to extend the brief analysis above, showing that racialised imperialism continues to supply the moral force for the continuation of international inequalities; the justification for countless first-world interventions; and the fear that fuels innumerable impositions of order. Again, I am not suggesting that the Blair government is involved in an overtly racist global conspiracy – in fact a certain kind of anti-racism is part of the discourse. However, the continuation of racialised *traditions* is decisive, in the sense that the Blair government has decided to continue the inequalities, interventions and impositions of imperialist and neo-imperialist development paradigms through numerous policies, practices and rhetorics. It is racialised assumptions, both historical and contemporary, that allow these injustices to continue and serve to give them their moral force.

BALANCING DEVELOPMENT AND STASIS: RACIST CONSTRUCTIONS OF TIME

The early twentieth century was a time of great debate in Britain about the meanings of race and racial difference, heavily informed by the struggle to retain imperial possessions against the rising tide of anti-imperialism. It is in this context that the first Colonial Development and Welfare Act was passed in 1929. Seven years previously, Lord Frederick Lugard's widely read and influential book, *The Dual Mandate in British Tropical Africa*, set out one important side of the debate. Britain, he asserted, had a responsibility to make the wealth of the tropics available to the rest of the world because 'the tropics are the heritage of mankind [sic]' (Lugard, quoted in Spurr, 1993: 28). Although the 'darker races' inhabited these places, it was only Europeans who knew how to fully exploit them. Indigenous people, therefore, had no right to resist the Europeans in doing so. The second part of Lugard's dual mandate was that Britain had a moral responsibility to protect the people of the tropics – as weaker and more vulnerable races – from excessive social disruption. In effect black people were excluded from entering into industrialisation and commerce in ways that might compete with British commerce.

Moreover, the dual mandate did not include either education or social welfare programmes, since either of these would only disrupt the 'natives'' traditional way of life (see Havinden and Meredith, 1993: 312). This version of internationalism turned Britain's economic imperative to keep these territories under British control into a moral imperative. The world's resources simply had to be taken out of the control of black people and controlled by whites for the greater good of all humanity. Black people were to provide the cheap labour to make it happen.

This conservative racist construction contrasted with forms of racialised developmentalism that were cohering around the Commonwealth ideal during the First World War. Developmentalists opposed ideas of fixed racial difference as the moral foundation of the British Empire, and argued instead for the Empire as an instrument for the evolution of the 'backward races', arguing that the higher evolution of the white races, as represented by the English as the highest, was not so much a question of their 'breed' as of their institutions:

> In the course of the last few thousand years the people of Europe have distinguished themselves from those of Asia, Africa, America and Oceania by their higher capacity for adaptation ... The English had advanced further than the other nations of Europe in replacing the personal authority of rulers by laws based on the experience of those who obeyed them and subject to revision in the light of future experiences (Curtis, quoted in Rich, 1986: 62).

It was the responsibility of the British Empire, through its Commonwealth ideals and institutions, to bestow this rule of law upon 'backward races' in order to advance their development.

After the Second World War, these ideas of racial evolution through the adoption of first-world institutions formed the cornerstone of the international development discourses put forward by the Bretton Woods institutions, particularly in the group of ideas known as modernisation theory, and elaborated most famously in W. W. Rostow's *The Take-Off into Self-Sustained Growth* (1956).[6] Rostow described five evolutionary stages of development, from 'traditional society' (which largely described the societies of the world as they were 'discovered' by Europeans) to maturity (which largely described European societies). All countries would naturally follow this same path, unless they were blocked by distortions (flawed policy choices for example, or reactionary cultures). Development policies were aimed at pushing 'backward' or 'developing' countries more quickly from one stage to the next, and often integral to this approach were complex explanations as to why third-world societies were *not* developing in the prescribed way – why there was relative stasis. Although the language had now changed from 'backward/undeveloped races' to 'backward/undeveloped countries', the racialised temporal and spatial dichotomy between development and stasis remained intact.[7]

Even though modernisation theory has been formally subject to much criticism, most notably from dependency theorists, the dichotomy between development and stasis continues to inform Blairite development discourse. Third-world countries appear as static in their poverty, and third-world governments appear incapable of the kind of independent action that might lead to their own development. First-world intervention is seen as the only means of development for those whose status as 'developing' never seems to end.

Throughout the EWP, third-world countries are repeatedly pictured as static. The 'challenges' of third-world poverty are described in snapshots, frozen in time:

> Some 1.3 billion people ... continue to live in extreme poverty ... They feel isolated and powerless ... (EWP: 10).

> Over 1.3 billion people do not have access to safe water. Eight hundred million people are hungry or malnourished (EWP: 24).

> an estimated 150 million primary age children do not go to school (EWP: 25).

Where there is change, it is itself accompanied by stasis:

> The overall proportion of illiterate adults has been falling but the uneducated children of today will be the illiterate adults of tomorrow' (EWP: 25).

Or it amounts to change for the worse: the same situation – only more so.

> The second half of the twentieth century has seen unprecedented changes in the size, structure and setting of the world's population ... Ninety-five percent of the current growth is in developing countries, least well-equipped to cope with the consequences (EWP: 27).

Any change deemed positive is to be brought about by the first world. EWP is full of animating pictures of development 'challenges' and 'responses', and phrases that are replete with active verbs in future tenses, emphasizing purpose:

> Great progress has been made and more is possible if *we* build on this experience (EWP: 12, my emphasis).

> We will treat water as both a social and economic good ... (EWP: 24).

We will support policies and projects for which poor people are the immediate and direct beneficiaries ... (EWP: 29).

Third-world governments are seen as potential agents of development, but only in partnership with first-world governments. Otherwise they make 'policy errors' (EWP: 9), or are 'not committed to the elimination of poverty' (EWP: 39). They do not seem to have learnt from past development failures and moved on, as first-world governments have, into a new era of synthesis and balance. They must be made to move, otherwise, according to this discourse, they will not move at all.

There is clearly something quite constitutional and fixed about the inability of these spatially very separate third-world countries and governments to join the same time frames as the developed world. What is preserved here from older imperial discourses is judgement about others which by implication ascribes stasis to fixed and ingrained features – which operate with all the necessary determinacy of theories of racial difference – even where they are social or cultural in character.

ERASING THIRD-WORLD AGENCY
Britain's role in providing aid is highly visible within its development discourse, but the agency of governments and non-governmental groups in third-world nations is erased. Where third-world economies have in fact experienced growth, independent policy choices on the part of governments are also erased in (at least) three ways.

First, their agency is hidden away behind the rhetoric of a natural development that is taking place along the lines of the Rostowian idea of 'stages of growth'. So, for example, some countries are deemed unsuitable as 'partners' for Britain: 'because [they] have *progressed* beyond the *stage* of their economic development where we would be justified in making available substantial concessional financial resources' (EWP 2.23: 39, emphasis supplied). Although, in the document's own terms, these countries are 'successful', success does not arise from independent third-world agency (choices backed up by action), but occurs, rather, through a progression that is held to be 'natural', but is defined by the first world.

Second, 'successful' third-world agency is hidden behind first-world agency, so that it is pictured as mere compliance or obedience to first-world policy prescriptions:

> The experience of recent years in the most successful developing countries has clearly demonstrated the value of maintaining a sound fiscal balance and low inflation. Equally it has shown the value of promoting more open and less regulated domestic and foreign trade (EWP: 18).

These 'values' correspond to the policy recommendations of the international financial institutions (IFIs). Independent agency is appropriated as first-world agency, the third-world governments having merely executed the prescriptions of first-world managers.

Third, the policy choices of third-world governments who have deliberately chosen to go against policy prescriptions are nonetheless represented as compliance. So, for example, we are told that in the 1980s: 'in much of Asia growth was robust, reflecting long-standing investment in education and generally sound economic policies' (EWP 1.4). 'Sound' or 'sensible' economic policies in the EWP consistently means those advocated by the IFIs – an open economy alongside 'a framework of law and regulation within which people can exercise their rights' (EWP: 16). But the phrase 'generally sound' belies a discrepancy that was the subject of intense debate in the late 1980s and early 1990s. Writers like Amsden (1990) have demonstrated that in fact the Asian 'tigers' (Taiwan, Singapore, Hong Kong and South Korea) experienced growth as a consequence of intense state regulation – which 'distorted' prices, used tariffs to protect the home market, subsidised inputs and controlled big business. Furthermore, their governments were often extremely authoritarian and anti-democratic, creating a labour force that was highly educated in terms of the application of new technology, while being politically relatively powerless. The path chosen was very far from that prescribed in the first world – it was defiantly deviant and yet outstandingly successful in terms of economic growth.

BALANCING POWER AND 'PARTNERSHIP'

The EWP introduces with great fanfare the concept of 'partnerships' to describe its relationships with third-world countries. This concept has, in fact, a long history in British governmental discourses of international development, stretching back to the immediate aftermath of the Second World War. At that time, the Labour government re-packaged the empire, in order to try to reconcile British opinion and US pressures. At a time when many citizens were returning from overseas having fought hard for the retention of British colonial possessions, it sought to maintain a consensus in favour of empire, while attentive to an increasingly powerful US government, which combined an old grudge against British imperialism with new competitive neo-imperialist aspirations of their own (Darwin, 1988; see also Rich, 1986). 'Partnership' at this time was not at all about the British government sharing international power with independent third-world governments; rather, it was about maintaining unequal power relations whilst seeking to share international power and status with the key 'partner' – the USA.

This suggests that we might read the return of the rhetoric of partnership within Blairite discourse as not so much a signal to third-world governments of the British government's desire for mutual acceptance and equality, but more as a signal to other powerful members of the international community of Britain's desire to continue the inequalities of power that contribute to its status in the world. Certainly, partnerships are elaborated as thoroughly unequal relationships. The British government plays the 'adult' role of disciplinarian and provider to third-world governments, who seem to be children, presenting 'challenging' behaviour. Britain stipulates the terms and conditions under which it will enter into partnership, stating moreover that it will only enter into partnership where it 'has the influence to play a positive role' (EWP, panel 14: 39). Crucially, Britain retains the right to assess and evaluate the performance of its 'partners', and to decide when and how to give 'partner' governments more liberty to decide independently how aid money should be spent:

> Where we have confidence in the policies and budgetary allocation process and in the capacity for effective implementation in the partner government, we will consider moving away from supporting specific projects to providing resources more strategically in support of sector-wide programmes or the economy as a whole (EWP: 38).

The terms and conditions that Britain demands for its money are set out as a kind of contract with a list of bullet points introduced by the words: 'We would expect partner governments to: ... ' (EWP: 39). The document also lists those to whom Britain will refuse 'partnership': countries which are not poor enough, or any government which 'is not committed to the elimination of poverty, is not pursuing sound economic policies or is embroiled in conflict' (EWP: 39); to which are added 'countries in which the UK is not well-placed to make an effective impact, where others [multilateral institutions or other bilateral donors] must *lead*' (EWP: 39). This construction of partnership is a formal display of power that carries as its moral force echoes of 'trusteeship' – the racialised assumption that third-world countries must be controlled and led by the first world for their own good. Partnership is therefore as much about the new Blair government asserting itself as a powerful first-world government as it is about establishing new developmental relationships with third-world governments.

IN THE BALANCE?

'Partnership', as we have seen, emerged at the point at which old imperial power was fundamentally challenged both by the USA and by impending decolonialisation. Under the terms of this first partnership, indeed, the empire was to disappear. In a similar way today, the re-emergence of the discourse of partnership is a reaction to the threat of a greater loss of power.

Development has become an extremely competitive arena for the buying and selling of international influence, and Britain is increasingly unable to compete with other donors for centrality of influence in third-world countries. In fact, in recent years Britain has been forced to all but withdraw from some middle-income countries in order to focus its development assistance on fewer recipients, given that, 'we have limited financial and human resources' (EWP: 39). The moderation of this statement masks the frank admission made by the last Conservative government. As FER put it, Britain ...

> ... is unlikely to be able to 'afford' the size of programme which would buy it greater influence in [the middle-income regions of] south-east Asia, Latin America and CEE/FSU. Middle-income countries have enough resources of their own and enough interest from other donors (who are likely to get substantial returns on their investment) that the British government would have to outbid others in order to buy influence. This it cannot afford to do.

It therefore recommended focusing aid on fewer countries (FER: 104).

Due to its need to form alliances for greater strength on the world stage, Britain has increasingly had to merge its development assistance with that of other donors. Most of the policy-based grants and loans with which the British government is involved happen in the overall context of the European Union (EU), or of the structural adjustment programmes of international financial institutions' (IFIs) – in particular those of the World Bank and the International Monetary Fund. Policy-based loans from the IFIs are characterised by 'policy conditions designed to increase the probability of repayment' (Mosley, 1992: 129). British programme aid can either be 'co-financed' with the IFIs – in which case IFI conditionality applies directly – or 'co-ordinated' with the IFIs, meaning that:

> the programme aid grant is not linked to specific Bank actions but is generally conditional on the progress of the adjustment programme ... this is normally defined by an IMF arrangement being in place and staying on track (Sandersley, 1992: 58).

Despite the impression that terms and conditions are set independently by Britain (see EWP: 39), the IFIs define the conditions to which third-world countries are meant to comply, and these conditions are very much associated with the ability to repay as well as with longer-term macroeconomic agendas. As Sandersley puts it:

> Donors rely on the [International Monetary] Fund and [the World] Bank to do the running and make the important judgements as to when the time is ripe for a programme to be brought to their Boards, and that the resulting package is sufficiently substantial and the 'best' one available in the circumstances (Sandersley, 1992: 62).

This is one reason why, in the first section of the EWP, so much emphasis is placed on conforming to internationally agreed development targets (e.g. EWP: 19-21).

Moreover, the relative freedom of choice of third-world countries in a competitive aid situation, however constrained, can no longer in practice be denied. Trading relationships with Britain are not the primary focus of many former colonial countries (Segal: 1994), and the bargaining power of aid recipient governments can vary according to the market. Those who are selling influence may have some limited space to make decisions in their own favour if the conditions are right – for example if there is competition for what they are selling, or if the buyer is ignorant of or intimidated by the situation. Furthermore, the history of what is called 'conditionality' (the tying of aid to definite conditions) shows that it is far from easy to ensure that donor countries will achieve the results or influence they have paid for. Weighed and balanced against intra-national political and economic considerations, recipient governments often find that they cannot or need not make the policy changes that the donor countries have specified. As Maingot (1994) points out in the context of the small island states of the Caribbean and their complex inter-relationships with the superpower on their doorstep, even the most ostensibly weak states do have some room to negotiate situations in their favour, if they are shrewd and flexible enough.

Maingot argues that Caribbean political leaders have been able to negotiate in their own favour, despite attempts to constrain them, by using three main strategies. Firstly, they have recognised that all sovereign states are always to some extent constrained, just as individuals always exercise their freedom in the context of societal constraints; and they have sought to work out how best to maximise the advantages and reduce the costs of those constraints. Secondly they have tried to understand and manipulate the geopolitical situation in which the US finds itself at any one time, particularly through highlighting shared interests. And, thirdly, they have recognised that the US is 'an open system', which means that there is a possibility of ...

> ... skilful use or mobilisation of the transnational networks created by immigration and racial and ethnic allies in the metropolis. This can result in their participation in the setting of the bilateral and multilateral agenda of the region's international relations, as well as influencing the nature of the language of the diplomacy of those agendas (Maingot, 1994: 246).

Thus Blair's development policies have to operate in an environment where they are in competition for influence with other powerful states, and where the market for influence confers some bargaining power on those to be influenced. The marginal power that aid-receiving governments can exercise, however, does not gainsay our larger arguments, especially those about the power that is sought by donors, and the unequal nature of the partnerships proffered

RESTORING THE BALANCE? THE IMPERIAL LEGACY AS RESOURCE AND LIABILITY

It is clear that the government is involved in a balancing act between the needs and priorities of many 'partners' in an interdependent world. At best the 'fulcrum' position claimed in the EWP is one of 'influence', not of power or domination. But it is in this context that the government has continued to draw on a discourse of development that constructs imaginary relationships between donors and recipients on imperial lines. Indeed, as our argument might predict, this rhetoric has acquired an exaggerated force in the face of the Bush government's tendencies to unilateral action, and its repeated breaking of international 'partnerships' and agreements. The more British power weakens in the face of its most powerful 'partners', the stronger the imperial residues appear in political rhetoric.

Thus, in Tony Blair's well-known speech to the Labour Party conference of October 2001, in the middle of the anti-terrorist moment, all the familiar imperial images re-appear. Britain again is at the centre, between the USA and Europe, part of an 'international community' certainly, but the key element in its orchestration. Again, there is a deep polarisation between third-world victimhood and first-world agency. A stereotypical 'Africa' is 'a scar upon the conscience of the world'. Moreover:

> The starving, the wretched the dispossessed, the ignorant, those living in want and squalor from the deserts of northern Africa to the slums of Gaza, to the mountain ranges of Afghanistan: they too are our cause.

'We' respond to 'our' cause by rescuing 'them':

> This is the moment to seize. The kaleidoscope has been shaken. The pieces are in flux. Soon they will settle again. Before they do, let us reorder this world around us.

This 'heroic' drawing on racialised traditions, as with the parallel use of anti-terrorist rhetorics, strengthens the government's grip on global power in the short term by giving it an influence – at least a certain 'moral' leadership – in relation to Bush's USA, the partners in Europe and the wider 'international community'. In the long term, however, insofar as New Labour continues to embrace, in the international field, the dominant neo-liberal solutions of the IFIs, the US government and the big corporations, it will only compound the long-term global inequalities that are still on the increase in the twenty-first century (see Wade, 2001). If the Blair government really wants a mission, it could be to make its own decisive break with racialised imperialism, and to use any influence it has not just to alleviate extreme poverty, but to push for a fundamental redefinition of the balance of global power.

NOTES

1. Throughout this chapter I will be referring to the first world and the third world. Although these terms may appear offensive or archaic, I have chosen them over the other available terms for two main reasons. First, despite the diversity of these countries and the fracturing of the non-aligned movement in recent years, both of which have led many to abandon the term (see for example Bayart, 1991, and Westlake, 1991), 'third world' retains the hope of a possible 'third way' with more prominence given to the perspectives of that majority of the earth's population which sees mainly the underside of progress, or in other words: 'all those nations which, during the process of formation of the existing world order, did not become rich' (Abdalla, quoted in Thomas, 1992). It was with this hope in mind that third-world leaders began to use the term in the post-independence years. By using the term 'third world' within a critique of unequal development relationships, and recognising the understandable souring of the post-independence optimism with which it was first coined, my aim is to reassert the positive oppositional spin of the term. Second, although 'third world' took on a pejorative connotation in relation to the 'capitalist first world, communist second world, everyone else third world' split of the Cold War era, I would rather draw attention to the process of pejoration itself, and to the unfair discourses which surround it, than bury these unequal relationships under a mound of euphemisms.

   Most alternatives to first-/third-world ('developed'/ 'developing'/ 'undeveloped'/ 'underdeveloped'/ 'less developed' or 'advanced'/ 'backward') reinforce the idea that some countries are a model to which others must aspire. The geographically-inspired 'north' and 'south' appear to be neutral, but geography is not always as neutral or simply descriptive as it looks. Finally, although my work does draw on the legacy of dependency theories, the terms 'centre/periphery' suggest a relationship that is too fixed in a general sense. Although these terms do highlight a general theory of expropriation, they do not allow for the reciprocity which, though generally unacknowledged, is immanent in the development discourse, nor for the ways in which the discourse contains possibilities for decentring the first world. (See Thomas, 1992: 2-6 for a more in-depth analysis of the differences between these terms).

2. The Aid and Trade Provision (ATP) – which was designed to support projects which were 'of particular industrial and commercial importance to the UK' (Overseas Development Administration Information Department, 1992: 1) – has been discontinued, largely as a result of the very public scandal around the Pergau hydro-electric dam project in Malaysia. In November 1994 the British government was taken to court by the World Development Movement, and was found guilty in the High Court of acting illegally in abusing the provisions of the 1980 Overseas Development and Co-operation Act (see Chinnock et al., 1995: 93). What's more, studies carried out in the years immediately preceding the

rise of the Labour government concerning the economic effects of the ATP have found that this approach in fact brought very few real economic benefits for the UK economy as a whole (see Chinnock et al, 1995: 94).

3. The EWP emphasises that efforts are being made to reduce the levels of aid tying, although it is worth noting that previous governments have recognised that aid tying reduces the effectiveness of aid and have been looking into ways to mitigate its effects since 1965 (see Ministry of Overseas Development, 1965: 26). The FER in fact describes research which shows that 'general untying, either in the EU or the OECD, would be greatly to Britain's advantage, and that even unilateral untying would, over the longer term, have small benefits to the British economy' (FER: 124). In particular the FER observes that, although there would be short-term political opposition from the British businesspeople who currently benefit from tying, Britain would gain much in international prestige if it were to untie aid, because at the moment its levels of aid-tying are heavily criticised by the rest of the donor community.

4. See dependency theorists such as Cardoso (1982) and Frank (1966), as well as critiques such as Palma (1981).

5. Post-imperialism does not mean that imperialism is dead and buried, but invites a consciousness of what that history means in the present. As Hall puts it: 'one of the principal values of the term "post-colonial" has been to direct our attention to the many ways in which colonisation was never simply external to the societies of the imperial metropolis. It was always inscribed deeply within them – as it became indelibly inscribed in the cultures of the colonised (Hall, 1996: 246).

6. Bretton Woods institutions are those coming out of the meeting of heads of state at Bretton Woods in July 1944 to manage the post-war world order, namely the International Bank for Reconstruction and Development (the World Bank), the International Monetary Fund, the UN and the General Agreement on Tariffs and Trade (GATT) (see Hewitt, 1992: 222-4).

7. The blurred distinction between race and nation, as seen in phrases like 'this island race', has been a potent source of racialised conflict in European countries, suggesting that black immigration entails a loss of racial purity in European countries racialised as white (see for example Gilroy, 1987).

REFERENCES

Amsden, A. (1990) 'Third world industrialisation: global fordism or a new model?', in *New Left Review*, 189, July/August: 5-31.

Bayart, J.F. (1991) 'Finishing with the idea of the Third World: The Concept of the Political Trajectory', in J. Manor (ed.), *Rethinking Third World Politics* London: Longman.

Bhabha, H. (1994) *The Location of Culture*, London: Routledge.

Blair, T. (2001) Speech to Labour Party Conference October (printed in full *Guardian*, 3.10.01).

Bowen, H. (1998) 'British conceptions of global empire, 1756-83', in *The Journal of Imperial and Commonwealth History*, 26, 3: 1-27.

Brah, A., M. Hickman and M. Mac an Ghaill (eds.) (1999) *Global Futures: Migration, Environment and Globalization*, Basingstoke: Macmillan.

Brodber, E. (1988) *Myal*, London: New Beacon Books.
Cardoso, F.H. (1982) 'Dependency and Development in Latin America', in T. Shanin (ed.), *Introduction to the Sociology of Developing Societies*, Basingstoke: Macmillan.
Chan, S. (1988) The Commonwealth in World Politics: A Study of International Action 1965-1985 London: Lester Crook.
Chinnock, J., Curtis, M. and McFarlane, I. (1995) 'United Kingdom' in ACTIONAID (eds), *The Reality of Aid 1995: An independent Review of International Aid*, London: Earthscan.
Chambers, I. and L. Curti (eds.) (1996) *The Post-Colonial Question: Common Skies, Divided Horizons*, London: Routledge.
Darwin, J. (1988) *Britain and Decolonisation: The Retreat from Empire in the Post-War World*, Basingstoke: Macmillan.
Department for International Development (1997) *Eliminating World Poverty: A Challenge for the 21st Century*, London: The Stationery Office.
Escobar, A. (1995) *Encountering Development: The Making and Unmaking of the Third World*, Princeton: Princeton University Press.
Esteva , G. (1992) 'Development' in W. Sachs (ed.) *The Development Dictionary: A Guide to Knowledge as Power*, London: Zed Books.
Frank, A. (1966) 'The Development of Underdevelopment', *Monthly Review*, September: 3-17.
Gilroy, P. (1987) *There Ain't No Black in the Union Jack*, London: Hutchinson.
Hall, S. (1993b) 'Old and new identities, old and new ethnicities', in A. King (ed.), *Culture, Globalization and the World System*, Basingstoke: Macmillan.
Hall, S. (1996) 'When was the post-colonial? Thinking at the limit', in I. Chambers and L. Curti (eds.), *The Post-Colonial Question: Common Skies, Divided Horizons*, London: Routledge.
Havinden, M., and D. Meredith (1993), *Colonialism and Development: Britain and its Tropical Colonies 1850 –1960*, London: Routledge.
Hewitt, T. (1992) 'Developing countries – 1945 to 1990', in T. Allen and A Thomas (eds), *Poverty and Development in the 1990s*, Oxford: Oxford University Press.
JanMohamed, A. and D. Lloyd (eds.) (1990) *The Nature and Context of Minority Discourse*, Oxford: Oxford University Press.
Jess, P., and D. Massey (1995) 'The contestation of place', in D. Massey and P. Jess (eds.), *A Place in the World? Places, Cultures and Globalization*, Oxford: Oxford University Press.
King, A. (ed.) (1993) *Culture, Globalization and the World-System*, Basingstoke: Macmillan.
Lefebvre, H. (1991) *The Production of Space*, Oxford: Blackwell.
Maingot, A. (1994) *The United States and the Caribbean*, London: Macmillan.
Manley, M. (1987) *Up the Down Escalator: Development and the International Economy: A Jamaican Case Study*, New York: Andre Deutsch.
Massey, D., and P. Jess (eds.) (1995) *A Place in the World? Places, Cultures and Globalization*, Oxford: Oxford University Press.
Massey, D. (1999) 'Imagining globalization: power-geometries of time-space', in A. Brah, M. Hickman and M. Mac an Ghaill (eds.) *Global Futures: Migration, Environment and Globalization*, Basingstoke: Macmillan.

Mosley, P. (ed.) (1992) *Development Finance and Policy Reform*, London: Macmillan.

Mosley, P. (1992) 'A theory of conditionality', in P. Mosley (ed.), *Development Finance and Policy Reform*, London: Macmillan.

Noxolo, P. (1999) '"Dancing a Yard, Dancing Abrard": Race, Space and Time in British Development Discourses' (unpublished Ph.D thesis, Faculty of Humanities, Nottingham Trent University).

O'Callaghan, E. (1993) *Woman Version: Theoretical Approaches to West Indian Fiction by Women*, New York: Macmillan Press.

Overseas Development Administration (1995) *Fundamental Expenditure Review* (unpublished report).

Palma, G. (1981) 'Dependency and Development: a critical overview', in D. Seers (ed.), *Dependency Theory: A Critical Reassessment*, London: Frances Pinter.

Rich, P. (1986) *Race and Empire in British Politics*, Cambridge: Cambridge University Press.

Said, E. (1994) *Culture and Imperialism*, London: Vintage.

Sandersley, P. (1992) 'Policy-based lending: an ODA perspective', in P. Mosley (ed.), *Development Finance and Policy Reform*, London: Macmillan

Sangari, K. (1990) 'The politics of the possible', in A. JanMohamed and D. Lloyd (eds.), *The Nature and Context of Minority Discourse*, Oxford: Oxford University Press.

Spurr, D. (1993) *The Rhetoric of Empire: Colonial Discourse in Journalism, Travel Writing, and Imperial Administration*, Durham and London: Duke University Press.

Taylor, P. (1991) 'The English and their Englishness: "a curiously mysterious, elusive and little understood people"', in *Scottish Geographical Magazine*, 107, 3: 146-161.

Taylor, P. (1995) 'Beyond containers: internationality, interstateness, interterritoriality', in *Progress in Human Geography*, 19, 1: 1-15.

Thomas, A. (1992) 'Introduction', in T. Allen and A. Thomas (eds.), Oxford: Oxford University Press.

Wade, R. (2001) *Is Globalization Making World Income Distribution More Equal?*, London: LSE Development Studies Institute.

Westlake, M. (1991) 'The Third World (1950-1990) RIP', in *Marxism Today*, August: 14-16.

Worsley, P. (1999) 'Culture and development theory', in T. Skelton and T. Allen (eds.), *Culture and Global Change*, London: Routledge.

13. Mowlam, Mandelson and the broken peace: Northern Ireland and the contradictions of New Labour

Beatrix Campbell

On Good Friday 1998, a year after the election of the Labour government, a peace agreement (the Agreement) was signed in Belfast. The Agreement was hailed as one of the government's greatest achievements, and a personal triumph for New Labour's first Secretary of State for Northern Ireland Mo Mowlam and for Prime Minister Tony Blair. Yet, as so often with New Labour, democratic reform grounded in movements in civil society was to be checked by more traditionalist and authoritarian forces in government and state. Northern Ireland reveals with particular clarity the diverse forces struggling for sway within New Labour's magnetic field – forces refracted, in this case, through the first two New Labour Secretaries of State, Mo Mowlam and Peter Mandelson. In their tenures, which spanned the signing of the Agreement (1998) and the establishment of the new Northern Ireland government (1999), Mowlam and Mandelson came to personify diametrically contradictory tendencies within New Labour.

Their differences appeared especially over the warrants of the Agreement's founding spirit, which included a new culture of rights, de-militarization and the de-commissioning of weapons, reform of the police and security state, and recognition of the British state's complicity in assassinations. Equality and a new culture of rights were bequeathed directly by the terms of Agreement, and the constitution it inaugurated is documented below. The contested areas – policing and security, militarism, and the nature of the history of state collusion – were to be addressed within the spirit of the Agreement's 'new beginning' for Northern Ireland. These are the areas explored in this chapter, alongside the different approaches of Mowlam and Mandelson

Mowlam's pragmatic social progressivism infused her approach to the renovation of Northern Ireland and her efforts to represent all its people. This distinguished her from her predecessors, from Northern Ireland's new First Minister David Trimble (who performed unswervingly as a

221

unionist First Minister), and from her successor Peter Mandelson. Mandelson's authoritarian populism was comfortable with the security state and sympathetic to the Unionist leader, and led to the breakdown of the peace process. (It is interesting, but beyond the scope of this chapter, that these differences were repeated later – during President Bush's 'war on terrorism' and the invasion of Iraq. Mowlam's social progressivism converged with her anti-colonialist opposition to the war; Mandelson's authoritarian populism found expression in his support for Blair's 'new imperialism' (see Noxolo and Johnson, in this volume) and for the US as the fulcrum of global power in the new millennium.)

BACKGROUND TO THE AGREEMENT

Many of the conditions for the Agreement, even a template for it, were in place before 1997. Three of these conditions were especially important: first, the longer history of the emerging coalition for peace in Northern Ireland itself; second, New Labour's prior commitment to devolution generally; and, finally, the achievement and contradictions of New Labour's own hegemony within the Labour Party.

The making of the equality agenda

During the time of the Troubles it was customary for the principles of equality to be practically breached and semantically traduced: discrimination against Catholics was simultaneously practised and denied. Thus nationalism and republicanism were invigorated in the 1970s less by an affinity to the republic south of the border and more by the quest for equality and justice. For unionism, on the other hand, 'so-called equality' denoted a 'republican agenda'. Women's Coalition members Monica McWilliams and Kate Fearon have cautioned that the peace process did not necessarily reconcile unionism to a culture of rights or to constitutional nationalism. Rather, 'the emergence of constitutionalism *and* a culture of rights' enabled unionists to feel that their right to remain within the UK was secure. This then enabled the Ulster Unionist party (UUP) to concede 'a rights agenda in an environment in which they have denied the need for such rights' (McWilliams and Fearon, 1999). A cross-community dynamic underlay the Agreement's adoption of what it called 'the right to equal opportunity in all social and economic activity, regardless of class, creed, disability, gender or ethnicity'.

An important focus for these processes had been the labour movement, simultaneously enemy and practitioner of inequality. By the 1980s some of the most powerful trade unions were forced to face their own complicity in discrimination (against women and against Catholics) – under legal and international pressure. This challenged everyone: employers, the government, trade unions. In 1984 the Nobel peace prize-winner Sean MacBride had introduced what became known as the MacBride Principles. These adapted good, anti-discriminatory practice from the US (where it was targetted on racism), and took the form of securing equality measures through contract compliance, using the power of the purchaser or investor as a progressive, pro-active power. Public employees' leader Inez McCormack became a MacBride signatory. The principles were endorsed in Dublin, and by Labour in opposition at Westminster. The Thatcher government declared the Principles illegal, while a New York court declared them legal. Some powerful trade unionists, however, instead of embracing the Principles as an external tool of internal reform, joined the British Conservative government's delegations to the US to oppose anti-discrimination initiatives.

But the evidence of inequality was stark – unemployment among Catholics was 'well above the level observed in the worst-hit regions in mainland Britain ... and considerably higher than any disadvantaged ethnic minority in mainland Britain' (Rowthorn and Wayne, 1988). In the 1980s, catholic male unemployment, at 35 per cent, was two and a half times greater than Protestant male unemployment. As Chris McCrudden has argued, the campaign for the MacBride Principles began to fill, however partially and inadequately, 'the political vacuum caused by the failure of Northern Ireland's political institutions to address the issue adequately' (McCrudden, 1999).

By 1989, Conservative governments were under pressure, particularly from Europe and the US, to monitor and mainstream equality policies. Labour in opposition sought to push beyond anti-discrimination law and to impose on government departments a duty to promote equality and monitor progress, a proposal that the government refused to incorporate into statute. In 1993, however, guidelines were introduced for all Northern Ireland policy-making. They were the Policy Appraisal and Fair Treatment Guidelines (PAFT), a bureaucratic instrument that was to acquire extraordinary resonance among unions, women's organisations and a plethora of voluntary organisations (McCrudden, 1999).

'PAFT' entered the language of trade unionists. Inez McCormack noticed that the acronym acquired a life of its own, even becoming a verb in activist vernacular. When the award-winning human rights organisation, the Committee on the Administration of Justice, began to organise briefings for community organisations and the voluntary sector, it led to the birth of a loose 'equality coalition' (McCrudden, 1999); members included human rights campaigners, the public sector workers' trade union Unison, the Women's Support Network, the robust disability movement, and Northern Ireland's small in number but energetic ethnic minorities. This was one of the few anti-sectarian movements not to position itself outside or above cultures of difference, and it became what Mary Holland described as 'a parallel peace process', in many ways as important as the talks at Stormont (Holland, 1998). As McCrudden explained in an influential paper, 'the new approach envisaged equality and anti-discrimination as part of the ethos of decision-making across *all* spheres of government – in short, to mainstream fairness issues in public policy' (McCrudden, 1998). Mainstreaming, supported by rigorous monitoring, required the 'participation of those with an interest', and this was decisive – the participation of government and civil society in a dynamic dialogue. This was the background to the equality provisions in the Agreement.

The equality and social need provisions of the Agreement *were* popular, not least among parties closest to dispossessed working-class neighbourhoods in both unionist and nationalist territories. They were secured by these parties' active presence as negotiators. Their spirit infused the Good Friday Agreement and also extended to a Pledge of Office, which brought the equality duty 'to the service all of the people of Northern Ireland equally'. According to Professor of Jurisprudence, John Morrison, this had ...

> ... the potential to establish the foundation of a society where participation in a public civic space can take place in conditions of real equality, and where unjust differentials in power, from whatever source, public or private, can be addressed in an emancipatory project, which may have a tremendous resonance world-wide (Morrison, 1999).

New Labour and devolution

A second condition of the Agreement was Labour's policy on 'devolution'. Along with constitutional reform, it became the *marque* of New Labour's first term, and a focus of internal resistance and early disappointments. The new government bowed to the neo-nationalist consensus that had been consolidated by two decades of Toryism – and de facto Scots and Welsh disenfranchisement at Westminster. But devolution did not inaugurate a new constitutional paradigm: New Labour's approach was ad hoc and tactical, avoiding the re-positioning of England and Britain within a newly constituted archipelago, and merely reacting to irresistible movements in Northern Ireland, and powerful ones in Scotland and Wales, where political culture was left of centre and relatively unimpressed by New Labour's vaunted 'Third Way'.

Blairism simultaneously conceded and controlled devolution: it swiftly introduced legislation launching new governments in Edinburgh and Cardiff. Northern Ireland, however, presented a different challenge. While devolution there was also seen as necessary, its restoration after almost thirty years of the Troubles and direct rule from Westminster depended on a settlement that would both end the armed conflict and guarantee new terms of political engagement.

Devolution affected New Labour's Northern Irish profile. It made the party attractive to unionism as a way to resolve the 'democratic deficit' created by direct rule from Westminster. Labour's commitment to inclusivity in the peace process guaranteed unionism's place at the table. This was attractive to a unionism disillusioned with British Conservative governments, and encouraged it to soften its resistance to accommodation or power-sharing with nationalists, and to move into a new mindset: only an historic compromise with nationalism could release it from an adhesion to British rule that yielded little or no self-respect. In any case, republicanism's shift from abstention to assiduous participation in the political process (including representation in local government) left unionism with no immunity from power-sharing. Inclusivity and power-sharing were made more attractive for unionism by the Agreement's pledge that Northern Ireland's constitutional integrity as part of the UK could change only by consent. Trimble saw this as unionism retaining its veto (Trimble, 1998).

New Labour's hegemony

By 1997 New Labour and its new prince Tony Blair were enjoying unprecedented hegemony as the modernising agent in a Labour Party that had been routed by Thatcherism. I want to stress, however, the mixed political character of New Labour, which made it subject to contradictory tendencies, well illustrated in its gender politics.

New Labour in office was rewarded by a key sign of the modernisation of the 1980s – the successful campaigns to get more women into the House of Commons. Yet the macho megalomania of its leadership minimised their impact on the archaic and rowdy culture of the Commons. Regimented in the power-dressing livery of New Labour's dress code, these women were dubbed 'Blair's Babes'. Mo Mowlam (along with Clare Short) was one of the few leading women to break with these constraints (interestingly, they were also among the few women to have power bases outside the New Labour court). Thus Mowlam's modernising politics came from a particular strand within the Labour Party.

Tony Blair's coterie emerged in the early 1990s from the centre right, but was the beneficiary of Neil Kinnock's centre-left modernising mission. I have argued elsewhere that this group had tendencies that were both abject and authoritarian (Campbell, 1997). Successive electoral defeats had demoralised the social-democratic impulse in the party. New Labour subsequently emerged not so much as an ideology but as a coup, mesmerised by Thatcherism's *élan* and in recoil from the radicalisms proliferating in the party since the 1960s. The mission was to centralise the party's democratic structure and cement the leader's 'unquestioned control' (Hughes and Wintour, 1990). The modernising project, steered by Tony Blair and his allies, was re-incarnated as 'New Labour'. Mandelson, though disengaged from the rank and file, was one of its architects. Mowlam, a popular presence amidst the rank and file, had been a long-standing lieutenant of the modernisers. The newly remodelled party, 'reformed' and often 'hollowed out' (see Tincknell in this volume), brought its own contradictions to the handling of Northern Ireland. As we shall see, the very different *modus operandi* of Mowlam and Mandelson confirm that New Labour is no unified block or strategy.

Labour's massive electoral victory had opened up a big opportunity for a peace settlement in Northern Ireland. John Major's Conservative government had been paralysed by its precarious majority, and by its dependence on nine Ulster Unionist MPs. His political misfortune had effectively empowered the marginal Unionists and enabled them to impose their veto on the peace process. Labour's election, with a massive Parliamentary mandate, released the government from this dependence on unionism, and this, together with its commitment to modernising and reform, activated ambitions for a settlement.

NEW WOMAN, NEW BEGINNING: THE MO MOWLAM EFFECT

Undoubtedly the appointment of Mowlam as Secretary of State brought an unprecedented tone to the peace process. During direct rule from Westminster, the civil servants at Northern Ireland Office (NIO) reigned. The NIO culture was infused by the security ethic and a paranoia towards the equality coalition. It dominated local politicians, for whom the civil service had little respect, and could over-ride appointed Ministers for Northern Ireland, who usually had only a fleeting and often reluctant responsibility for their posts.

Mowlam was a middle-of-the-road social democrat, who personified the shift away from the formidable authority of Methodist respectability within the Labour tradition. She admitted to having lived a 'messy' personal life before her partnership with Jon Norton, a banker who later turned to painting. She was renowned for indiscriminate cuddles. She acknowledged that she'd smoked cannabis and that, unlike President Clinton, she'd inhaled. And she was game: she appeared hilariously on Graham Norton's camp comedy TV show in 1999, descending a staircase escorted by two golden men dressed only in loincloths, to officiate at the marriage of two dogs. She was the antithesis of the Christian moralism – not to say misogyny – of the men's movement that ran New Labour. She was an academic, with a relaxed (rather than religious) approach to morals and a pragmatic commitment to social justice. She represented pragmatic social progressivism within New Labour.

Her raunchy vernacular and affectionate manners extended not only to the aristocrats who sojourned at the Secretary of State's official residence, Hillsborough Castle, but also to the woman in the street, and to former combatants among both loyalists and republicans whom, she agreed, had to be engaged in the settlement and the new polity. She acquired a reputation as a raggedy saint amidst a besieged population, previously habituated to towering, posh patricians, dispatched to do time in Northern Ireland. She was remarkably popular – though she was not to the liking of patriarchal, conservative unionism, or to the jealous god of New Labour. For a British Secretary of State, Mowlam was unusually familiar with the territory. For all these reasons, she was the first Secretary of State who was not sequestered by Northern Ireland securocrats and civil servants – even though she sometimes seemed unable or unwilling to assert her power against the hostile NIO, who were not above leaking or briefing against her. Her chutzpah appeared to be exemplified by her readiness to go where Secretaries of State had feared to tread, whether it was a community centre in the republican inner city Falls, or the neighbouring loyalist Shankill. This confidence was consummately expressed by her visit in 1998 to the Maze Prison, the most fortified in Europe, to meet loyalist prisoners who were turning against the peace process. 'It was really of very little importance what was said – it was the act itself that held the meaning for them' (Mowlam, 2002).

Her progressive presence was detectable before and after the election, and within and after the Agreement itself. Before the 1997 general election she had already lent her endorsement to the movement for 'a statutory duty for government bodies to take equality of opportunity into account through more rigorous enforcement of the PAFT guidelines' (Mowlam, 1997). This was in opposition to the NIO which, shortly before the election, and knowing the likely outcome, launched what McCrudden describes as a sustained attack on PAFT (McCrudden, 1999). Her support for *statutory* rights and duties aligned her with the equality coalition.

It is clear that anxieties about this in Downing Street and the NIO included the fear of any 'read-across' from the Agreement eastwards over the Irish Sea – any application of the same principles to England. The NIO fought to mute it in the translation into legislation, and when the legislation came before Parliament it had a difficult passage. Secretary of State Mowlem defended the integrity of the Agreeement in the legislation however. Thus the outcome of these battles, Section 75 of the Act, requires public authorities to have 'due regard' – a significant duty – to the need to promote equality between persons of different religious beliefs, political opinions, ethnicities, sexual orientations, ages, marital status, ability/disability, between persons with and without dependants, and between men and women generally. This duty was to be followed through by impact assessment and monitoring. Mainstreaming, suggests McCrudden, had arrived.

Neither New Labour nor Mowlam created the Agreement's rights provisions – they were the fruits of a coalition between social activists and scholar activists, who had enlisted the resources of both state and civil society to yield 'huge change' in Northern Ireland. But, once alerted to their erasure in the translation into legislation, by statist and sectarian impulses, Mowlam used her power against the NIO to protect the mainstreaming that had – almost – arrived. The Agreement was finally signed in Spring 1998, and the referendums north and south of the border, which overwhelmingly endorsed it, harvested the ingenuity of its multiple participants and processes.

It is important to stress the centrality – and vulnerability – of the equality and rights agenda in the initial moves towards ending the Troubles. The Agreement scripted a unique culture of governance, which required the active engagement of civil society, *envisaging a new dialogue between direct and representative democracy*. The discipline of equality and human rights inscribed in the Agreement was incorporated in the institutional duties given to the new Northern Ireland state and its mechanisms of governance. These bureaucratic instruments contained the fascinating potential to 'move away from absolute notions of statehood, sovereignty, and territorial integrity, through devices of consociational government, cultural provision, human rights protections, and cross-border connections' (Bell, 2002). The duties of the new state transcended, and indeed transformed, the orthodox definition of Northern Ireland's problem. Thus, for example, the representation of the Troubles as the problem of armed republicanism – perpetuated through the debate about de-commissioning – found no echo in the agreement itself. De-commissioning and disarmament were to be part of a parallel process; paramilitary disarmament was to be part of the de-militarisation of Northern Ireland. The Agreement was innovative, potentially transforming, and beloved among its advocates. Its appeal crossed parties and communities. 'It is a thing of beauty', said Gusty Spence, the loyalist former Ulster Volunteer Force combatant from the loyalist community in the Shankill, whose imprisonment for the murder of a catholic in 1966 is described by some as 'starting' the Troubles, and whose passion for the peace process in the 1990s lent vital loyalist support to the ending of it.

Yet the Agreement remained vulnerable. The British government was under intense pressure from unionism to enforce linkages between the de-commissioning of arms and just about anything, particularly the creation of a new executive and the participation of republicans. Though this had been the major demand brought by unionism to the peace process, it was not written into the Agreement. Rather, a de-commissioning deadline was offered by Tony Blair as a last-minute personal codicil to encourage unionism to sign up to the deal; and indeed insistence on de-commissioning remained a hallmark of his approach. But, of course, it was the rules of democracy that the peace process had to reform. Mowlam, by contrast, while acknowledging the necessity for disarmament, also appreciated the high risks being faced by the negotiators, not least those closest to the paramilitaries. Nor – unlike Blair – did she traduce the energy and imagination republicans and nationalists had brought to the peace process.

THE NEW MAN – OLD TIMES: MANDELSON AND RECUPERATION

Peter Mandelson was Tony Blair's main man, a confidante, a king-maker in the beau Blair's court, whose reputation ranged from 'the prince of darkness', a malevolent and petulant fixer, to a witty and cosmopolitan exponent of the short-lived Third Way. He designed Neil Kinnock's 1987 election campaign, as the Labour Party's communications director, and left Kinnock deeply disappointed when he became Tony Blair's adviser after winning the parliamentary selection for Hartlepool – an unlikely proletarian constituency adjacent to Blair's Sedgefield. Mandelson and Philip Gould, New Labour's pollster, were perhaps the most eloquent exponents of the populist discourse of New Labour and its invocation of traditional power.

Mandelson's appointment as Northern Ireland Secretary of State came less than a year after his resignation in disgrace as Secretary of State for Trade and Industry. His fleeting exile from Blair's court was clearly intolerable, perhaps for the Prime Minister too, but his appointment was a response to David Trimble's hostility to Mowlam. The First Minister had routinely short-circuited Mowlam and taken himself directly to the 'top man' in Downing Street. And appeasement of the unionist leader had been accompanied by a toxic campaign of briefing from the NIO and Downing Street. Northern Ireland's most popular Secretary of State *ever*, the ambassador of new times, had become the subject of furtive complaint as a brain-damaged, scruffy, foul-mouthed sloth, an affront to the strait-laced respectability of unionist culture. Unionism was one of the most unreconstructed political cultures in the archipelago: intensely patriarchal, it had few women representatives, and its organised social base lay in the exclusive, secret and sexist regiments of masculinised Protestantism, the Orange Order.

Mandelson's appointment was represented as a gift to unionism. Here was Blair's envoy, a *man* unionism could do business with, a man who had assiduously courted the unionist establishment. His regency at Hillsborough proved to be brief but devastating – a regression to the *ancien régime*. His rapport with the security state was not untypical of secretaries of state, but after Mowlam's open-mindedness and accessibility, his methods startled those who encountered him. In contrast to Mowlam, Mandelson asserted New Labour's impatience with human rights discourse, and with Northern Ireland's lively NGOs and social movements. His main aim, it seems, was to sustain Trimble's leadership of the perilously fractured UUP, and to escort the reluctant party towards participation in a power-sharing, devolved government. Preserving Trimble had long been a New Labour aim, and had been shared by Mowlam, though qualified by her commitment to inclusivity. The new Secretary of State, however, did not disguise his function as a friend of unionism. Many observers close to the process were exasperated by the IRA's cliff-hanging refusal to de-commission without simultaneous de-militarisation by the British; but they were also shocked by the British government's acceleration of the crisis. Mandelson's most spectacular achievement was to force the collapse of Northern Ireland's first experience of devolved, power-sharing democracy, the Assembly and the executive.

When Mandelson arrived in Northern Ireland at the end of 1999 he was confronted by unionism's refusal to participate in the new government without IRA arms de-commissioning. As David McKittrick noted, 'practically everyone in Ireland', together with an international body set up to consider the issue, knew that this was 'an exam the IRA could not pass', even though it had ceased armed conflict (Mallie and McKittrick, 1996). Furthermore, de-militarisation also applied to the British Army, which had refused to make a symbolic gesture (Macintyre, 2000). In this admittedly difficult situation, Mandelson did in the end succeed in selling a deal to the UUP, but only at the cost of adopting Trimble's timetable – de-commissioning had to be delivered by February 2000, or Trimble would withdraw from the Executive. In February 2000, the deadline derived from Trimble's timetable was reached, without his conditions having been met, and Mandelson accordingly suspended the newly created Northern Ireland assembly. This crisis left the Irish government aghast – it was furious with IRA procrastination, but also with the British government's unilateral destruction of the new Assembly, which it regarded as constitutionally questionable (Kennedy, 2000).

The pro-Agreement parties complained bitterly that Mandelson had refused to meet with them to avoid the crisis. Though he appeared to be honouring the Prime Minister's personal pledge on decommissioning made to Trimble, he was also re-asserting British authority. Although the Assembly was the creation of an international treaty between Westminster and Dublin, although it was endorsed by a massive majority both sides of the border and in Washington, the wishes of all these parties were brushed aside in a destructive gesture that confirmed the subordination of the people and the residual potency of the unionist veto. Here was a Secretary of State behaving like a colonial Tory, an exemplary Tory for some unionists.

The difference between Mowlam and Mandelson was the difference between 'new beginnings' and the 'old tradition'. Unison's Inez McCormack observed that, unlike Mandelson, Mowlam had understood that the NIO and securocrats were not neutral. But Mandelson's choreography of the suspension of the Assembly had followed the UUP's agenda on de-commissioning. The precipitation of the crisis and the collapse of the Stormont government was recidivist, a dramatic re-alignment of New Labour, and a re-assertion of the colonial habit.

RESISTING REFORM ON POLICING AND STATE COMPLICITY

The reform of the RUC and the security state was promised, though not prescribed, by the Agreement. Again it was Mowlam who took the initiative. Because the 92 per cent Protestant RUC was beyond the reach of internal reform, she appointed an International Commission on Policing, chaired by former Conservative minister Chris Patten, a 'left' Tory, who had himself been exiled to Northern Ireland by Margaret Thatcher.

Patten's Commission proposed that the police must be representative, unarmed and accountable (Patten). A time-tabled recruitment programme was to ensure that a third of the police service would be of catholic origin and all officers were to swear an oath of commitment to equality and human rights. Patten criticised the Special Branch, the security section of the RUC, as a 'force within a force', urged action to deal with it, and recommended ending the power of the Secretary of State and the NIO over policing. However, by the time the legislation emerged from the secretive lair of the security-state in the NIO in the early summer of 2000 (and with Mandelson now in post), Patten had been shredded: the oath was to be for new recruits only, shielding bigots already in the force; the recruitment programme was reduced; and the Secretary of State's powers were actually increased. By excluding anyone with a 'criminal' record from participation in local police partnership boards, including combatants in the Troubles, by retaining the powers of Chief Constable and the Secretary of State to block investigations, and by refusing the details of Patten's plan for a Policing Ombudsman, the Bill traduced Patten's principles of representativeness and accountability. The Committee on the Administration of Justice, an internationally-renowned human rights organisation, concluded: 'there is no way the Chief Constable could be held to account'. Brendan O'Leary described the bill as 'a fundamental breach of faith, perfidious Britannia in caricature. It represents Old Britain; it was drafted by the forces of Conservatism' (O'Leary, B. 2000). Seamus Mallon complained bitterly in the House of Commons on 6 June 2000 that the government 'takes the report … espouses it then emasculates it'.

It is believed that the NIO's director of security David Watkins and the Chief Constable guided the drafting of the bill. Certainly, elected Members of the Assembly complained that they could not engage Mandelson. The Secretary of State again appeased unionism and the RUC, and also created a grave crisis for the government, alienating the nationalist communities and irritating allies in Dublin and Washington. Mandelson simply did not appreciate the fundamental importance of this issue for nationalists and republicans, and their desire, as Seamus Mallon put it, for nothing less than 'huge change'. Policing was the Geiger counter for measuring the government's good faith in implementing the Agreement's 'new beginning'. It was the key to the stability of the new dispensation.

Perhaps the consequences of the old police regime, the failure of reform, and the deeper long-term complicities of the British state, were most clearly revealed in the handling of illegal killings: Britain could hardly represent itself as a disinterested broker and simultaneously acknowledge its complicity with armed loyalism in the lawless killings of 'the enemy' – Catholics and republicans. Yet, by the late 1990s an awesome archive of evidence had accumulated showing that the British state had been complicit in the assassination of progressive lawyers, killings that fundamentally breached of one of the basic conditions of democracy: the independence of lawyers and the judiciary. Suspected collusion – whether organised or informal – not only assailed the state's duty to uphold the right to life, but also menaced the right to legal representation and lawyers' independence from the state. Yet these assassinations have not been satisfactorily investigated. (See especially the cases of Rosemary Nelson and Pat Finucane, both fearless defence lawyers who had received many death threats from serving RUC officers, and were eventually killed: British Irish Rights Watch, 1998; Davies, 1999; Lawyers Committee for Human Rights, 2002; Campbell, 2001).

In the face of government resistance to investigating such deaths, Mowlam announced at the end of 1997 a public inquiry into the Army's killing of unarmed citizens during a banned peaceful protest in Derry's Bogside on Bloody Sunday 1972 (Mowlam, 2002). However, much of the process has been obstructed by the Special Branch, and Sir John Stevens' long-delayed inquiries attracted sabotage and political fudging. New Labour's responses to the persistent bias of policing and to state promotion of assassination in Northern Ireland have thus been complex and rarely transparent.

Thus Blair's vaunted challenge to the 'forces of conservatism' did not extend to one of the most conservative and masculinist redoubts in the British Isles. When it came to a choice between the interests of a corrupt state and the interests of democratic renovation New Labour balked. It interpreted its responsibility as a balancing act between rival traditions, rather than a duty to reform discredited but fortified flanks of the secret state. This meant that New Labour was once more positioned on the side of the unionist state and against the victims' relatives and critics of a corrupt security service. As so often, a line was drawn in the promotion of justice in Northern Ireland at precisely the point where the complicity of Westminster, Whitehall and the British state had to be faced. New Labour therefore appeased unionism, rather than helping it to confront its own history and embrace the 'new beginning'. The interrogation of this cruel and corrupt history could have helped the Northern Irish in particular and the British in general to come to know themselves, and, in knowing themselves, to change.

'PERFIDIOUS BRITANNIA'

Paradoxically, it was a peripheral place, an unloved relic of greater Britain that offered a context in which the New Labour could have manifested its newness. Or at least its difference from the forces of conservatism and colonialism. Peace and a pluralist polity were the necessary alternatives to either unionism's failed Protestant state or the hallowed 'narrow ground' of the centre. There could be no return to unionism's majoritarian tyranny. And the centre could not accommodate the penumbra of peace-makers – including former combatants – whose participation was vital to ending the Troubles and creating a new political culture.

This episode was as revealing about New Labour as about Northern Ireland. The mercurial political personas of Mo Mowlam and Peter Mandelson showcased the unstable tensions between Labour's social progressivism (Mowlam) and authoritarian populism (Mandelson), devolution and a pluralist polity and centralising neo-colonialism, modernisation as cultural and political renovation and modernisation as managerialist rapport with traditional power and the construction of a broad coalition versus the holding of a narrow political space.

Mowlam brought a style and substance that derived from cultures that were either marginal to Labourism or repudiated by it, from her gender, her generation, her class and her career as an academic. Her knowledge of Northern Ireland's political geography released her from the control of the Northern Ireland Office and the securocrats. Her social progressivism recognised that the state and civil service was not neutral and had to be the subject not just the broker of change. This distance enabled her to engage respectfully with demonised *dramatis personae*, and with activists who for the first time felt that a British minister was accessible. Unlike Mandelson, Mowlam did not perform power.

By contrast, New Labour's authoritarianism, its populism, its jealousy of movements within civil society, its dependence on the state apparatus, its fatal attraction to power and finally its emergent 'new imperialism' were expressed through Mandelson. Gay and apparently metropolitan, he did not share the particular laddishness of the New Labour court, but he also recoiled from the new social movements and the 1970s radical sexual politics that had shaken both old and new Labours. Northern Ireland was his route back to the Cabinet from exile. He courted the unionist establishment whose distaste for Mowlam was simultaneously patriarchal and patrician. He squandered Mowlam's popular base and followed the usual British preference for the 'narrow ground' of the centre – a mirage in Northern Ireland. As an ambassador for the Prime Minister, he could rely on a political intimacy never enjoyed by his predecessor, and this added value, a veritable treasure chest, to his social capital.

This did not, however, bring with it an appropriate modesty of engagement with the Republic of Ireland, a country that, despite perfidious Britannia's best efforts, had refused to die. Dublin's rennaissance, its autonomy as a sovereign state, and as Britain's post-colonial *partner* in the peace process, did not always seem to register in the big-power temperament of the Mandelson-Blair partnership. They steered hard towards the politically conservative, managerialist flank of New Labourism. Hence the tactical commitment to Trimble's survival, the adhesion to the state and the status quo and the primacy given to unionism's priority of 'security' and the securocrats' suspicion of civil society. Similarly, Mandelson was a patrician rather than a popular figure, with a scarcely disguised disdain for the new social movements, the equality coalition, human rights advocates and parties close to the paramilitaries – all constituent parts of the tumult of transition, the movement for 'huge change'.

Mowlam's style and strategy, simultaneously an exception and an embodiment of the engaging newness of New Labour, both promised success, seemed to articulate New Labour's insecurity about its own power. Mandelson, by contrast, exemplified the grandiosity of New Labour's dominant faction and its deployment of its power in the service of existing power.

Overall, and despite some audacious manoeuvres, New Labour has proved neither willing nor able to re-position the British state within the process of reform in Northern Ireland. The effect of this has been to quell renovation and the drama of self-discovery on both sides of the Irish Sea, for Northern Ireland's secrets were the secrets of the *British* state. New Labour's hegemony ultimately ensured that the Agreement's egalitarian disciplines would not be allowed to travel across borders and over the sea, where inequality was growing and political engagement was declining. Once more Britain inured itself against the 'winds of change' blowing from the post-colonial settlement on the edge of the archipelago. While New Labour's pragmatism certainly encouraged a supple intervention in the peace process, in the end it fatally evaded the bigger tensions between *stability* and *change*.

REFERENCES

Adams, G. (1999) 'To Cherish a Just and Lasting Peace', *Fordham International Law Journal*, Vol 22, No 4, New York.

Bell, C. (2002) *Peace Agreements and Human Rights.* Oxford, Oxford University Press.

Blair, T. (1996) 'The Northern Ireland Peace Process', in *New Britain*, London, Fourth Estate.

British Irish Rights Watch (1998) *Finucane Murder Summary*, London, BIRW.

British Irish Rights Watch (1999) *Justice Delayed: Alleged State Collusion in the Murder of Patrick Finucane and Others.* London, BIRW.

British Irish Rights Watch and Committee on the Administration of Justice (1999, 11 Feb) Press Release, London and Belfast.

Campbell, B. (1995) 'Old Fogeys and Angry Young Men: A Critique of Communitarianism', *Soundings*, No 1, Autumn, London.

Campbell, B. (1999, 17 March) 'Suddenly in Lurgan', *The Guardian*.

Campbell, B. (2001, 19 May) 'Who Killed Rosemary Nelson?', *The Guardian*.

Davies, N. (1999) *Ten-Thirty-Three*, Edinburgh, Mainstream.

Holland, M. (1998 12 March), *Irish Times*.

Hughes, C. and Wintour, P. (1990) *Labour Rebuilt: The New Model Party*, London, Fourth Estate.

Jones, N. (2001) *Control Freaks*, London, Politicos.

Lawyers Committee for Human Rights (2002) *Beyond Collusion: the Security Forces and the Murder of Patrick Finucane*, LCHR, New York.

McCrudden, C. (1999) 'Mainstreaming Equality in the Governance of Northern Ireland', *Fordham International Law Journal*, Vol 22, April, New York.

MacIntyre, D. (2000) *Mandelson and the Making of New Labour*, London, Harper Collins.

Mallie, E. and McKittrick, D. (1996) *The Fight for Peace: The Secret Story Behind the Irish Peace Process*, London, Heinemann.

McWilliams, M. and Fearon, K. (1999) 'The Good Friday Agreement: A Triumph of Substance over Style', *Fordham International Law Journal*, Vol 22, No 4. New York.

Morrison, J. (1999) 'Constitutionalism and Change: Representation, Governance and Participation in the New Northern Ireland', *Fordham International Law Journal*, Vol 22, No 4. New York.

Mowlam, M. (1997 25 Feb), *The Independent*.

Mowlam, M. (2002) *Momentum*, London, Hodder and Stoughton.

O'Leary, B. (2002, 15 June), *The Guardian*.

O'Leary, O. and Burke, H. (1998) *Mary Robinson: The Authorized Biography*, London, Hodder and Stoughton.

Trimble, D. (1998, 17 April) Speech to Northern Ireland Forum.

Trimble, D. (1999) 'The Belfast Agreement', *Fordham International Law Journal*, Vol 22, No 4. New York.

14. Washington's favourite: Blairism and the 'blood price' of the international

Richard Johnson with Deborah Lynn Steinberg

INTRODUCTION

Several authors in this volume have argued that New Labour is an internally diverse political formation. In this chapter we focus attention on one axis of these differences: the tension between the national and the transnational. This involves giving priority to those tendencies in New Labour that we term 'Blairite'.[1]

By Blairism, we mean the political forces, rhetorical repertoires and social alliances clustered around the Prime Minister himself and his Office in Downing Street. Blairism is centrally – and often very explicitly – a politics associated with global forces, global interests and global social alliances and linked to international organisations and policies. It takes its agenda – and much of its rhetoric – from this larger transnational sphere. This affects its relation to national institutions and local movements, particularly to those we can call 'national-popular' (Gramsci, 1971). Blairism is, in a very particular sense, a 'cosmopolitan' politics. Typically, as we shall argue here, national-popular elements are to be controlled, 'reformed' or 'modernised'. Politics bcomes a means for transmitting transnational requirements to national agents. Blairism represents, therefore, a fundamental re-positioning of national politics, without, however, as the excesses of globalisation theory might suggest, rendering them redundant.

The nation state is, rather, a vital link in transnational chains of power. Political elites must win power there to secure an international presence. They must represent and articulate both national and transnational interests. We have two strikingly different examples of this negotiation in the figures of Tony Blair and President George W. Bush. Blair has used his long-term domestic political capital to become an international statesman, aspiring to 'reorder this world around us' (Blair, 2.10.01).[2] Bush's shaky electoral beginnings were rescued by the attack of 11 September 2001 through which he established himself – in the years immediately after the attack – as an all-American hero-

President, installing also the neo-conservative agenda of his circle. Thus Blair drew on his national successes to project himself internationally, while Bush used his world-wide 'war on terrorism' to establish himself nationally. As we shall see, these differences underlie their complementarity in diplomacy and war.

Articulating the national and the transnational is a two-way process. Transnational demands and dynamics must be 'sold' to the nation, while convincing versions of 'national interest' are woven into international projects. During the 'war against terrorism' and the war against Iraq, it has been easier for Bush than for Blair to make these links. While the US public was rebounding from the unfamiliar experience of victimhood, Blair was forced into excesses of spin and an implausibly long chain of argument to link British national interests to the twin towers and to Iraq. On the eve of invasion, for instance, he agreed with a BBC interviewer that Britain must be 'prepared to send troops to commit themselves, to pay the blood price' for the American alliance (Blair, 6.9.02).

This admission, and the widespread recognition today that Saddam Hussein's Iraq was not a threat to Britain, has opened up a line of critical assessment that has focused on the costs of international ambitions, especially to the nation. Included here are the lives lost and young men wounded or traumatised, but also the diversion of resources from peaceful uses, the strengthening of fear, terrorism and militarism worldwide, and the erosion of democratic institutions and civil rights in the name of a spurious security. Blair has been attacked, from left or right, for neglecting 'domestic' issues and 'sacrificing' the nation. Yet he is right to stress the transnational dimensions of politics today, their human or global scale. The old division, between 'home' and 'foreign' policy (e.g. 'Home Secretary' and 'Foreign Secretary' in Britain) no longer works today. Every nation's future is transnational. If this is so, appraisal must not halt at national boundaries. We must investigate Blair's version of the transnational or global too.

We start with looking more closely at the idea of the transnational state and how this might fit Blairism. We then analyse Blair's rhetorical deployment of 'globalisation' as a keyword in his speeches. We ask what 'global' means exactly in Blairite theory and in practice, and whose 'universality' it encapsulates. We consider how Blair represents and positions the British state and its peoples within this global politics. Throughout this, we will consider both the outward projection of power in military and diplomatic manoeuvres (before and after 11 September 2001) and the subordination of domestic politics to this global emphasis. We stress the vulnerabilities as well as the strengths of this extended political formation.

BLAIRISM AND THE TRANSNATIONAL STATE

In debates about globalisation and international political economy the idea that the state and its power function at transnational as well as national levels is now commonplace. In one version of this argument, Robert Cox, a founder of the so-called 'Italian' or 'Gramscian School' in International Relations, has applied some of Gramsci's insights about hegemony to international processes (e.g. Cox, 1981; Cox and Sinclair, 1996). Cox's work is of interest here because of the long engagement of cultural studies with Gramsci's ideas. It suggests ways of bridging a long divorce between the cultural and the economic analyses of power.[3]

Cox's version of 'the internationalisation of the state', however, refers not only to supranational organisations like the World Bank, the International Monetary Fund (IMF) and the World Trade Organisation (WTO), which lay down rules for national policies, but also to tensions within national states themselves. Some parts of nation states have a transnational orientation. As Cox puts it: 'The internationalisation of the state gives precedence to certain state agencies – notably ministries of finance and prime ministers offices – which are key points in the adjustment of domestic to international economic policy' (Cox, 1981:146).

Moreover parts of the state that grew up to promote narrowly national interests have come to be subordinated to 'the central organs of internationalised public policy'. Cox cites old-fashioned Ministries of Labour or Industry, once preoccupied with labour relations and national manufacturing. To this we might add those ministries associated with education, health, social welfare or law and order. Even the more outward looking parts of government, concerned with finance, trade, aid and development and war and diplomacy do not necessarily take their agenda from outside. Although always involving cross-national relations, they can be pursued primarily according to 'the national interest.' It is arguable, for instance, that Thatcherite foreign policy foregrounded national interests in this way – and that this has changed under Blair.

These state developments are linked to long-term changes in the international economy; they institutionalise economic interdependence and dependence. The huge growth of transnational corporations means they more than rival some national states in their wealth and political clout. There is the closest of relations between 'international policy networks' and 'big business'. Together these form 'a new informal corporative structure' overshadowing those parts of economies that are 'nationally oriented'. Cox sees this process as also affecting class formation, so we can speak of a 'transnational managerial class' with 'focal points of organisation' in IMF or OEDC, but also among executives of multinational corporations and those who manage the internationally-oriented sectors within major nation states. This transnational managerial class may also coincide with the social formation discussed elsewhere in this volume as the (gendered) 'superclass' (see Johnson and Walkerdine chapter in this volume).

There are many indications that Blairism is somewhat separate from the rest of government, dominant within it and distinctively oriented towards the international. Blair's own political style has often been called 'Presidential'. The frequency of his travels around the world have often been a subject of comment. His oratory expresses a highly personal vision of the nation in the world and of his own mission, reiterated all the more insistently in the face of opposition. In political terms, his circle is large and powerful enough to constitute a faction – the hegemonic faction indeed – in New Labour's larger constellation. Institutionally, the prime minister has huge powers of patronage, including rewarding loyal MPs with office. His circle has instant access to public media, and is uniquely close to the secret 'inside' of government, crucially the military and the Intelligence Services, though these relationships are not without tensions. Another feature of this power and partial autonomy is the large-scale employment of special advisers and communication experts or 'spin doctors', who are more or less independent of the civil service and are immune from parliamentary responsibility and, usually, scrutiny. The government currently employs 70 such advisors, at the cost of £5.4m a year. This is a three-fold increase since 1997, suggesting it is a distinctively New Labour feature. Of these advisors, no less than 38 work in or for Number 10 Downing Street. Some of them – famously Alistair Campbell, the Director of Communication until his resignation in 2003 and Jonathan Powell, the Chief of Staff – are as influential and better rewarded, than many Cabinet ministers. Nowhere is this Blairite hegemony more obvious than in 'foreign affairs'. With the advice of Powell, David Manning (who became British Ambassador in Washington) and key military figures, Blair himself has come to dominate the foreign policy arena, especially on matters of going to war. According to Kampfner (2003), Downing Street in many ways has displaced the Foreign Office as the key locus of decision-making in this sphere.

The complex relationships between prime-ministerial power, the civil service, special advisors and the most authoritative news media entered evident crisis in 2003 around the government's gross exaggerations of the threat posed by Iraq's so-called 'weapons of mass destruction'. Aside from widespread public scepticism, government claims were openly contested by the more usually compliant British Broadcasting Corporation and by some weapons experts, and queried more discretely within the security services themselves. The evidence given to the Hutton Inquiry, set up on a narrow brief to investigate the suicide of Dr David Kelly the leading British expert on Iraq's weaponry, was important in showing the extent of Number 10's controlling ambitions. Although 'intelligence' about Iraq clearly had its own limits, its public presentation was dominated by the overwhelming imperative of justifying the war. The (con)fusion of spin and intelligence was signalled by Campbell's chairmanship of the Joint

Intelligence Committee, the government's key link to the secret services, and by his resignation when the whole strategy came under public scrutiny. Crucially, for our argument, this affair concerned the relation of national interests to international ambitions. Saddam Hussein's very modest armoury was presented as an immediate threat to two of the most powerful and best armed nations in the world. Implausible though this claim was – and remains – a project of regional and world dominion had somehow to be squared with the much more modest scale of national interest, not to mention international law.

Another feature of the Blair circle is its close connections with big business, the very rich, and, generally, with uninhibited aspects of capitalist 'enterprise'. The more 'respectable' end of this link is represented by the relationship with Lord Sainsbury, head of one of the largest supermarket chains in Britain, a minister and major funder of New Labour; the less respectable was represented by Lord Eccleston through whose influence with Number 10, including a £1million donation to the Labour Party, Formula One motor racing was temporarily exempted from a ban on tobacco advertising. Then there is the list of wealthy personal benefactors, including the evangelical pop star Cliff Richards and the Italian newspaper proprietor Prince Girolamo Strozzi, whose gifts have included holiday facilities used by the Blairs. There is a longer list of wealthy people who have given substantial sums of money to the Labour Party and been rewarded with honours bestowed at the prime minister's discretion. (For a recent instance see Sir David Garrard's £200,000 uncovered by the Electoral Commission and reported in *The Guardian* 13.8.03.) Blair has also sought surprising political alliances with the media tycoon Rupert Murdoch, the Italian prime minister/media mogul Silvio Berlusconi, and of course the neo-conservative Republican President of the USA, with his close links with oil and other corporate interests. The very close relationship with Peter Mandelson, a key organiser of New Labour, has something of the same character, since Mandelson himself has twice fallen foul of financial scandal and twice been exiled from government, once in connection with another scandal-dogged Labour politician businessman, Geoffrey Robinson. In spite of this, Mandelson continues to be a major spokesman for Blairism (see also Beatrix Campbell's chapter in this book). These entanglements sit somewhat askew with Blair's own self-image as a particularly erect public figure.

Much the most significant evidence for Blairism's business orientation lies in the content of policies and the forms of their rhetorical framing. Just as Naomi Klein has argued that branding is a distinctive feature of corporate capitalist culture, so the style of New Labour's politics can be understood as a kind of political re-branding (Klein, 2001). New Labour has been redefined as a party friendly to business, while retaining, as we shall see, a certain 'idealism'. This business-friendly party also deploys keywords from a socialist past like 'social justice' and 'community'. Just as corporations hide exploitative labour relations behind their evocations of style and consumer identity, so Blairism's 'realist' edge – cf his rather consistent neo-liberalism; and see especially *Blair's Wars* (Kampfner 2003) – is softened by his 'idealism'. As in the case of branding, these rhetorics are very audience specific, very 'targeted', socially and spatially. Blair's idealism, like much branding discourse, addresses audiences 'at home' while often concealing the detail of global exploitation which happens elsewhere, particularly in East or South.

We will discuss Blair's idealist rhetoric in more detail later, but his realism is clearest in speeches to corporate and state managers and investors, at home or abroad. In Japan he says: 'A modern Britain, a Labour Britain, is offering more – a better skilled and educated workforce, better infrastructure, and a macroeconomic environment more conducive to sustained investment' (Tokyo, 9.1.98). In the Hilton Hotel in Chicago, he recalls the US origins of the British retail chain Selfridges and urges mutual inward investment (Chicago, 22.4.99). In South Korea, he presents Britain as 'the gateway for Asian investment in Europe' (Seoul, 19.10.00). To an audience of scientists and managers in the biotech industries (but not to workers and professionals of the National Health Service), he is happy to stress that Britain should be 'the bridge between the European and US healthcare markets' (London, 17.11.00).

In these moments, while not altogether dropping his 'national' identifications and invitations, Blair also speaks as a kind of general manager for collective capital. He points the way to good investments, he hails a less regulated, more uniform and profitable future and he offers almost every aspect of social provision and scientific discovery for commodification and profit. In Gramscian terms, he is a new type of 'organic intellectual' or 'director' for transnational economic interests. In all this, however, we would be better to speak not only of 'he' or of 'Tony Blair' but also of 'the Blair figure', recognising in this odd term that he is not only an individual but a kind composite political author, a particular embodied person; he has his own masculine styles and bodily resources and vulnerabilities, but is also a product of many hands and minds, formed in dialogues with the different constituencies with which he allies. It is to such representations and policies, especially of the global, that we now turn.

BLAIR'S GLOBAL RHETORIC

'Globalisation' is a favourite Blair word, particularly emphasised in a series of speeches delivered at home and abroad in 2000 and early 2001, during a period of renewed public expenditure, and before the preoccupation with terrorism and war took over after September 2001. The theme of these speeches was 'the choices I believe Britain faces'. Yet Blair's 'choices' are paradoxical:

Round the world, virtually irrespective of a country's state of development, the choices, however tough, are at least clear. As the old left/right
ideologies recede into memories of the 20th century, the 21st century
posits a set of fairly clear rules to follow on that road to success. These
rules originate in the forces of globalisation and technology. No matter
where you are, the global economy is where you do business; and technology will transform the business you do (Seoul, 19.10.00).

So these are not choices between alternatives exactly, since the age of
alternatives – of left and right – is over. They are not really choices at
all. What Blair says we have instead are 'fairly clear rules to follow', and
that it is 'the forces of globalisation and technology' which prescribe
future actions, however hard and unpalatable in the short-term this so
called 'choice' may be:

> Economic reform, the willingness to change is the absolute essence of
> future prosperity. Reform is hard but right and will succeed. Failure to
> reform will inevitably lead to failure. There is no escape from this rule.
> We can see what it is we need to do (Seoul, 19.10.00).

Blair uses this argument in a wide range of applications. It applies to
nations naturally: 'successful nations, round the world, are flexible
enough and adaptable enough to change as the world changes around
them'. It applies to the European Union, which is also positioned as a
potentially resisting 'local' within the dynamics of global change. It too
must turn from past introspection to face the future process of globalisation, a 'challenge that has to turn it outward' (Warsaw, 30.5.03). Thus
Britain can have a role in Europe, but only if Europe respects certain
conditions, hence 'our commitment in principle to go in' but also to
'structural reforms in relation to Europe' (London, 26.6.03).
    Blair preaches the same message in Britain, Europe, E. Asia, Russia,
Eastern Europe, and even to the G8 richest countries, where he finds
everyone talking about 'reform', that is 'adapt[ing] and adjust[ing]
your public services and economies very quickly' (Evian, 4.6.03).
    On all these scales, then, policy is (properly) under the dominance
of globalisation as a process whose social, spatial and temporal features
are only lightly sketched. Although change is uncomfortable, Blair
always denies there are any contradictions or deep conflicts between
the different scales of policy. Speaking to a Polish audience, for example, he stressed that it was patriotic to be pro-European in Poland or in
Britain, but that the real 'task' is to re-shape and reform it, 'to with-
stand and then harness the force of globalisation' (Warsaw, 30.5.03).
    Typically he 'finds' – or rather seeks to construct – a consensus on
these issues. He calls this 'the coalition' or, better, 'the international
community', a ubiquitous phrase which transposes a key term of Third
Way domestic politics to the world. As at home, the main effect of this

is to tuck away major differences or conflicts and stress solidarities. 'Community' articulates a general human interest certainly, but it denies differences rather than dealing with them. In the international context it refuses any hint of 'multipolarity' in the world (e.g. Evian, 4.6.03). When major differences impose on policy, Blair still hastens to restore 'consensus'. In speeches in the aftermath of the Iraq war, when his 'coalition' dwindled dreadfully, he hailed UN Resolution 1483 (on Iraqi 'reconstruction') as evidence of 'the international community pulling back together again and working together'. His most optimistic production of potential world harmony, however, was his discovery of 'lasting good' out of 'the shadow of this evil' in the famously idealistic October 2001 speech to the Labour Party Conference, a few weeks after the attack on the twin towers:

> The critics will say: but how can the world be a community? Nations act in their own self-interest. Of course they do. But what is the lesson of the financial markets, climate change, international terrorism, nuclear proliferation or world trade? It is that our self-interest and our mutual interests are today inextricably woven together. This is the politics of globalisation (2.10.01).

This speech was a seeming high point in Blair's progressive world vision, winning plaudits from the left of his party. It argued for the 'international community' to tackle the issue of world poverty and debt, to address the state of Africa, attend to the environmental crisis and also wage war on terrorism and 'fanaticism'. A closer reading shows the characteristic splitting of idealist aims and realist means that runs right through his politics. Internationally, war and if necessary occupation (of Afghanistan, then of Iraq) are means to peace, prosperity and self-government, and a way of defending 'our way of life'. At home, testing children almost every year of their school lives and setting their teachers targets are means to 'the joy of art and culture and the stretching of imaginative horizons that true education brings'. Meritocracy and 'the reward of talent' are, as we have seen, the very contradictory 'means' to social justice and equality of worth. As he puts it himself, 'our politics only succeed when the realism is as clear as the idealism'. Blair's global idealism is addressed to those elements within the Labour Party that remain attached to social-democratic goals of social justice, or to humanitarian interventions abroad, or indeed to forms of working-class representation. For these audiences at least, idealism is a key feature of the brand.

This takes us back to the paradox of rules and choices, which is another example of the same ideal/real opposition. Here again, the ferocity of constraints matches the strenuousness of ideal imaginings, so that heroic efforts are required. Another favourite Blair phrase – 'huge challenges' – expresses this perfectly. The nation's pursuits are never modest; we seek success, greatness and exemplary performances, and we are haunted by failure or decline. It is important, in the footballing analogy, that Britain is 'a major player in Europe'; similarly, 'Britain and Poland can win in Europe. But we can't do it standing on the touchline' (Warsaw, 30.5.03).

But whose tremendous efforts, whose agency is evoked here? Agency is quite strictly reserved for certain spheres of action and to certain key agents. There is rather little scope for it economically. The global economy and its main dynamics – globalisation, liberalisation, the commercial direction and exploitation of scientific knowledges – are seen as fundamentally untouchable by critical agency. On the 'basis' of this typical New Labour economism, everything else must strenuously adapt to these realities, including all forms of social provision and human subjectivity. The heroism lies in this massive painful process of adaptation. We are told, again and again, 'it won't be easy. Nothing worthwhile ever is'. And that it must be managed – 'it will require more tough choices' (London, 14.3.01). Blairism is profoundly 'passive' in what it leaves outside the sphere of political agency; it is 'revolutionary' in the grandiose adaptations or assimilations it demands.

It is, however, only certain agents that have choices. Professional subjects and ordinary citizens are, as we have seen, put under intense pressures; while fuller (but not untrammelled) agency lies with government. For more popular agents, most choices that really matter have already been made, if not by government then by the process of global change itself. While governments are capable of clear long-term vision, the electorate is seen as suffering from myopia. This means that elections can be a difficult challenge for those who want to manage change. As Blair puts it:

> Both globalisation and technology bring change in people's lives. With change comes insecurity. Governments have to become managers of this change, a helping hand through it. But change is often resisted and always difficult. So the temptation for governments to slip back into short-termism is acute, especially given the pressure of elections. But we know where short-termism leads, it leads to decline (Seoul, 19.10.00).

So, as we argue throughout this volume, Blairism is a fundamentally elite, or managerial, form of politics, profoundly non- or anti-popular in the sense of disallowing popular agency. Globalisation, a version of the transnational, is integral to this spatial and social allocation of agency. The stress is on cosmopolitan initiatives by elites; the main duty of the citizens of the nation states is an active compliance.

Blair's relation to movements for global justice is the most relevant instance here (though see also Lisa Smyth's chapter in this book on the way the fuel crisis was managed). He misrepresents global justice movements, steals their slogans and spins their keyword – 'justice'. He argues that these movements are against globalisation as such: the 'demonstrators' (who have challenged him so directly at G8 meetings and elsewhere) are 'right to say there's injustice, poverty, environmental degradation', but the answer to these problems is always more, not less, globalisation. The task, as usual, is 'to use the power of community to combine it with justice' (Labour Party, 2.10.01). There is no question, apparently, of allying with popular global movements to put pressure on recalcitrant governments or corporations, nor any concept of alternative forms of globalisation.

WHAT IS GLOBALISATION? BLAIR'S GLOBAL VISION

Blair is an interesting politician because he has a worldwide vision and says he is concerned with 'the choices facing humankind'. He seeks to persuade us all to take the new reality of global interdependence on board. As we have seen, he develops a global agenda, embracing issues of poverty, the environment and (from September 2001) on military intervention against rogue states and terrorists. We can agree thus far: an adequate progressive politics today requires a vision as global as this, without refusing local initiatives.

How exactly does Blair define global interests? He is not an advocate of global citizenship, global government or new forms of humanitarian international regulation. He opposes global power in the shape of a reformed UN or a united Europe. His conception of the EU is a union of nations, not a federal superstate. The UN is more a source of legitimation than a locus of a power that might qualify national or imperial might. Blair can play the humanitarian card, and can seek international legitimacy, but this not primarily the way he sees the globalising dynamic.

Nor is he much concerned with the social and cultural themes that have preoccupied sociological theorists of the global, although Third Way politics shares the sociologists' fixations on modernity, the dynamics of change and the phenomena of emergence. There is a connection with social theory, but it is not as close as that of 'old Labour', with its tradition of empirical sociological research into social inequality, from the 1930s to the 1970s. Blairism, like much social theory, has a pronounced tendency to describe contemporary social change (often without much empirical grounding) as more or less a *fait accompli*. Blairite politics shares in common with much social theory a tendency to 'discover' key dynamics as necessities which demand a radically new political agenda – rather than to acknowledge that the discovery and description of such trends is often itself a form of intervention. In particular, Blairites follow Anthony Giddens in jettisoning all notions of capitalism as a worldwide, unstable and unequal social system and accept its dynamics with little critical thought. (For these affinities see especially Giddens, 1998, 2002.) They carry forward very little from earlier social(ist) theory, especially from Marxism or a left Weberianism. The problem is rather the classical liberal one – how to 'modernise' – that is, keep up with the new global challenges. In so far as Blairism belongs to this larger anglophone, sociological, 'modernising', Third Way tradition, with its characteristic substitution of passive social description for thoughtful critical engagement, we can say that Blair's universality is a thoroughly 'British', or even English, universality.

In his economic policies, however, Blair is a quite strict neo-liberal. He is strongly in favour of extending markets into public services. This is what he usually means by 'reform' which is gener-ally the price (to professionals and workers) of state investment in public services. Much of the money granted to 'public services' is therefore destined to end up in the pockets of those international capitalist corporations that are moving everywhere into previously public services, often through labyrinthine forms of sub-contracting. He is happy to woo the big corporations to take on health provision, water supply, transport infrastructure, the building and management of prisons, hospitals, schools, and detention centres for asylum seek-ers. In the schemes termed Private Funding Initiatives (PFI), for instance, corporations are given state support and conditions of unfair competition with what remains of public services to achieve this extension of capitalist commodity relations (Monbiot, 2000). Blair envisages a time when 60 per cent of retirement pensions will be funded privately. He is opposed to a 'social Europe', while steal-ing social-democratic language to redefine the social itself. He favours of course a 'flexible' Europe, ready to reform economically to meet the challenge of globalisation, and with a proper stress not on employment protection but on 'skills and education … through-out life' (Warsaw, 30.5.03).

Science and technology are also viewed within this neo-liberal frame. This is particularly clear in discussions of biotechnology – science's 'new frontier'. In a classically modernist stress, science is crucial to progress: 'It is science and moral judgement together that drive human progress. Scientific innovation has been the motor. Judgement the driver' (London, 17.11.00).

But here again realist science and ethical-political judgement, 'facts' and 'values', are split. Moral judgement should come after discovery; it should not limit or guide it:

> Let us get to the facts and then judge their moral consequences. There is a danger, almost without noticing it or desiring it, we become anti-science. The distinction I believe is this: our conviction about what is natural or right should not inhibit the role of science in discovering the truth; rather it should inform our judgement about the implications and consequences of the truth science discovers (17.1100).

Resistance to particular technologies – GM crops for instance – is therefore a kind of 'blackmail'. Such forms of resistance are also, 'realistically', self-defeating since Blair envisages Britain as the 'European hub' of biotechnology and as a 'bridge' for US corporations. There is no attempt to distinguish between the possible human benefits of some scientific advances and the sectional interests that drive much of biotechnology, the search for corporate advantage and control.

As we have seen throughout this volume, however, there are *distinctive* marks of Blair's neo-liberalism that distinguish it from the Thatcherite phase. First, there is the concern to translate and 'liberalise' all the key terms of socialism and Labourism rather than simply to bury them – and to re-articulate, rather than to defeat, Labour's older class constituencies. Second, there is the interest in producing subjects suitable for a neo-liberal future, including amenable, knowledgeable, skilful, but also proletarianised labour – labour, that is, that has lost much of its control of the nature and tempo of work. To these definitions we can now add a very distinctive emphasis on the global, which is closely linked to neo-liberalism too.

WASHINGTON'S FAVOURITE AND BRITAIN'S PLACE

Critics have often expressed surprise at how closely Blair has clung to the US alliance, especially to a president who moves to the right of his own politics. The US alliance has been the touchstone of his foreign policy even when it has threatened to wreck his long-term prospects at home. It seems to us, in explanation of this, that the US alliance is the most over-determined aspect of Blairite internationalism, and that it has many roots.

First, the US alliance is central to the way Blair understands the place of his own nation in the world. Britain should be 'at the centre of the alliances and power structures of the international community': it is a fulcrum or 'pivot' nation (see especially Noxolo's chapter in this volume). 'Although not today a superpower, Britain is a pivotal power in international relations' (Guildhall, London, 13.11.00). As we have seen, this centrality flows, in part, from the promotion of Blairite neo-socialism as a model for other nations to follow. Similar manoeuvres are attempted in relation to 'our own peace process' in Northern Ireland, in its applications to Israel/Palestine (e.g. Northern Ireland with Bush, 8.5.03), and the boast that Britain's 'multiculturalism' makes it the globalised nation par excellence (London, 28.11.01).

Britain's 'pivotal' status crucially refers, however, to the double relation with Europe and the United States, and to Blair's 'committed Atlanticism' (e.g. Canadian Parliament, 23.2.01). Sustaining this double relation is crucial both for Britain's centrality and for its national interests. This is why Blair fiercely opposes any conception of Europe as a counter-balance to US power in a 'multi-polar' world, and why the French, German and Russian opposition to the Iraq war and occupation were such tests for his politics. He sees no need to choose between Europe and the United States:

> The whole of my political philosophy is based on the fact that the choice is false in the end. We've got to get Europe, America, and, indeed, Russia working together. The reason for this is that our relations with America are vitally important; it is a strong historical relationship, but it is also based on values we share and common challenges we face.

> For Britain, the more I do this job, the more convinced I am, that for us, we have to keep both alliances in place because they are both vital for our own strategic interests (London, with Putin, 26.6.03).

The relationship with the USA is presented as a huge national asset, which it would be mad to throw away – 'many countries aren't fortunate enough to have the possibility of that strong relationship with both Europe and America'. He is therefore utterly committed to 'a Europe dedicated to upholding the transatlantic alliance' (Warsaw, 30.5.03). Although he has favoured the capacity of the EU to undertake military actions in its own right, the use of any joint military capacity should be strictly subordinate to the NATO 'partnership'.

Blair typically uses the term 'partnership' for grossly unequal relationships of this kind, whether in the domain of aid to the underdeveloped world or in relation to US/UK relations.

> We regard the United States as our allies and partners. We are proud of what we have achieved together against tyranny and in the defence of freedom, most recently in Iraq (Warsaw, 30.5.03).

'Partnership' disguises relations of dependence, which are in fact deepened by intensifying this kind of subaltern relation. (In this case Blair's conception of partnership seems to prevent him from recognising his own subaltern role; more usually the partnerships he proposes obscure his own dominant position.)

This partnership/dependence applies to trade relations but also to the military. Thus there is a close intertwining – set to increase with 'star wars' and British military reorganisation – of the military and coercive powers of the British and US states. This kind of relationship is evident in intelligence and surveillance, in the procurement of military hardware and technology (including nuclear), in the US bases and listening posts on British soil, and in the longer-term and many-sided re-shaping of the British services to be compatible with, and complementary to, the US military. This subordinated complementarity is precisely what the Pentagon looks for in its military allies – in the newer contributions of eastern European states for instance.

Other aspects of Blair's Americanism are related to his neo-liberalism. The USA is the world hub of neo-liberal ideology and of capital-ist consumption as a way of life. Blair is an uncritical supporter of this way of living. 'Our way of life' is one of the things, which, like Bush, he sees as stakes in the war against terrorism (Johnson, 2002).

Blair also adopts and adapts classic figures of US ideological politics, especially 'freedom' and 'the free world'. He weaves these 'American' terms into his more 'European' vocabulary of 'community', 'justice' and 'coalition'. His stance on terrorism and pre-emptive war has become indistinguishable from that of President Bush. Indeed, a study of his speeches over time, especially in transatlantic venues, shows him to have been a principled interventionist in the affairs of other states long before 11 September 2001 (e.g. Chicago, 22.4.99). In other areas of policy – in education, crime, the pursuit of civic 'decency' and 'welfare for work' – his government has borrowed from policies tried (and sometimes failed) in parts of the United States. It is hard not to see in Blair's stress on equality of opportunity, hard work and talent an angli-cised version of 'the American dream'. Certainly when he describes – to a Canadian rather than a US audience – 'the core package of our political canon', it includes not only 'democracy', 'individualism' and 'human rights', but also 'the primacy of the market as the engine of growth' (Canadian Parliament, 23.2.01). We might add that some char-acteristically US social pathologies – including gun crime, urban decay, family break-up, and chronic everyday insecurity – are also emerging consequences of neo-liberal 'Americanisation', often unaccompanied by the countervailing 'American' virtues.

In quite a strong sense, then, Blair's globality is a US universality. It is imagined certainly as Anglo-American, fruit of a long-term Atlantic alliance. In practice, Blair has given away much of his own political capi-tal, many of the social benefits of 'his' citizens, and even the blood of 'his' soldiers, in the service of an alliance with the Bushites. It is easy to see what the Bushites gain from this alliance: Blair's international profile, coalition-building aptitudes, ideological versatility, military back-up and ultimate compliance. No wonder he is Washington's favourite, enraptur-ing, it seems, even politically sophisticated US audiences.

An account of this relation would be incomplete, however, without its strongly imaginary character. This stems from Blair's personal idealism (and his public-school Christian background), and from larger imperial legacies in Britain. Both elements find expression in Blair's moral abso-lutism. Like Bush, but in a different register, Blair represents his greatest enemies – from terrorists to the leaders of rogue states – as absolute embodiments of evil, with whom there can be no negotiation, and whose motivation we should not, in the end, even seek to understand:

> Understand the causes of terror? Yes we should try, but let there be no moral ambiguity about this: nothing could ever justify the events of September 11, and it is to turn justice or its head to pretend it could ...

> There is no compromise with such people, no meeting of minds, no
> point of understanding with such terror. Just a choice: defeat it or be
> defeated by it. And defeat it we must (Labour Party, 2.10.01).

Here even a 'realist' knowledge of the other seems irrelevant, as
enemies are excluded from the human race. As Pat Noxolo argues in
this book, there is a distinctively imperial element in such constructions, which parallel those found in the discourses of aid and
development. Not only are rogue states mainly to be found in non-
white, non-western-European spaces; but the voices of complete moral
superiority which clear the way for the military forces are distinctively
imperial. It is now common knowledge that the neo-Conservative
group around Bush developed a systematic strategy for dominating the
world, partly to secure remaining resources, partly to pre-empt the
growth of rival powers. There is a kind of historical symmetry in the
alliance with a predecessor imperial power, especially one that retains a
military capacity and a willingness to go to war.

This militarism is one further strong continuity with Thatcher's
Britain. Blair has taken the nation to war, with or without UN and
popular support, in Bosnia, Kosovo, Afghanistan and Iraq – and has
involved the military in other struggles – peacekeeping in Sierra Leone
for example. All these wars – the pros and cons of which, in our view,
have varied widely – have been justified in the same morally absolute
terms. It is this kind of moral imagination – unable to distinguish understanding as knowledge of the other from sympathy for its causes – that
underlies what one ex-cabinet colleague (Clare Short) has called Blair's
'recklessness'. The refusal to understand – enemies especially, perhaps –
signals a suspension of political rationality (see also Kampfner 2003).

   There is also a strongly moral-imaginary element in Blair's typical
answers to what he calls 'anti-Americanism'. He insists on being the
'partner' of the US, not its 'servant' (London interview, 31.5.03). He
argues that the only way to influence the US government is to support
its projects but to influence its actions with 'our' (Europe's? Britain's?)
own principles. This, is another version of the splitting of principle and
realism, with Europe as the bearer of ethics and the US as a kind of
amenable but amoral beast, not too hot on the diplomacy. It is this
hope that draws Blair into being a facilitator for US power. The central
failure of his international career – his failure to draw the world and
even his own national public behind an Anglo-American invasion of
Iraq – revolved around a fantasy of British influence in the world, both
the power to influence the US government and the power to win the
world to its causes.

Blair's own ideals, stated in 2003, seem to be this:

> I think my attitude to this is you can construct an agenda which takes
> really seriously the issues of terrorism and weapons of mass destruction,

but adds to that then the Middle East, global poverty, climate change, the issues to do with, if you like, the concerns of other countries other than America, and I think that global agenda is there and can be accepted (London interview, 31.5.03).

The trouble is that the agenda itself is self-contradictory, mixing idealist aims for a better world according to broad human interests, with a realist (but not very farseeing) strategy to defend the privileges of the richer nations and the global elites. The Bushite agenda against 'international terrorism' and 'rogue states' is, predictably, only serving to produce more violent reactions among oppressed peoples and more defensive reactions in threatened states, including new attempts at nuclear armament.

Furthermore, pursuing terrorists (often loosely defined) everywhere and playing fast and loose with national and international law makes the pursuit of a different kind of world order less and less believable.

CONCLUSION

It is still too soon to say just how vulnerable Blairism will be to the political contradictions of its mediation between (Americanised) global demands and national interests. The Iraq war introduced a note of pathos into the public representation of a prime minister who knew that his international policies were deeply unpopular and that his war of persuasion was very widely disbelieved. Blair himself, though, still appears to believe that the invasion and corporate take-over of Iraq was fundamentally for the Iraqi people. Though deceptions have certainly been involved, he and many of his circle succeeded in persuading themselves that invasion was morally and realistically justified. This fits with our analysis of the Blairite international project, subsumed as it is within a US-centred version of the global force field. Yet the terrible unfolding disaster of the war and occupation in Iraq has also brought out the huge gulf between Blairism's idealist branding and its pragmatic realist underpinning, its crazily optimistic face and its hard pessimistic side.

While the credibility of Blairite politics in this sphere has been very deeply wounded, its political fate will also depend on the fortunes of its adversaries. It could be vulnerable to two forms of politics. The first would be a politics (of the left or of the radical right) that managed to bring together an opposing set of national-popular interests and symbols – whether in defence of the NHS or in a demand for greater international independence (and this could be in opposition to the USA and/or the EU). Since Blair is fundamentally right about transnational interdependence today, however, the longer, deeper challenge will come from a globalising politics of a different kind, one that aims at global justice, and seeks to transform or regulate existing capitalist dynamics; but this would also need to be a more broadly based politics, more concerned with human interests, and much more ecologically aware than most groups currently to the left of Blairism.

ENDNOTES

1. For the themes of New Labour as an alliance of rather different political tendencies and of Blairism as the hegemonic fraction of New Labour, see also the Introductions and Chapters 5, 6, 8, 11, 13 and 14 in this volume.
2. All speeches by Tony Blair referred to in the text are referenced at the end of this essay in date order.
3. On another occasion it may be useful to question Cox's reading of Gramsci, especially for its stress on institutions, and neglect of popular agency. This neglect is a serious one because unjust wars and unfair rules of trade have prompted large-scale and transnational popular opposition in South and North.

From www.number-10. gov.uk unless otherwise stated.

9.1.98, 'New Britain in the Modern World' (Tokyo).

13.1.98, 'Address to the North Atlantic Assembly' (Edinburgh).

22.4.99, 'Doctrine of the International Community' (Chicago).

19.10.00, 'Britain: Gateway for Asia in Europe' (Asia-Europe Business Forum, Seoul).

13.11.00, 'Britain's Choice: Engagement not Isolation' (Guildhall, London).

17.11.00, 'Biotechnology: Investing in the Future' (European Bioscience Conference).

23.2.01, 'Speech by the Prime Minister to the Canadian Parliament' (Ottawa).

14.3.01, 'Prime Minister's Speech on the Launch of the Employment Green Paper' (London).

2.10.01, Speech to the Labour Party Conference (printed verbatim in *The Guardian*, 3 October 2001).

28.11.01 'Speech by the Prime Minister at the Annual Meeting of the Network' (London).

28.6.02, 'PM: Press Conference at G8 Summit' (Canada).

6.9.02, 'Britain will pay 'blood price' – Blair', Interview with BBC, BBC News Online (http//news.bbc.co.uk).

8.5.03, Press Conference: PM Tony Blair and President George Bush ('Northern Ireland').

30.5.03, 'PM Speech on Europe in Warsaw' (Warsaw).

31.5.03, 'PM interviewed on Iraq, Weapons of Mass Destruction, Europe and Euro' (London).

4.6.03, 'PM says he is "100 per cent" behind Iraq evidence' at G8 Summit (Evian).

26.6.03, 'Press Conference with the Prime Minister and President Putin of Russia' (London).

REFERENCES

Cox, R.W. (1981) 'Social Forces, States and World Orders: Beyond International Relations Theory', *Millennium Journal of International Studies*, 10 (2): 126-155.

Cox, R.W., with Sinclair, T.J. (1996) *Approaches to World Order*, Cambridge: Cambridge University Press.

Giddens, Anthony (1998) *The Third Way: The Renewal of Social Democracy*, Oxford and Cambridge: Polity Press and Blackwell.

Giddens, Anthony (2002) *Where Now for New Labour?* London, Cambridge and Oxford: Policy Network, Fabian Society, Polity Press and Blackwell.

Gramsci, Antonio (1971) *Selections from the Prison Notebooks*, London: Lawrence and Wishart.

Johnson, Richard (2002) 'Defending Ways of Life: The (Anti-)Terrorist Rhetoric of Bush and Blair', *Theory, Culture and Society* 19, (4) 211-232.

Kampfner, John (2003) *Blair's Wars*, London: Free Press.

Klein, Naomi (2001) *No Logo*, London: Flamingo.

Monbiot, George (2000) *Captive State: The Corporate Takeover of Britain*, London: Pan Books.

Notes on Contributors

Beatrix Campbell is a visiting professor in the Centre for Gender and Women's Studies, University of Newcastle upon Tyne. Her publications include: *Sweet Freedom* (with Anna Coote, Virago, 1982); *Wigan Pier Revisited* (Virago, 1984); *Iron Ladies: why do women vote Tory?* (Virago, 1987) *Unofficial Secrets: Child Sexual Abuse – the Cleveland case* (Virago, 1988); *Goliath; and Britain's Dangerous Places* (Methuen, 1993).

John Clarke is Professor of Social Policy at the Open University. Drawing on a background in cultural studies, his interests have centred on the political, ideological and organisational conflicts around social welfare. Much of his recent work has addressed the role of managerialism in the remaking of welfare systems, including: *The Managerial State* (Sage 1997), co-authored with Janet Newman; *New Managerialism, New Welfare?* (Sage 2000), co-edited with Sharon Gewirtz and Eugene McLaughlin; and *Changing Welfare, Changing States: new directions in social policy* (Sage 2004).

Debbie Epstein is a professor in the School of Social Sciences at Cardiff University. She has published widely on sexuality, race and gender particularly in education. Her most recent book on these issues, co-authored with Sarah O'Flynn and David Telford, is *Silenced Sexualities in Schools and Universities* (Trentham, 2003) and *The Academic's Support Kit*, a six volume boxed set, co-authored with Rebecca Boden and Jane Kenway (Sage, 2005).

Chris Haywood and Mairtin Mac an Ghaill currently teach at the Faculty of Humanities and Social Sciences, University of Newcastle. They have just completed *Men and Masculinities: Theory, Research and Social Practice* (Open University Press).

Richard Johnson taught at The Centre for Contemporary Cultural Studies at the University of Birmingham from 1974 to 1993, and retired from his post as Professor of Cultural Studies at Nottingham Trent University in September 2004. He has written on Thatcherism (and education), nationalism and national identity, the anti-terrorist rhetorics of Bush and Blair, and masculinities and politics. He has recently completed a collaborative book about method in cultural studies: Richard Johnson, Deborah Chambers, Parvati Raghuram and Estella Tincknell, *The Practice of Cultural Studies* (Sage, 2004).

Ken Jones is Professor of Education at Keele University. He is author of *Education in Britain* (Polity Press). With other members of the education network of the European Social Forum, he is currently working on a book about neo-liberalism and education policy in Europe.

Joe Kelleher works in theatre and performance studies at Roehampton University. His current projects include a book co-edited with Nicholas Ridout, *Contemporary Theatres in Europe* (Routledge 2005), and a collaboration with Italian theatre-makers Societas Raffaello Sanzio, *The Theatre of Societas Raffaello Sanzio* (Routledge 2006).

Michael McKinnie teaches in the Department of Drama and Theatre Arts at the University of Birmingham. His research focuses on theatre and urban development, cultural theory and arts policy, and Canadian theatre. Recent publications include articles in *Theatre Journal*, *Essays on Canadian Writing*, and *Shakespeare in Canada: A World Elsewhere?* (ed. Diana Brydon and Irena Makaryk, University of Toronto Press).

Janet Newman is Professor of Social Policy at the Open University. She has worked extensively with public service managers experiencing the changes introduced within the modernising reforms of New Labour. She has also undertaken a range of research projects on these reforms, including projects on public service innovation, on partnership working, and on public participation. She is the author of *Modernizing Governance: New Labour, Policy and Society* (Sage 2001), and co-author, with John Clarke, of *The Managerial State: Power, politics and ideology in the remaking of social welfare* (Sage, 1997).

Pat Noxolo is a research associate with Leicester University. She is currently working on a project that explores the relationships between popular television drama and socio-spatial identities in Britain, New Zealand and Australia. More generally, her research focuses on the application of postcolonial theory and insights from cultural geography to discourses of international development and globalisation. Her thesis explored the racialisation of British governmental development discourses.

Liza Schuster is T. H. Marshall Fellow in the Department of Sociology at the London School of Economics. She was previously a Research Fellow in the Faculty of Humanities and Social Science at South Bank University, London. She is the author of *The Use and Abuse of Political Asylum in Britain and Germany* (Frank Cass 2002).

Lisa Smyth is a lecturer in the School of Sociology and Social Policy at Queen's University Belfast. She is the author of the forthcoming book *Abortion and Nation: the Politics of Reproduction in Contemporary Ireland* (Ashgate 2004).

John Solomos is Professor of Sociology in the Department of Sociology, City University, London. Before that he was Professor of Sociology in the Faculty of Humanities and Social Science at South Bank University, London, and he has previously worked at the Centre for Research in Ethnic Relations, University of Warwick and Birkbeck College, University of London and the University of Southampton. His two most recent books are *The Changing Face of Football: Racism, Identity and Multiculture and the English Game* (co-authored with Les Back and Tim Crabbe, Berg 2001); and *A Companion to Racial and Ethnic Studies* (co-edited with David Theo Goldberg, Blackwell 2002).

Deborah Lynn Steinberg is a Reader in the Department of Sociology, University of Warwick, where she teaches feminist, media and cultural theory. Her books include *Bodies in Glass: Genetics, Eugenics, Embryo Ethics* (1997); *Border Patrols: Policing the Boundaries of Heterosexuality* (with Debbie Epstein and Richard Johnson, 1997); and *Mourning Diana: Nation, Culture and the Performance of Grief* (with Adrian Kear, 1999).

Estella Tincknell is Associate Head of the School of Cultural Studies at the University of the West of England and has researched widely in the area of gendered identities and popular culture. She is the author of *Mediating the Family: Gender, Culture and Representation* (Arnold, 2005); and co-author of *The Practice of Cultural Studies* (Sage, 2004). She is also on the editorial board of *Body and Society*.

Valerie Walkerdine is Professor of Critical Psychology, Cardiff University. She has been researching aspects of gendered and classed subjectivity for many years.

Jeffrey Weeks is Professor of Sociology and Executive Dean of Arts and Human Sciences at London South Bank University. He is the author, co-author or editor of some twenty books, and has published numerous articles, mainly on the history and social organisation of sexuality and intimate life. Recent publications include *Invented Moralities* (1995), *Sexual Cultures* (edited with Janet Holland, 1996), *Making Sexual History* (2000), *Same Sex Intimacies* (with Brian Heaphy and Catherine Donovan, 2001), *Sexualities and Society: A Reader* (edited with Janet Holland and Matthew Waites, 2003), and *Sexuality* (2004).